THE MURRANJI TRACK

First published in 2007 by Central Queensland University Press

Second published in 2011 by Boolarong Press, Salisbury, Brisbane, Australia.

National Library of Australia Cataloguing-in-Publication entry

Author:	Lewis, D. (Darrell)
Title:	The Murranji Track : ghost road of the drovers / Darrell Lewis.
ISBN:	9781921920233 (pbk.)
Subjects:	Stock routes--Northern Territory--History.
	Droving--Northern Territory--History.
	Stockmen--Northern Territory--History.
	Murranji Track (N.T.)--History.
Dewey Number:	994.295

Typeset by Watson Ferguson & Company

Printed and bound by Watson Ferguson & Company, Salisbury, Brisbane, Australia.

THE MURRANJI TRACK

Ghost Road of the Drovers

Darrell Lewis

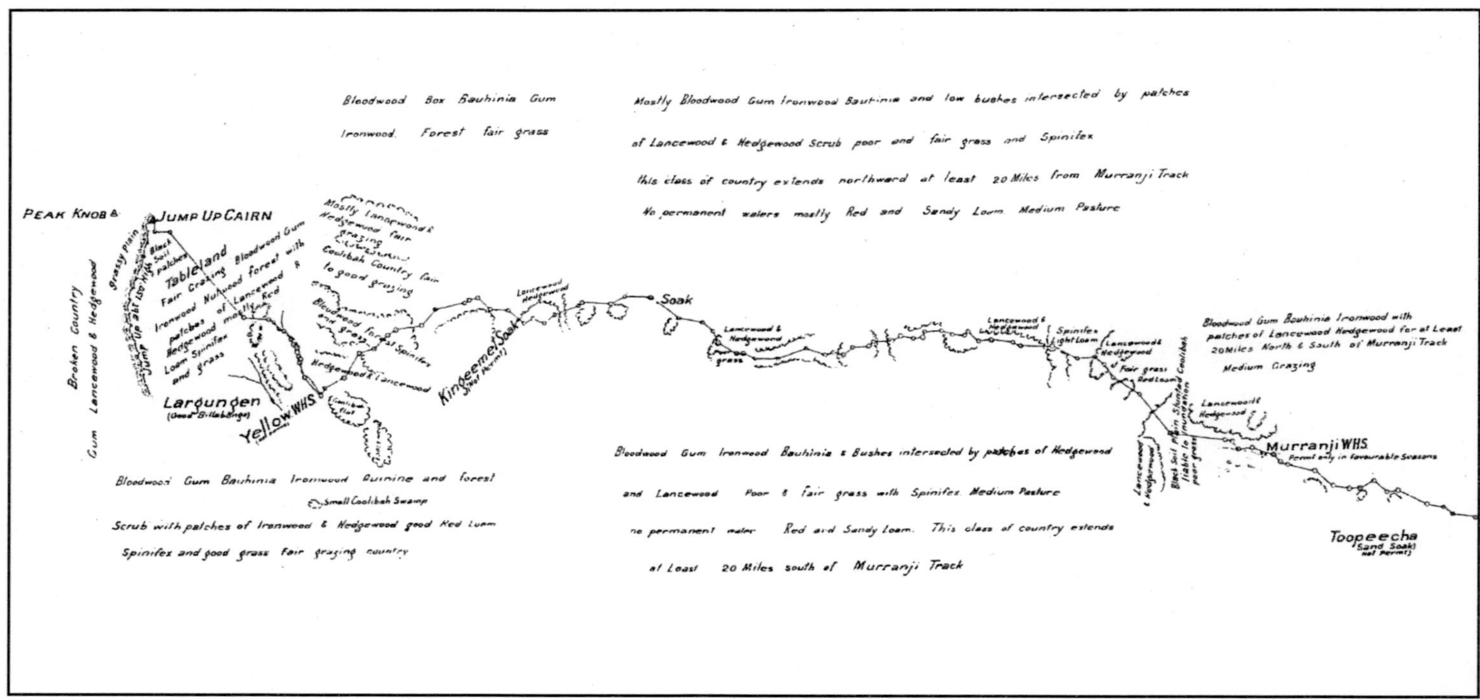

The Murranji Track from the Jump-up cairn to Murranji Waterhole, adapted from Scandrett's 1914 plan.

CONTENTS

Conversion Table

1 foot (12 inches)	30.5 cm	1 stone (14 lb)	6.3 kg
1 inch	25.4 mm	1 ton (2,240 lbs)	1016 kilos
1 yard (36 inches)	91.44 cm	1 centimetre	.39 inches
1 chain	22 yards or 20 metres	1 metre	39.3 inches
1 acre	.404 hectares	1 kilometre	.62 miles
1 mile (1,760 yards)	1.6 kilometres	1 square kilometre	100 hectares
1 square mile	2.5 square kilometres	1 square kilometre	.386 square miles
1 square mile	259 hectares	1 litre	.219 gallons
1 pint	.568 litres	1 kilogram	2.2 lbs
1 gallon	4.5 litres	1 pound (£)	$2 (in 1966)
1 lb	.45 kg		

FOREWORD

I have known Darrell Lewis for over twenty years, having first met him in 1984 when he was studying the rock art of the Victoria River District for his Masters degree. During most of this time I was the owner of Bradshaw station, and I came to know Darrell very well as he put in a lot of time on Bradshaw, exploring and documenting historic sites and recording the overall history of the Victoria River District. A glance at the reference list in any of Darrell's books or manuscripts shows that he is always meticulous and wide-ranging in his research, and his history can be relied upon to be authentic – unlike some of the other books on Northern Territory history where it is difficult to differentiate between truth and fiction.

And Darrell does not rely solely on archival research, but gets to know the country and, where possible, the people he writes about. Bradshaw homestead is only a couple of kilometres from the base of the 300 metre high Yambarran Range, and I clearly remember one of our staff running to the homestead one day in an extremely agitated state. He reported that there was a man walking down from the escarpment with a large scraggy beard, a very small swag on his back and carrying a rifle. This was Darrell, the bushman whom I got to know, not the academic known to people in the south. In this instance Darrell's wife had taken him by four-wheel drive to Wombungie, at the headwaters of the Fitzmaurice River, and had turned him loose with a swag and rifle. For about ten days he walked down the rugged and remote Fitzmaurice River valley and over the Yambarran Range to Bradshaw, a distance of well over 100 kilometres. He had lived off the land, eating Aboriginal bush tucker with which he is thoroughly conversant. Because of the time and dedication Darrell puts into his research I feel honoured to be asked to write the foreword to The Murranji Track.

At this point I should explain my credentials to speak about the Murranji Track at all. I first came to the Northern Territory in January 1953 when I arrived in Alice Springs. The following year I moved to the Barkly Tablelands and in nearby Camooweal I met a lot of the drovers of that time, including Walter Cowan, Stan Fowler, Bill and Mick Cussens, Jack Carroll, Bert Crouch, Don and George Booth, Clarrie Pankhurst, Jack Stewart, Les Griffiths, Mick Coombes, Charlie Robinson, John White and many others. A lot of these blokes were twenty or thirty years older than me, and the vast experience they had and the stories they told of the hardships they'd endured in years gone-by made me feel a relative newcomer, although in hindsight it's now 50 years ago. However, as Darrell's book shows there were drovers before them who had it even tougher, battling the elements and the problems of finding water for their stock in the days before there were windmills and bores along the Murranji Track. Noel (Piccaninny) Willetts and Bruce (Twenty one) Simpson were also boss drovers when I first came to the 'Weal, as it was known, but they are my age, a bit younger breed than the chaps mentioned above.

In 1956 I bought my own droving plant and was droving for the next eight years. My first jobs were to take mobs from Brunette Downs and Alexandria into Queensland, and my last mobs were 1250 Auvergne bullocks which I walked down the Murranji Track to Headingly near Urandangie in 1963, and 1250 Auvergne bullocks I walked to Avon Downs in 1964. Compared to the first old-timers who travelled the Murranji Track, the watering facilities were good in my day, but cattle still had to have a dry day between waters as the bores were an average of twenty miles apart, and we still had the problems of thick bulwaddy and lancewood scrub, hollow or 'drummy' ground and dark moonless nights where cattle could become spooky. It was essential to have your cattle full and content if they were to camp at night without rushing. Having your cattle full, that is not hungry, also stopped them eating the poisonous little Ironwood suckers which look so appetizing to hungry cattle, but are very poisonous, as referred to in Darrell's book

Through his painstaking research Darrell has been able to show the absolute necessity of opening up this stock route as it cut hundreds of miles off the old route to the Victoria River country, and thus saved many months of travel with stock. His book shows the lack of understanding and the ineptitude of many politicians and bureaucrats over the years, but also highlights the invaluable dedication of a few like Captain Bishop and Colonel Rose, who contributed greatly to the betterment of the cattle industry in the Northern Territory.

This book contains so much information and past history of the old stock route that it is very hard to highlight any one part as most interesting. The photos of the old watering places and 'bagman's gazette'; the old aboriginal history and stories of the first explorers; the first settlers and poddy dodgers all make fascinating reading. As in all books of this era there are the trials and tribulations and deaths of the pioneers.

It is a fact of life that none of us last forever and there are not many of us ex-boss drovers left who actually walked cattle down the Murranji. Pic Willetts and Twenty one Simpson whom I mentioned previously are both still in the land of the living, as are a number of our old ex-ringers including Benny Trindle, Luric Sowden, 'Bomber' Stacey, Keith Luscombe, Peter Costello and Eugene Kostin, and possibly many others of whom I have completely lost track. If not for people like Darrell putting this history on record much of it would very soon be lost forever. I consider this well-researched history of the places, people and events on the Murranji of great importance and a lasting memorial to the Murranji drovers. Once again I congratulate Darrell on a good job well done and hope all readers enjoy this book as much as I have.

Ian McBean
Bonalbo Station
Douglas Daly N T
January 2007

ACKNOWLEDGEMENTS

I first began research into the history of the Murranji Track in the early 1980s, but a survey of historic sites along the track which I carried out for the Australian National Trust (NT) in 1991 gave a great boost to this research. In the course of this survey I was introduced to the track by three Mudbura men – Nuggett Kiriyalangungu, Tobacco Jack, and Long Captain Marajala, and since then I have spoken with various men and women who were Murranji drovers, or who drove transport vehicles along the track, or who lived on stations in the region. These people shared their stories with me, and in many instances allowed me to copy their private collections of photographs or documents.

Among the former drovers I spoke with were Bill Cussens, Noel 'Pic' Willets (who took the last mob across the Murranji), Edna Jessop (nee Zigenbine), Ian McBean (who later became owner-manager of Bradshaw, Coolibah and Innesvale stations), Eugene Kostin, Reg Hart, Rodney Watson, Scotty Watson, Mick Coombes, Kelly Dixon, Charlie Yeeda, Dick Scobie (who was also the pioneer and owner-manager of Hidden Valley station on the Murranji) and Charlie Schultz (who drove cattle across the Murranji a number of times and was also the owner-manager of Humbert River station).

Betty Burrowes, whose father Charlie Phillott took the sixth mob of cattle across the Murranji, kindly provided me with a copy of a photo of her father's droving team on its way out to VRD in 1903. Marie Mahood, who in the 1950s was a correspondent for *Hoofs & Horns* magazine, the storekeeper on VRD in 1950, and with her husband Joe was pioneer of Mongrel Downs in the Tanami, shared her photos with me, as did Bert Mettam, a former policeman who was based at Timber Creek in the 1950s and who was a regular contributor to *Hoofs & Horns* magazine under the pen name 'John Stockman'. The legendary Edna Jessop, Emily Pankhurst, Charlie Schultz, Ros Fraser, Ernie and Pauline

Rayner, Joyce Scobie and Maggie Lilly all provided photos from their private collections.

Others I spoke with who had strong connections to the Murranji were Sid Hawkes, who opened the Top Springs store in the early 1950s and thus developed a good knowledge of the Murranji; Mick Bower, who was a ringer on Birrindudu, Nicholson, Limbunya, Nutwood Downs and Manbulloo, and who did a droving trip across the Murranji in 1955 with Mick Cussens; Syd Jones, who drove transport trucks across the Murranji in the 1950s; and Dave Napier, a former stock inspector who was based at Top Springs and who gave me several of the original Drover's Schedules. One of these is reproduced in this book, and the originals have since been deposited at the Northern Territory Archives.

As with almost all historical studies, the staff in various archives were most helpful, particularly Françoise Barr and Kathy Flint at the Northern Territory Archives and Wendy Tabrett at the Stockman's Hall of Fame in Longreach. Vern O'Brien, former Director of the Northern Territory Lands Department and Stuart Duncan at the Office of the Placenames Committee in Darwin both assisted with maps and documents, as did Greg Coleman at the Department of Primary Industries and Fisheries in Alice Springs, who in 1991 gave me access to a number of important files of Murranji documents.

Others who contributed in various ways were David Nash, a linguist, and historian of the northern Tanami, and Stan Jones, manager of Gordon Downs from 1954 to 1964. And last but not least, my thanks go, as usual, to my wife, Deborah Rose, who gave her love, support, advice, and companionship on many a bush trip into the Murranji country, and elsewhere. She has always been and continues to be an inspiration, and this book would not have been the same without her.

PART ONE

The Birth & Death of the Track

INTRODUCTION

'OUT ON THE MURRANJI'

Wild dogs howl and hedge-wood groans,
A night wind whistles in semitones,
And bower-birds play with human bones
Under a vacant sky.
The drover's mob is a cloud of dust,
The drover's mob is a sacred trust
Where devil says 'Can't!' and God says
'Must!'
Out on the Murran-ji.

Hedge-wood writhes in the dark o' night,
Ant-hills glimmer a ghostly white,
The cattle are galloping mad with fright
From where the dead men lie.
The drover's mob is a fateful trust,
The life of a ringer less than dust,
When God says 'Can't!' and the Devil says
'Must!'
Out on the Murran-ji.[1]

The Murranji: a waterhole, a track, a region – a legend. For some a place of strange beauty,[2] for others, a 'sinister soundless scrub'.[3] Home for Aborigines for thousands of years, but a place of dread for white Australian travellers of little more than a century. The Murranji wasn't particularly long – only 240 kilometres – but of all the hard stockroutes in Australia it gained one of the fiercest reputations, and became known to early drovers as the 'Death Track'[4] or the 'Suicide Track'.[5]

Great 'jungles' of dense bulwaddy and lancewood scrub made it difficult to control cattle as they passed through.[6] 'Drummy' ground, prowling dingoes, weird sounds made by branches rubbing together when the wind blew and, in the early days, attack by Aborigines, all combined to make the cattle nervous. If they rushed (stampeded) it was almost impossible for drovers to head them, and they risked serious injury or even death if they tried. Bouts of fever were common and until the bores were put down the waters were unreliable – some of the great dry stages in Australian droving history occurred on the Murranji.

The story of the Murranji stockroute is a story of determination in the face of neglect and indifference. For years requests were made for the Government to provide water supplies, to clear the scrub, to wipe out poisonous plants, to establish stock reserves, and for years nothing was done. Meanwhile, the drovers kept droving. When water was finally provided there was constant neglect of the bore facilities. Requests for the water supply to be upgraded and for other improvements were frequent; droughts came and went, bores broke down, cattle rushed, reports were written and recommendations were made, but as ever, improvements were painfully slow to come.

Through it all, in spite of it all, the drovers took their cattle across the Murranji, and beyond. Ironically, sixty-odd years after the first big herds moved eastwards along the Murranji and only a few years after the last major improvements were established, the droving era ended. Possibly a million cattle walked across the Murranji Track. Now, only the worn out bores, and the story, remain. Today there are relatively few Australians who have visited the region and although renowned in outback folklore – 'the Ghost Road of the Drovers'[7] – most wouldn't know where it is.

Considering its legendary significance, the Murranji waterhole (or waterholes) is relatively insignificant. It's not some large, deep, lily-covered and pandanus-lined tropical oasis abounding with fish, turtles and crocodiles. J. K. Little who rode the Murranji Track in 1897 described it as a 'soup-basin depression'[8] while popular author Ernestine Hill, ever quick to paint a dramatic word picture, described it as, 'no more than rain-water shallows in grey clay, seventy yards across…Rimming the waters are wizard box-trees hundreds of years old, mal-formed dwarfs of the kindly coolibah, and their snaky reflections'[9] (plates 1 & 2). Echoing Hill's account, George Farwell, who visited the waterhole in about 1950, was of the opinion that, 'To call it a waterhole is almost an act of courtesy,'[10] and he described it as,

> *three smallish depressions, ringed about by stout but extremely dwarf coolibahs. Their tortured shapes seem almost to have acquired a living expression of the tragedies they have witnessed in sixty or more years. It is by no means an idyllic scene, even when the Murranji is full. Empty, as we saw it, the place has an oppressive atmosphere, with the crowded ranks of dwarf coolibahs, the dead limbs and trunks on its bare grey bed, and no sound of birds.*[11]

The Murranji *Track* is easily defined. It extends from Top Springs in the north-west to Newcastle Waters in the south-east to – 145 miles in the old measure – but defining the Murranji *region* isn't so easy. Its east-west dimensions are clear, but to the north and south the borders are ill-defined. For the purposes of this book I've chosen to define the north-south extent of the Murranji region as the area covered with the dense lancewood[12] and bulwaddy[13] 'scrubs' that give the Murranji Track its distinctive character (plates 3 & 4).

Some fifty kilometres to the south of the Track, this 'dismal dreary forest' of explorer Stuart's experience[14] gradually blends into the almost limitless sand plains and scrubs of the Tanami Desert. Forty or fifty kilometres to the north, the bulwaddy-lancewood country is gradually replaced by the dry open savanna-woodlands that are dominant in the higher rainfall 'Top End' of the Territory.

CHAPTER 1

THE MURRANJI THROUGH THE AGES

Key features of the present-day Murranji are relative flatness, scarcity of surface water, and in particular the extensive swathes of bulwaddy-lancewood scrub. For those who've never seen these thickets, George Farwell provides a graphic description:

> *No one who has not seen the bullwaddi [sic] can appreciate its savage nature. It spreads its many upward-growing limbs very close to the ground, and is so tough you can never bend it, and can break it only when it is close to dying. Its branches have spikes like iron that cut deep into flesh and can impale a beast rash enough to collide with it at speed. It is not a tree, but something out of a medieval torture chamber! Ask any drover who has had to ride after cattle that have rushed through that scrub, and his descriptions will be rather more exhaustive and lurid than this. The lancewood, despite its name, is not so aggressive. It is a thin, straight-growing acacia, almost as slender as a tribesman's spear, but again it grows so thickly as to make the passage of a mob of cattle difficult*[15]

Take away the bulwaddy and lancewood, and the Murranji would've been no more difficult, or legendary, than many other inland stockroutes. From time immemorial the Murranji has been flat and relatively waterless, but it hasn't always supported the same mosaic of arid woodland and grassland seen there today.

The most comprehensive environmental reconstruction for this part of Australia is that of the geomorphologist, Jim Bowler.[16] His studies have found that between about 60,000 and 40,000 years ago Lake Woods, on the south-eastern side of the Murranji, was more than ten times larger than it is today, evidence that rainfall in the region was much greater than at present. In fact, Lake Woods was then one of the largest freshwater lakes in the world. It may have begun to shrink about 35,000 years ago and by about 20,000 years ago it was dry.

Drying out of the region was a response to the onset of the last ice age when vast amounts of the world's water were trapped in great ice-sheets, and sea levels were much lower. At this time conditions in Australia were generally cooler and drier; the desert core of the continent was bigger and more arid, and major vegetation zones were pushed outwards.[17] Continental Australia was then much larger and the Murranji, now about 300 kilometres inland, was 700 to 800 kilometres from the coast.[18] At this time the Murranji region would've been a very fierce place indeed. It was probably completely waterless and covered with arid shrublands, grasslands and spinifex, and the bulwaddy and lancewood scrubs that now characterise the region probably grew far to the north.

As the ice age ended and the world warmed, wetter conditions returned. By about 10,000 or 12,000 years ago the climate was probably much like that of today and it's remained fairly stable since then, so the particular ecosystem now seen in the Murranji is likely to be up to 10,000 years old.

Much of the Murranji region is flat, almost featureless country – the Sturt Plateau[19] composed of plains and undulating hills so low that in the areas covered with the bulwaddy and lancewood scrubs, views are almost non-existent. From Sturt Plain, an extensive area of open grassland on the south-east end of the Murranji (plate 5), several watercourses – Bucket Creek, Ross Creek and Goocheegoochena Creek – flow south into Newcastle Creek and on into Lake Woods. The western edge of the dense bulwaddy-lancewood country is marked by a 'jump-up',[20] a sudden change in the level of the country (plate 6). The stretch of country between the Sturt Plain and the jump-up is the heartland of the Murranji – largely waterless, featureless, and home to the densest thickets of lancewood and bulwaddy. In this area there are only short creeks which peter out within a few kilometres.

West of the jump-up the topography and vegetation changes dramatically. There, a maze of creeks combines to form Armstrong Creek which drains low country at the head of the Victoria River. Instead of relatively flat terrain there's stony, broken sandstone and limestone country. By the time Top Springs is reached about thirty kilometres from the jump-up, the bulwaddy and lancewood has given way to savanna grasslands, and the flat-topped hills and black-soil basalt country that characterise much of the Victoria River district.

The Murranji region straddles the interface between the wet monsoonal coastal zone and the drier inland desert country. The monsoon rains arrive in summer, a period of extreme humidity and extreme heat, while winter is usually completely dry. The position of the Murranji means that fluctuations in intensity of rainfall or shifts in the north-south extent of the monsoon cause considerable variations in annual rainfall. Whether the rains are massive or meagre is of little consequence to natural water supplies. Apart from extremely short-lived waters that appear immediately after rainfall – shallow claypans or gilgais – there are very few surface waters on the Murranji and none of them are permanent. For six to eight months of the year the Murranji is virtually waterless, and during this time it constitutes an arid forest.

CHAPTER 2

ABORIGINES

Very little is known about Aboriginal occupation of the Murranji in the times before European settlement. Flakes and stone tools – spearheads, adzes and grindstones – can be found on surface scatters throughout the region, but most of these are of types known to date from within the past 3-5000 years.[21] Aboriginal occupation of the Murranji is, of course, likely to have occurred much earlier than 5000 years ago. To the north there's evidence that people have been living continuously in Arnhem Land for about 50,000 years,[22] while to the south there's evidence for human occupation of Central Australia up to 25,000 years ago during the intensely arid conditions that existed at the height of the last glacial period.[23] Whether Aborigines in the Murranji region were able to survive there during the extreme conditions of 25,000 years ago remains to be determined, but it's probable that they have inhabited the area during wetter periods over an immensely long time – perhaps many tens of thousands of years.

Contrary to long-established belief among Europeans, the name Murranji doesn't refer to a water-holding desert frog[24] and it doesn't belong to the waterholes that now bear this name. According to Mudbura elders, Murranji Waterhole consists of a series of four main depressions, each with its own Aboriginal name – *Narlwan*, *Mulmulka*, *Panganyi* and *Pututji* – but all four names may be referred to collectively as *Narlwan*[25] or *Mulmulka*.[26] The word 'Murranji' doesn't exist in the Mudbura language. However, Mudbura elders say a small soak near No. 10 Bore is known as *Murruynjalangu*,[27] (more like Mooroonjalyoong to an untrained ear[28]), so 'Murranji' is almost certainly a European corruption of this name. It should be noted, however, that some neighbouring groups refer to Mudbura desert country in terms of *kajangarna*, the burrowing frog[29] ('*wartaanji*' in Mudbura language[30]), so it's likely that confusion has arisen between the name of the waterhole, the soak, and the 'country of the burrowing frog'. However it happened, the name 'Murranji' is now firmly fixed as the name of the waterholes. Most white people pronounce the name 'Mah-ran-jie' though 'Moor-an-jie' would perhaps be more appropriate and indeed, some elderly long-term white residents of the Victoria River country say it this way, perhaps influenced by hearing Aborigines pronounce the name.

European records from the first century of settlement provide little more than a fragmentary and sometimes inaccurate picture of Aboriginal society in the Murranji country. However, land claims lodged under the Northern Territory's *Aboriginal Land Rights Act (1976)* led to a number of intensive studies in the 1970s and early 1980s,[31] and combined with studies of Aboriginal groups elsewhere, these provide a reasonable understanding of traditional life in the Murranji.

At European contact most of the Murranji was occupied by people speaking the Mudbura language. Another language group, the Jingili, occupied a small part of the region in the east and north-east. These language-groups appear to have shared virtually identical cultural systems and as the Mudbura occupied the greater part of the Murranji, including all of the Murranji Track, discussion is restricted to this group.

Mudbura people speak a language that is the most eastern member of the Ngumbin sub-group of languages, and the most northern of the large Nyungic group of languages common to a large part of the Northern Territory and most of Western Australia, including the Western Desert.[32] They are divided into three clans distinguished by minor differences of dialect, and inhabiting three distinctive habitats – the *Pujurruny* people of the eastern Murranji stockroute (Sturt Plateau), the *Kuuja* (limestone) people from the limestone country on the upper reaches of the Armstrong, Townshend and Cattle Creeks, and the *Yalarra* people who lived on the eastern banks of the Victoria River south of Armstrong Creek.

Through thousands of years of collective hunter-gathering experience the Mudbura came to possess an intimate knowledge of their country, a knowledge that enabled them to survive in a difficult and seasonally harsh region. They probably followed a pattern of land use common in arid Australia; when rains replenished soaks and filled ephemeral waters they would've scattered throughout the region to exploit otherwise inaccessible resources. As these waters dried up they would've retreated to longer-lasting waters and, in extreme circumstances, probably fell back on permanent water bodies such as those at Newcastle Waters, Top Springs or the Victoria River.

Mudbura country was crisscrossed with footpaths or 'pads', observed and in many cases used by early Europeans in the area.[33] Apart from the few semi-permanent waterholes, the Mudbura knew locations where water could be obtained from soaks (*nankuna*) and trees (*karrinpiri*).[34] The best description of the soaks or wells in Murranji country is provided by Billy Linklater, who was in the region in the very early 1900s:

> *They used to dig these wells with sticks and their naked hands, and made a sort of a ramp down which they could walk to the water… They had a crude but effective way of timbering them and always removed the soil dug out and scattered it over a wide area at some distance from the well. In an area distinguished chiefly for its aridity it paid to make any water supply as inconspicuous as possible.*[35]

These wells were usually covered with branches and grass to keep out animals and birds, and as Linklater suggests the shafts sometimes were angled to make access easier, and to prevent evaporation from the sun shining directly on the water[36] (plate 7).

Mudbura Aborigines say that trees holding water can be identified at night-time because something they describe as 'like lightning' hovers or flashes over them. Once this is seen people can go there the next morning and cut into the base of the tree to access the water.[37] Bill Harney learnt about these 'water trees' from Jingili people, and later published the following description of how the trees collected water and how they were located and used by Aborigines:

> *This Karimbi [sic] is really rainwater that has been caught during the rain time through an opening at the tree fork, generally of a bloodwood tree, and over the years it has accumulated till as much as fifty gallons of water can be tapped from a single tree. The method of detecting the water is first to tear the bark off each side of the tree: then, with the ear pressed close to one side, a hard rap is given to the opposite side with a stone. Should water be in the tree a gurgling noise is made by sound waves passing through the water to the ear, but if no water is within a hollow sound is given out.*
>
> *When Karimbi is found a small hole at a knot place is made, and out of this a stream of water, slightly woody if it has been there a long time, will flow, to be always plugged up again after use so that it may be conserved for the future.*[38]

With their intimate knowledge of the location of these trees and their skill at finding them the Aborigines could, if they desired, travel long distances in the driest of times. In 1913 when all surface waters in the Murranji country were dry a group of Aborigines travelled over 150 kilometres from Daly Waters to the Top Springs area, and on the trek they 'subsisted on water got out of hollow trees.'[39]

In common with many Aboriginal groups elsewhere, Mudbura people believe that the present 'shape' of the physical and social world was established by 'Dreamings', creative beings that were active during a time referred to today as the 'Dreaming'. Some Dreamings were active in localised areas while others travelled great distances across the land. Whether localised or travelling, it was these beings who provided the pattern for all aspects of life, including social organisation, regional rituals, and trade and marriage relationships. They also left signs of their presence on the landscape. Particular trees, rocks, waterholes, open swathes through the scrub, and so forth, are believed to have been created by one or another of these beings and to still retain that being's creative power.[40] Being arid country, many Murranji Dreaming sites are places where water can be found. Such places attracted Europeans and Aborigines alike, so many European historic sites are also Aboriginal Dreamings and archaeological sites.[41]

The distribution of sites created by localised Dreamings provided the basis for clan organisation. The Mudbura were and still are divided into patrilineal clans that are identified with and responsible for sites within particular areas of land. People trace their ancestry through their parents and grandparents to the ancestral beings believed to have created these sites. The sharing of common ancestry is the basis of clan membership.

Travelling Dreamings provide the common element linking the different clans, and on a broader scale, linking different language groups; all members of all the 'countries' through which a Dreaming passes share a relationship with that Dreaming and, therefore, with each other. Among the major travelling Dreamings that pass through the Murranji from the west are the 'Two quiet snakes', Galah, and Storm bird.[42]

Spiritual affiliation to land is most obvious in people's relationship to Dreaming sites which include almost every natural feature – trees, waterholes, soaks, rocks, creeks, etc. In addition to group affiliations there are also personal affiliations. For example, during the Murranji land claim a number of bulwaddy trees were identified by claimants as 'name trees' for particular individuals.[43] That is, particular trees and particular individuals possess the same name and are related through Dreaming.

Before Europeans settled in the region Mudbura people made regular and widespread use of fire. Explorer Stuart in the early 1860s made constant reference to distant smoke, burnt areas and actual fires lit by the Aborigines.[44] Apart from the use of fire as a weapon against enemies (including European explorers) and for warmth, light and cooking, it was used to assist in hunting and inter-group communication. Fire was probably important in maintaining the open areas around and within the bulwaddy-lancewood scrub. Indeed, it's been suggested that much of the open grassland encountered by the explorers and early settlers in many parts of Australia was the product of millennia of Aboriginal burning.[45] This traditional burning didn't suit the early settlers who wanted the grass preserved for their cattle, and their attempts to stop the Aborigines from firing the country was probably a major reason for conflicts erupting.

In the Newcastle Waters area Aborigines resisted the arrival of the whites and their cattle in their lands (plates 8 & 9). One of Stuart's men shot and wounded an Aboriginal man who attacked him near Newcastle Waters in May 1861.[46] When the overland telegraph line was constructed in 1871-72 Aborigines twice attacked travellers at Newcastle Waters,[47] and hostilities were such that the telegraph station at Powell's Creek was built of stone, without windows but with loopholes for rifle fire.[48]

There was another attack on travellers at Newcastle Waters in 1875,[49] and in August 1883 a teamster was murdered at Lawson Springs, immediately south of Newcastle Waters.[50] Three weeks later a party of settlers and police set out in search of the teamster's killers and thirty-five kilometres 'east by north' from Newcastle Waters the party was attacked by up to seventy Aborigines. No whites were injured, but at least two Aborigines were believed to have been severely wounded before all of them escaped into an area of bulwaddy scrub.[51]

News of these fights, woundings and killings, and of conflicts in neighbouring regions would quickly have spread to Aborigines throughout the Murranji region, and created a universal attitude of hostility towards all Europeans. At the Yellow Waterholes in 1897, 'prowling natives threw a two-pronged wire spear amongst the horses' belonging to two travelers. The spear hit the best horse in the mob of twenty-three, and injured it so badly that it had to be shot.[52] In his old age Billy Linklater recalled that in 1900 Aborigines at the Yellow Waterholes attacked 'Mulga Jim' McDonald and another man named Hardcastle. According to Linklater, Hardcastle was speared in the chest, but lived for another two years before succumbing to the effects of the wound.[53] Linklater also recalled an incident at the Yellow Waterholes in 1894 when 'Some packers from the Cook Town country' escaped a shower of spears unharmed.[54] Linklater himself was attacked 'about twenty miles west of the Yellow Waterholes.' Camping out one night with Jim Campbell from Illawarra station, Aborigines threw spears into their mosquito nets. Both men escaped unharmed because they'd suspected an attack and spent the night sleeping away from their nets.[55]

Once the Aborigines learnt that spears and boomerangs were no match for rifles they kept to the desert country outside the Newcastle Waters lease, but whenever the waters they were using failed they had no choice but to come in to the permanent waters on the station. When this happened they hid themselves in camps in the Ashburton Range and speared cattle as opportunity allowed.[56] To try and prevent the cattle spearing, towards the end of the 1890s station manager Steve Lewis encouraged the Aborigines to camp near the homestead, and gave them an occasional 'worthless beast'.[57] However, M.A. Radford, who was manager by 1902, believed this policy had failed because cattle were still being speared. When Aborigines came in from the desert towards the end of 1902 he tried to get them to go to the Powells Creek telegraph station where they'd be given Government rations. Some went but Radford noted that, 'there are some which the brightest vision of free flour will not, for some reason draw them down there, so I thought it best to let them remain where they are hoping for early rains to take them back to their old haunts.'[58] He warned them not to kill or disturb the cattle and apparently they heeded him, probably because, for reasons which are unknown, one of them had recently been shot dead by Mounted Constable Kean.[59] When the rains finally arrived Radford ordered the blacks back into the desert.[60]

In the Victoria River region and at Elsey station to the north-east, station camps were established by 1902-1905.[61] Radford was replaced as manager by mid-1904 and it's likely that the new manager, Harry Grainger, established similar camps on Newcastle Waters around this time. By the time large-scale droving began along the track the dangers of Aboriginal attack probably had diminished because the majority of Mudbura people were living in station camps and learning to work for the whites.

Some people chose to remain in the bush, out of fear of the whites or for other reasons, and during each summer wet season when station work was suspended the station Aborigines were free to go 'walkabout', perhaps to join their bush relations. Bill Harney claimed that some of those who stayed in the bush managed to take advantage of their status as traditional owners of the land to gain access to desired European goods. According to Bill, 'On the Murranji track, many years ago, the Mudbura aborigines with their families lived beside each main water and levied tribute from the aboriginal stockmen and drovers who passed that way.' He also described a ritual in which the local people 'introduced' Aboriginal stockmen from other tribal groups to the country to prevent them becoming sick or dying.[62] Similar rituals are still practiced today in various parts of the Top End.[63]

The last bush people 'came in' during the 1930s,[64] but until relatively recently Mudbura people regularly walked across the Murranji country to Victoria River Downs (VRD) during the wet season to fulfill ceremonial obligations, visit relations, obtain or give wives and to exchange trade goods.[65] The goods they traded included spear and knife blades of stone, quarried near Newcastle Waters, hooked and conventional boomerangs cut from bulwaddy branches on the Murranji, and goods from other areas such as red ochre quarried on Banka Banka station. These items were exchanged for bamboo spear shafts from the Daly River region and pearl shells from the Kimberley coast, all of which were carried back to be used or traded in turn with groups further inland.

While the 'footwalk' days are over, the traditional relationships are still functioning. Mudbura people have strong marriage ties with Victoria River communities, and make regular visits by motor vehicle to stay with relations and to perform rituals including young men's initiation (*Marntiwa*) and 'Big Sunday' (*Kajirri*). In addition, they still make boomerangs which they trade with VRD people for bamboo spear shafts[66] (plate 10).

CHAPTER 3

THE FIRST WHITE MEN

Aborigines were, unequivocally, the original pioneers of the Murranji Track. It was Aborigines who found the keys to the Murranji – the ephemeral waterholes, the soakages, and the places where wells could tap deeper underground supplies – and it was Aborigines who discovered the most well-hidden waters of all, the reservoirs of the precious fluid trapped inside hollow trees.

When Europeans set out to explore beyond the frontiers they were entering what was to them a blank space beyond the edge of the known world, almost a physical and mental void. To the Aboriginal inhabitants intimately acquainted with local flora, fauna, topographic features and climatic conditions, this 'blank space' was the centre of the world. For them, it was the Europeans who were the unknown. Courageous as the European explorers undoubtedly were, they were following in the footsteps, often literally, of the Aborigines. This isn't to detract from the achievement of the first Europeans to make the crossing who, looked at in their own context, were brave, tough men. But it *is* undeniably the case that thousands of years before Europeans first probed the fringe of the Murranji, Aborigines had explored the region, adapted to its particular conditions, adapted it in turn, and made it their home.

In 1855-56, A.C. Gregory led a party to trace the course of the Victoria River.[67] His expedition travelled west and north of the Murranji country and didn't encounter the dense bulwaddy and lancewood scrubs of that region. That pleasure was left for John McDouall Stuart in 1861 and 1862. Stuart set himself the task of crossing the continent from south to north and made three attempts before achieving his goal.[68] In the vicinity of Lake Woods during his second trip (1861) he discovered 'a small-leaved tree much resembling the hawthorn, spreading out into many branches from the root; it rises to upwards of twenty feet in height.'[69] This new tree, 'as thick as a hedge',[70] was initially known to Europeans as 'hedgewood' but eventually became known as 'bulwaddy'.[71] Together with lancewood it forms the dense thickets that characterise much of the Murranji country. Stuart encountered one of these thickets the next day. His attempt to pass through it was a failure and he described how,

> *The scrub we were compelled to return from was the thickest I have ever had to contend with. The horses would not face it. They turned about in every direction, and we were in danger of losing them. In two or three yards they were quite out of sight. In the short distance we penetrated it has torn our hands, faces, clothes, and, what is of more consequence, our saddle-bags, all to pieces. It consists of scrub of every kind, which is as thick as a hedge.*[72]

A week later Stuart discovered and named Newcastle Waters on the south-eastern edge of Murranji. During the next month he tried to find a way north-west to the Victoria River, but came up against waterless bulwaddy-lancewood scrubs time and again. Each scrub seemed worse than the last, and he grew to hate them. His descriptions of the difficulties of travelling through the Murranji bush are the most graphic on record and they almost certainly became the basis for the later European view of the Murranji as a dangerous, forbidding region. They are worth quoting on both counts. Beginning on May 30th 1861, Stuart wrote that,

> *We went into a terrible thick wood and scrub for eleven miles and a half, without the least sign of a change – the scrub, in fact, becoming more dense; it is scarcely penetrable... Nothing to be seen but a fearfully dense scrub all round.*[73]

On June 10th:

> *From here the country seems to be a dense forest and scrub... The whole journey...has been through a dense forest of scrubs of all kinds – hedge-tree, gum, mulga, lancewood, &c. We have had great difficulty in forcing the horses through it so far; they are very tired. It is the thickest scrub I have yet been in... I fully expected to have got water to-night from the recent rains, but there is not a drop.*[74]

June 11th:

> *we again entered the forest thicker than ever. At eleven miles it became so dense that it was nearly impenetrable. The horses would not face it; when forced, they made a rush through, tearing everything we had on, and wounding us severely by running against the dead timber (which was as sharp as a lancet) and through the branches... Not a drop of water have we seen*[75]

June 12th:

> *This is the third long journey by which I have tried to make the Victoria in this latitude, but have been driven back every time by the same description of country and the want of water. There is not the least appearance of rising ground, or a change in the country – nothing but the same dismal, dreary forest throughout; it may in all probability continue to Mr Gregory's last camp on the Camfield.*[76]

June 14th:

> *We then entered a thick wooded country, of the same description as the western forest, being equally thick, if not thicker, and as difficult to penetrate... Not a drop of water have we seen since leaving Newcastle Water, a distance of about thirty miles, except a little rain water about three miles east of it.*[77]

June 15th:

> *Started at 7.30 am... through another ten miles of very thick forest, the thickest we have yet seen... It has been very heavy travelling, over rotten ground, and tearing through a thick wood and scrub, which has skinned our legs from the knees to the ankles and caused no little pain.*[78]

On June 16th 1861 Stuart decided make a final attempt to get to the Victoria River by skirting the southern edge of the dense waterless bush. He later reported that, 'This is very disheartening work. I shall proceed to the south, and try once more to round that horrid thick western forest; it is now my only hope; if that fail I shall have to return.'[79] He failed. Forced back by extremely dense bush and lack of water, Stuart conceded defeat and returned to Adelaide.

In 1862 on his third and successful attempt to cross the continent, Stuart travelled north of Newcastle Waters, reaching and naming Frew's Waterhole, Howells Ponds and Nash Spring.[80] From these waters he again tried to cut north-west to the Victoria River, including a foray thirty kilometres north-west of Nash Spring which must have taken him fairly close to Murranji Waterhole,[81] but each of his attempts failed because of dense scrub and lack of water. Eventually he gave up trying and instead skirted the eastern edge of the Murranji country, and continued northwards to reach the coast at Van Diemens Gulf.[82]

When Stuart and his men first reached Newcastle Waters and began trying to get through to the Victoria River they found signs of Aborigines wherever they went – distant smokes,[83] footprints,[84] abandoned campsites,[85] marked trees[86] and tree burials.[87] On several occasions Stuart followed Aboriginal footpads, hoping they'd lead to water and perhaps reveal the way through the dense scrub,[88] and at least once this strategy paid off. Heading west from Howell Ponds on May 8th 1862 Stuart,

> *struck a native track, followed it, running nearly north-west, until nearly 3 o'clock p.m. when we came upon a small water hole or opening in the middle of a small plain, which seems to have been dug by the natives, and is now full of rain water. This is apparently the water that the natives pointed to, for their tracks are coming into it from every direction.*[89]

Occasionally the explorers met the Aborigines themselves who were sometimes friendly and sometimes hostile.[90] For example, at Newcastle Waters on May 26th 1861 'seven natives, tall, powerfully made fellows' were at first threatening, then friendly, and then later attacked one of Stuart's men who was out alone duck hunting. In defending himself this man was forced to shoot and wound one of his attackers.[91] Strangely, the following year at Nash Spring some of Stuart's men 'had been visited by the natives…They were hugging Frew and King, for whom they seemed to have taken a great fancy; they were old, young and children.'[92]

The only other explorer to go anywhere near the Murranji region was Alexander Forrest.[93] On his way from the Kimberleys to the overland telegraph line in 1879, Forrest passed about 130 kilometres north of the future Murranji Track. He didn't encounter the 'horrid forest' that obstructed Stuart, and during the last three days before he arrived at the telegraph line, he described the country as,

> *one vast level plain, fairly grassed, and thickly wooded with gums, acacia, and scrub. We came across numerous dry swamps... For eighty miles now, we have been travelling over country of the same description, all well-grassed, and the horizon as level as the sea. Here and there are a few clay swamps*

> *which no doubt hold water in the winter time, but today we have neither seen a drop of water, nor any place that would be likely to hold it for long*[94]

With the end of official exploration, discovering the secrets of the Murranji – its hidden waters and pathways – was left to the settlers, drovers and other travellers who were soon to flood into the new lands.

CHAPTER 4

PIONEERING THE TRACK

Work on the overland telegraph between Adelaide and Darwin began in 1870.[95] The line followed closely the route established by Stuart, and hard on the heels of the linesmen came the first settlers. For more than a decade European activity remained largely confined to the telegraph line, or to areas further to the east and south-east. Newcastle Waters wasn't stocked until 1883[96] so until this time Mudbura people could largely avoid contact with whites. Likewise, the Victoria River country wasn't stocked until 1883[97] and until then there was little incentive for white people to attempt to cross the Murranji.

A number of land-seeking and prospecting expeditions entered the Victoria River region before it was settled, including land seekers Sullivan and McDonald who examined the Victoria River, Sturt Creek and Hooker Creek country in 1878,[98] prospectors Saunders and Johns who crossed from west to east in 1882,[99] and another group of land seekers led by Billy O'Donnell who travelled east from Springvale (Katherine) in March 1883.[100] All these parties passed north or west of the Murranji region, close to the relatively well-watered route discovered by Gregory in 1856. On their return from examining Sturt Creek Sullivan and McDonald tried to head eastward to Powell Creek. They passed beyond the eastern end of Hooker Creek, but before they reached the Murranji country dry conditions forced them north, back to the Victoria River.

With the stocking of the Victoria there began a regular traffic into and out of the region. Initially, the only practicable route in or out from the telegraph line was via Katherine, more or less on the route used by Gregory, Sullivan and McDonald, Saunders and Johns, and O'Donnell. For travellers from South Australia or Queensland who were heading for the Victoria River or Kimberley, this involved a circuitous loop to the north. It was obvious that if a more direct route could be found, that is, a route through the 'horrid forest' between Newcastle Waters and the Victoria River headwaters, the distance could be reduced by hundreds of kilometres.

Like the explorers, the European pioneers of the Murranji also followed the footsteps of Aborigines. In fact, some went one step further and actively sought out local Aboriginal guides with the knowledge to lead them to water and access routes across the region. For example, one group of travellers, 'managed to find it [Murranji Waterhole] through following up the blacks' foot-pads.' When a group of Aborigines at the waterhole fled at their approach, two of the Europeans tracked them over thirty kilometres to a soakage where, 'they coaxed a boy to go with them...to act as guide'.[101]

The earliest documented European crossing of the country between Newcastle Waters and the Victoria River – not necessarily along on the future Murranji Track – was made in 1885 by two men, George Hedley (or Headley) and Morgan (or Moore),[102] who were heading for the newly discovered Kimberley goldfield.[103] Nothing is known about Morgan's background, but Hedley was an early drover who'd previously been involved in 'dispersing' Aborigines and who 'pioneered' an important track – long a major Aboriginal trade and walking route[104] – across the northern Barkly Tableland in about 1880.[105]

There are very few records of Hedley and Morgan's trip. One is in a series of articles Gordon Buchanan wrote in 1921-22 about his father, Nat Buchanan, later put together and published as *Packhorse and Waterhole*,[106] while the other is a brief item published in the *Northern Territory Times* in August 1885:

> *On June the 18th, Mr. G. R. Hedley and Mr. Morgan arrived here, having come direct overland from Charters Towers to Powell's Creek, and thence from North Newcastle to the Victoria River cattle station. They had a rather rough time of it coming over owing to the scarcity of water on several long stages. At one time they had to do seventy miles without water.*[107]

Whether Aborigines were involved with this crossing is unknown. Later in 1885, on his way to the Kimberley goldfields Barney Lamond attempted a crossing, probably somewhat to the south of the present Murranji Track.[108] Taking local Aborigines to guide him to soakages, almost all of which were dry, he was able to penetrate only 125 kilometres before lack of water drove him back. Lamond and his party then continued on via the conventional track through Katherine.

Several successful crossings were made the following year, including the first that clearly followed the major portion of what was later to become the Murranji Track. Gordon Buchanan in his book *Packhorse and Waterhole* correctly attributes the first crossing to Hedley, but incorrectly puts the date of the crossing as 1886.[109] He states that 'Greenhide' Sam Croker was the next over, making his crossing in about June 1886,[110] but it may be that Croker passed south of the Murranji.

Croker was a renowned bushman who'd been a member of W.O. Hodgkinson's 'Nor'-west Exploring Expedition' in Queensland in 1876-77.[111] Together with Nat 'Bluey' Buchanan he opened up the Barkly Tableland in 1877 and was one of the men who helped Bluey bring the first cattle from Queensland to Glencoe station in 1878-79.[112] In 1883 he was in charge of the first cattle taken onto Buchanan's Wave Hill station where he stayed on to become the first manager.[113] In 1892 while working as a stockman on Auvergne station he was shot dead by Charlie Flannigan,[114] a man of mixed European and Aboriginal descent who later achieved the dubious distinction of being the first man hanged in the Northern Territory.[115]

In 1886 Croker started out on the tracks of some cattle that had strayed south-east from Wave Hill. He followed them right through to the overland telegraph line 'aided by showers on the way',[116] but he made his crossing farther to the south than Hedley, where the 'hedgewood' wasn't as thick.[117] It's likely that Croker was aided or encouraged by knowledge of Hedley and Morgan's crossing, either from reading the newspaper account cited above, or from personal acquaintance, but he also had the help of Aborigines.

Writing in 1901 C. Hemphill, who'd stocked country in the Renner Springs area in the 1880s,[118] recalled that Sam Johnson (Sam Croker), 'mustering with two black-boys', followed some cattle across to Tomkinson Creek, just north of Tennant's Creek. He then 'took the cattle back to Wave Hill with others mustered at Corella Downs, Eva Downs, Anthony Lagoon, Buchanan Downs, and Newcastle Waters'. Hemphill remarked that, 'The whole secret was that Sam had blackboys who could show him the different waters without hesitation.'[119] There's a traditional Aboriginal walking route between Cattle Creek on Wave Hill station and Lake Woods on Newcastle Waters station, and it's been suggested that Croker's Aboriginal guides took him along this route.[120] With the cattle he'd followed from Wave Hill and the various strays he picked up on the tableland stations, Croker had about 150 head, and on his return trip he met his boss, Bluey Buchanan, at Powell Creek[121] (plate 11). Buchanan, one of Australia's most famous bushmen, spent almost his entire life opening up new country across half the continent.[122] With him when he met Croker were his son Gordon, Archie Ferguson (later fatally speared on

Lochnagar station in Queensland), Mick Barry and Willie Glass.[123] Buchanan and his men had just come across from Queensland with a hundred horses, bound for Wave Hill.

Some rain had fallen a few days earlier and for several mornings there'd been white frosts, so Croker and Buchanan's party decided to try to make a shortcut and get their livestock across the Murranji. With the assistance of local Aborigines they began their attempt in July 1886, and the following is a brief description of the trip, set down by Gordon Buchanan thirty-six years later:

> *A short camp was made between Frew's Pond and Newcastle, while Sam Croker made a preliminary investigation. Meeting some friendly blacks they took him to Murrinji [sic] Waterhole, about 50 miles out, and now for the first time visited by white men.*
>
> *The whole camp was then brought on in two days and a night, and after a short rest at Murrinji, the same blacks, having been well fed, piloted the party to the Yellow Waterholes, over another 50 miles' dry stage. Thence to Armstrong Creek, a tributary of the Victoria, was a short distance, so the blacks were rewarded and parted with. These were the first stock through this dry belt, and they opened up the Murrinji route*[124]

A few months after Buchanan's trip a party taking a mob of horses to the Kimberley goldfield also made it across the Murranji – or at least, the claim was made by one member of the group, Charles Goodliffe, sixty years after the event.[125] Apparently unaware of the previous crossings, Goodliffe believed he and his companions were the first whitemen to make the trip. Strangely, they didn't see the tracks of Buchanan's cavalcade which the records suggest included over 250 head of cattle and horses. Whatever might lie behind Goodliffe's 'oversight', and accepting that it is a true account, his is the most detailed description of a crossing made before the best route became common knowledge, and it illustrates the difficulties and dangers of seeking a path through the Murranji region when it was still effectively unknown to Europeans.

According to Goodliffe, the manager of Newcastle Waters showed his party a map which indicated a considerable saving in distance if they could travel to Halls Creek directly west of the station. He also told them he'd heard from local blacks about a desert waterhole called Murranji, and Goodliffe's party managed to find it by following Aboriginal footpads. While based at Murranji Waterhole they obtained local Aboriginal guides, and with them different members of the group then made forays to the west to try and find other waterholes. Even with guides, on several occasions these men were close to dying of thirst. Eventually Goodliffe, one of his men and an Aboriginal guide found a way through to a rockhole at the head of Armstrong Creek. They then returned to Murranji Waterhole and brought over the rest of the party and their mob of horses. The fact that they missed the Yellow Waterholes suggests that their guide didn't want to show them these holes, or that they were dry.

In later years two other names appeared in connection with claims of Murranji crossings *before* Hedley's trip of 1885. In 1905 Drover John 'Jack-Dick' Skuthorpe published a letter in the *Northern Territory Times* in which he claimed to have crossed the Murranji in June 1878 and made his way through what was then totally unsettled country to the mouth of Ord River.[126] Elsewhere he apparently claimed that a tree at the Murranji Waterhole marked 'JS' over '1878' and still to be seen there in 1905 had been marked by him when he made the crossing.

Skuthorpe doesn't appear to have provided a reason for his trip or named any associates who could verify his story.[127] At the time that he made his claim he was embroiled in a personal dispute via newspapers and magazines with Hely Hutchinson, a drover-cum-journalist from a well-known Queensland family who wrote under the pen-name 'H7H',[128] and who was in the Victoria River-Murranji region in 1905-06.[129] According to Hutchinson, Skuthorpe's story was debunked by Paddy Cahill, a very early resident of the Top End, a renowned buffalo hunter, and at the time manager of Delamere station north-west of the Murranji.[130] Cahill told Hutchinson that a man named Jack Scanlon had marked the tree at Murranji Waterhole in 1878 and had then continued west to the Victoria River. He said that Skuthorpe first saw the tree in 1904 and took advantage of the fact that he had the same initials as Scanlon to claim that he'd been there in 1878.[131]

There's no documentation for either Scanlon or Skuthorpe crossing the Murranji to the Victoria River country in 1878, but Skuthorpe had made such a claim well before 1905. In the *Australasian Pastoralists' Review* of February 1893 a 'country subscriber' said he'd bought an old horse from 'Relics' Skuthorpe who told him he'd 'ridden that horse and another out 1000 miles to Ord River, 200 miles up river, 150 miles down, spelled six weeks, and was only away a fortnight.'[132]

The epithet 'Relics' came from another rather dubious claim Skuthorpe had made years earlier. In 1881 he announced that in unsettled country west of Glenormiston station (Qld) he'd seen a tree marked 'L' and recovered the journals of the long-lost explorers Ludwig Leichhardt and Leichhardt's brother-in-law, Augustus Classen.[133] He sought a payment of £6000 for the journals, but the Queensland Government wouldn't agree to this until it had seen the journals.[134] In spite of considerable public pressure Skuthorpe never produced the journals and as a result was accused of fraud, labelled by one critic the 'champion truth-teller of Queensland',[135] and became known as 'Relics'.[136]

Leichhardt's journal aside, it should be noted that Skuthorpe could well have been in the Top End at an early date. In 1905 he claimed that thirty-two years earlier he'd helped D'arcy Uhr bring a mob of cattle to Palmerston (Darwin), which would've placed him in the Territory in about 1874.[137] D'arcy Uhr brought the first mob of cattle from Queensland to Palmerston (Darwin) in 1872 and was in Darwin in 1873 and 1874,[138] but there's no contemporary or near-contemporary documentation of him being associated with Skuthorpe at any time. Perhaps the most curious aspect of the entire story is the readiness with which Hely Hutchinson accepted Cahill's story about Scanlan while rejecting Skuthorpe's claim, rather than querying both.

CHAPTER 5

THE FIRST TWENTY YEARS

The crossings of Hedley and Morgan, Croker, and perhaps Goodliffe's party showed that it was possible to traverse the Murranji country, but it was the crossing made by Bluey Buchanan and Sam Croker that established the Murranji as a packhorse road. During the depression of the 1890s it wasn't economically viable to send cattle overland to the eastern states – if any had been sent it would've cost more to do so than the sale price received – so for eighteen years after the Murranji Track was established no cattle were sent east, and the Track was used almost exclusively by travellers rather than drovers.

When Buchanan and Croker set out to cross the Murranji in 1886, many miners were taking the conventional route to the newly opened Kimberley goldfield. Gordon Buchanan who was with his father on this trip later wrote that many of them passed their camp between Newcastle Waters and Frew's Pond on their way via the Katherine, with 'one and all predicting disaster to us by the shorter route,'[139] but once the Track was opened it was used 'by many diggers en route to the Halls Creek gold rush'.[140]

Early sources refer to the track as 'the old Kimberley diggings road'[141] or 'the old Kimberley Track',[142] which suggests that some of the heaviest traffic occurred during the first few years when miners were still rushing to the Halls Creek goldfields. Unfortunately, none of the miners appear to have left a record of their experiences on the Murranji, and other sources are similarly mute. The Kimberley rush subsided almost as fast as it began, but a small number of travellers continued to use the Track through the late 1880s and 1890s.

Within a year of the Track being opened wagons were taken over and these gave it greater definition. Other wagons followed, but the order of their crossing and whether some of them actually made the crossing at all is unclear. Writing in 1945 to Alf Martin, the manager of VRD, an early Victoria River stockman, Walter Rees, recalled that, 'Mulligan was the pioneer of wheel traffic from the telegraph line via Newcastle Waters, Murringi [sic] and Armstrong Ck to the Victoria.'[143] In an article in *Walkabout* magazine in 1950 Rees provided slightly more information: 'The first wheel traffic over the route from Newcastle Waters to Armstrong Creek was in 1887. John Mulligan, McCloskey and Dave McCoy brought teams across and opened the track.'[144]

The John Mulligan mentioned by Rees was a teamster who was in the Victoria River district by 1886, moving goods between the Victoria River Depot and VRD.[145] In 1895 he and another teamster, George Ligar, were involved in a famous incident in Jasper Gorge where they were attacked and badly wounded by Aborigines. Besieged at their wagons for two days, Mulligan and Ligar eventually abandoned the loading to their attackers and rode 100 kilometres to Auvergne station to get medical attention for their wounds.[146]

Rees's claim is in opposition to Ernestine Hill who claims that, 'A man named Prosser took "the first pair of wheels across" in 1887, a bullock-wagon.'[147] Hill goes on to say that 'Big Jim Kennedy from Camooweal took two wagons across and sold them to Mulligan'. In yet another account, in 1940 Billy Linklater claimed that the Murranji Track was opened for wheeled vehicles by Big Jim Kennedy who took two wagons across in 1891.[148] Linklater added that Landrighan and Cranwell crossed in 1894 with a wagon each, and then Tom Deacon crossed with two horse teams.

About six months after Deacon, and in days when white women and children were almost unheard of in the north, Joe Bridge, his wife Deborah and their three children travelled from Normanton to Halls Creek in a covered wagon.[149] They crossed the Murranji in 1895 and sixty years afterwards an account of their experiences was published in *The Quirindi Advocate*. Crossing the Murranji is said to have been,

> *a nightmare of 220 miles. In the mornings, when Joe Bridge was away mustering the horses, the wife and three children would get into the waggon; Mabel [the eldest daughter] would have the gun, Mrs Bridge would not touch it, so the 12-year-old girl had to be prepared to defend the family should they be attacked by blacks whilst the father was absent.*[150]

By way of interest, in 1921 a 'sectional committee of public works' travelling by motor car attempted to drive across 'Murray's track' from Wave Hill, 'but found it quite impassable for even a dray, so had to return to the Katherine,' their cars 'badly strained over the rough tracks'.[151] Two years later Michael Terry and his mate Dick Yockney drove a car across from the Newcastle Waters side, and found 'a sort of general avenue had been cleared through the scrub' (plates 12 & 13). Going down the jump-up was very difficult though within a year or two a cutting was put in which made negotiating it much easier.[152] They made their crossing in 1923 during a privately funded adventure trip across northern Australia.[153]

Although the Murranji Track is now remembered primarily as a stockroute, with a few exceptions its discovery came too late to be of much use in stocking the western stations. This had largely been accomplished between 1883 and 1886, and in any case, the unreliability and wide spacing of the waterholes severely reduced the attractiveness of the Murranji route.

The exceptions or possible exceptions are as follows. In July 1887 eighty-three bulls purchased by VRD from Lawn Hill and Mayvale stations (Qld) were reported to be at Powells Creek and about 'to take the new road to the Victoria station, straight out, instead of having to go round by the Roper.'[154] Denison Downs station on Sturt Creek was taken up by William Stretch, Lewers, Weekes and J.S. Foster in 1887, and they set out the following year from Normanton, Queensland, with 750 head to stock the station. On the 1700 kilometre trek they lost about 200 head from redwater fever,[155] and according to Hely Hutchinson they travelled their cattle over the Murranji Track.[156] Years later this claim was confirmed by Tom Traine who said he'd acted as their guide.[157]

In 1889 Walter Gordon overlanded 1400 head of cattle from Queensland to Lilamoora station in west Kimberley, losing one third of the mob from tick fever while crossing the Northern Territory.[158] It's unknown whether these cattle were taken across the Murranji, but if there was water on the Track this is quite likely. A man named McDonald purchased 1000 bullocks from Newcastle Waters station in 1892, 'for Western Australia'.[159] Whether these were taken across the Murranji is unknown, though this seems likely.

In 1899 the firm of Connor, Doherty and Durack (CD&D) set itself up as an agent to buy east Kimberley and Victoria River cattle to supply the expanding southern goldfields market.[160] M.P. Durack set out to organise purchases for the company, and this included travelling over the Murranji to Newcastle Waters to seek cattle there. He bought 672 head from that station and sent them back over the Murranji in charge of Drover Fred Mork[161] (plate 14).

Mork was an 'ace drover' who'd been on many epic droving trips, including with Buchanan on his big cattle drive from Queensland to the Territory in 1881,[162] and a trip with D'arcy Uhr taking cattle from Queensland to Newcastle Waters in 1885.[163] He was persuaded to 'go the back track against his own inclination', and the Track got the better of him.[164] The cattle rushed and he lost almost 100 head, missing or killed,[165] and he later described it as 'one of the hardest trips he had ever done with cattle in the Northern Territory'.[166] Durack believed the rush occurred because of Mork's habit of saving money by employing mostly Aboriginal stockmen,[167] but the experience of drovers over the next sixty-eight years suggests that he was probably wrong.

All of the cattle purchased by CD&D were sent over 3000 kilometres by ship from Wyndham to Fremantle, and the company continued to buy cattle from stations on the eastern side of the Murranji for some years. The years 1900-1902 were very dry and cattle from these stations were overlanded via Katherine,[168] but the 1902-03 wet season was good and Newcastle Waters, Hodgson Downs and Elsey each sent 1000 head of bullocks westward across the track.[169]

Lastly, Inverway station was taken up by the Farquharson brothers in about 1896, but they had to work for some years to build up their finances before they could stock their lease. Early in 1902 they brought the first cattle onto Inverway,[170] 700 head supposedly overlanded 3000 kilometres from the Inverell district of New South Wales.[171] Once again, it's unknown if they brought their mob across the Murranji Track, though this seems highly likely (plate 15).

CHAPTER 6

'OUT WHERE THE DEAD MEN LIE'

When Bluey Buchanan and Sam Croker set out to cross the Murranji in 1886 it's clear that the Murranji country was already considered a dangerous place, entered only by madmen and fools, a reputation probably originating with Stuart's original account and amplified by local experience since settlement. Buchanan's discovery of the Murranji and Yellow Waterholes opened the way across the Murranji and while in his case the dire predictions of the gold seekers didn't eventuate, others who followed weren't always so lucky. Both waterholes were unreliable; they could be dry shortly after the wet season, or they could hold water until after mid-year. Travellers who used the Track gambled on the hope that there would be water in the holes; some lost the gamble and died of thirst. In addition there were the dangers of Aboriginal attack, of becoming ill or injured far beyond help, and even of drowning. Each of these dangers claimed victims and the forbidding reputation of the region grew, and soon claims of large numbers of deaths along the track began to appear – up to twelve men at Murranji Waterhole and twenty or more along the entire Track.[172]

For example, in 1899 M.P. Durack wrote to a South Australian Government minister offering to sink two wells along the Murranji, saying that 'too little facilitation is given to the traveling public in the north, owing to which, has been the sacrifice of <u>many</u> lives'.[173] Hely Hutchinson who traversed the track in 1905 claimed that, 'The dry stage between Newcastle River and Yellow Waterholes is dotted with little brown mounds, sad witness to the awful fate that overtook the poor fellows whose mortal clay occupies them.'[174]

In the 1990s long-time resident of the Murranji region, Dick Scobie, claimed there were nine men buried at Murranji Waterhole and that a number of marked trees were visible in his time, but he made no record of the names and the trees are now gone.[175] Former drover Rodney Watson believes he saw about twelve graves and a number of marked trees when he first visited Murranji waterhole in 1946.[176]

Charlie Schultz, owner of Humbert River station for forty-four years and occasional drover, saw two graves at Murranji Waterhole – one about 400 metres south of the holes and another a short distance to the west and off the road about sixty to eighty metres – and he'd heard there were eight or nine more there. In a letter he wrote to the Chief Veterinary Officer in 1948 he suggested that the graves should be identified and given place-markers because,

> *One could class them as pioneers, and we have a lot to be thankful to them for, some are only drovers cooks or ordinary drover's hands, but the fact remains they died under some shady tree and with their boots on, and buried wrapped up in their swags, right where they died – it being the only home they ever knew, or property they owned.*[177]

Unfortunately Charlie's suggestion wasn't acted upon.

When Sid Hawks established a store at Top Springs in the early 1950s he heard the local legends and came to believe there were sixteen or seventeen graves along the Murranji, but an old man he met at Top Springs claimed, 'That bullshit of seventeen that Hawky's got is wrong…there were over twenty people died on the Murranji.'[178]

Apart from these generalised statements about total numbers, over the years more specific claims have been made about deaths on the Murranji. Ernestine Hill tells of a man named Beale who walked from Oodnadatta and died between Murranji and the Yellow Waterholes, and in 1938 Allan Fleming wrote of a man and his wife who set out to walk from Queensland to the Kimberley goldfield with their possessions loaded on a wheelbarrow. Somewhere near the Yellow Waterholes the man died from fever, and after burying him his wife pushed the barrow herself the remaining 680 kilometres to Halls Creek.[179]

One persistent story concerns the deaths of a number of men abandoned by a boss drover. As with all such 'legendary' stories, the details vary significantly and are sometimes contradictory; some may in fact contain elements of two stories. A version provided by writer George Farwell tells of three men dying after being left by a boss drover and he says the circumstances of their deaths inspired Louis Esson to write *The Drovers*, a one-act play in which a drover faces the dilemma of what to do with one of his men fatally injured during a rush.[180]

Ernestine Hill also tells of three men who died of fever after being left to fend for themselves by a drover who she says was known ever afterwards as 'Murdering Charley', and who never again worked in the north.[181] Cattleman Frank Willmington spoke of three men buried on a small sand ridge near Camel Soak, about five kilometres west of Murranji Waterhole. He said that one of the dead men was 'Catfish Tommy', the first man in charge of Catfish, an outstation of Wave Hill. Willmington didn't say that these men were abandoned by a boss drover, and if he knew the circumstances or dates of their deaths this wasn't recorded.[182] It's possible that they were the same men as those in Farwell's story.

Sid Hawks said he saw a tree at Murranji Waterhole which bore the names of six men who died of fever at the one time. According to Sid,

> *Seven men were in a droving team, and two got fever, and they stopped at Murranji bore. And two others had it during the night. And they decided they'd rest there...and one decided he would ride to Newcastle, and he set off on a horse and the horse broke down when he was ten mile from Newcastle Waters. And he finished running in himself and got the police, and they came back in a T model Ford. And...they found the whole six men were dead.*[183]

Sid intended to punch these names onto a sheet of metal to preserve them in case the tree died, but unfortunately he never did and the tree is long gone.[184] This is the only story which claims that six men died together on the Track, but Sid was over ninety years old when he told his story so his memory may have been faulty.

When Norm Whatley worked on Mornington station in the Kimberley in 1949-50 the manager, Jack 'Smiler Smith', told him he'd been on a droving trip across the Murranji in the 1920s when the boss drover and another man died from fever. He said that he (Smith) and the cook then took the cattle on to Newcastle Waters and beyond.[185]

In the early 1960s when Clarrie and Emily Pankhurst were droving through the Murranji they saw a tree at Murranji Waterhole which had the initials of three men and the date 1926 carved on it[186] (plate 16). Clarrie believed these were men who'd perished of thirst, along with their mob of cattle. Such a dramatic event is unlikely to have gone unreported, but there's nothing in the historical record to confirm it.

As well as stories of deaths there are stories of near misses. In one example from the early 1920s, some drovers crossing the Murranji saw a delirious man walking past their camp. The man was perishing for water and had tried to end his suffering by cutting his throat. The drovers poured water over his wrists for an hour before giving him a drink and bandaging his throat, and then took him on to Newcastle Waters.[187]

In spite of the claims of legend, the contemporary historical record provides solid evidence for only four deaths at Murranji Waterhole and a total of nine along the entire Murranji Track. The first recorded death occurred in April 1896. Thomas Holden, alias Thomas Smith, drowned in Murranji Waterhole while trying to retrieve some ducks.[188] His death was reported at Gordon Creek police station by his mate, a man calling himself Thomas McDonald but who was in fact Ben Bridge, a horse-stealing and jail-breaking fugitive from New South Wales and Queensland justice.[189] Four years earlier in northern New South Wales, Bridge had sold some racehorses that weren't his own in order to pay a debt. He then stole the horses from the purchaser in order to return them to the rightful owner, but was caught and sentenced to six years jail. Soon afterwards he escaped from Murundi jail and cleared out into Queensland.[190]

At Burketown, 2000 kilometres to the north, Bridge was again arrested for horse stealing, and while being held there the jail burnt down, 'some say from the inside, some from the outside'.[191] Once again he managed to escape and next turned up 1100 kilometres to the west, in the east Kimberley-Northern Territory border country. There he kept out of sight of the law for some years, but eventually was recognised by Western Australian police and after an extensive manhunt he was arrested late in 1899, extradited to New South Wales and sentenced to six months jail.[192]

The police went out to Murranji Waterhole after Bridge's report, but were unable to find Holden's body,[193] and this led to some 'ugly rumours' about the cause of Holden's death and Bridge's role in it.[194] However, about the same time that Bridge was captured (1899), drover Fred Mork was at Murranji Waterhole with some cattle. The hole was dry and in it Mork discovered human bones, presumed to be those of Bridge's long dead mate, Thomas Holden.[195]

In the first half of 1899 a man named Daniel Sheahan died on the Murranji Track. His death is mentioned by Ernestine Hill who states that he 'is buried at the head of Armstrong Creek,'[196] and it's also documented in the Timber Creek police journals. The police gave no cause of death, and the only information about the location is in the entry for June 23rd when the manager of VRD reported Sheahan's belongings as being 'at Murranji'.[197]

Ernestine Hill also mentions a man named Murdock McLeod drowning in Armstrong Creek after 'doing a perish' on the Murranji.[198] This implies that McLeod died on the Armstrong Creek section of the Murranji Track, but in fact he drowned about twenty kilometres from Pigeon Hole, well beyond the Track, in about April 1904.[199]

On December 15th 1905, the Timber Creek police reported receiving 'Correspondence re Edward Connolly & blackboy dying at Murrangi [sic] – 63 Miles head of Armstrong Creek.'[200] This entry suggests that in 1905 two people had either gone missing, presumed dead on the Murranji, or that remains of one or both had been found. However, a series of reports in later years completely confuses the picture. In April 1908 the *Northern Territory Times* reported that Drover Walter Rose had found human remains on the Murranji Track.[201] Because he 'was rather noted for his remarkably small hands and feet', the remains were initially identified as those of a drover named Hussey or 'Young Ozzy' who'd gone missing on a trip from Eva Downs to Victoria River. Later in the same report the name 'Hussey' was corrected to 'Ernest Ezzy', although 'the man known by some as Hussey is believed to be identical with Ezzy'.

For reasons that are not made clear, but probably because Ezzy later turned up alive,[202] the police eventually decided that the remains weren't those of Ezzy, but were really those of the Aboriginal man who'd been working for 'Connelly' (Connolly). This Aboriginal was said to have died after a fall from a horse, but where this information came from isn't revealed in the police accounts. According to the police Connolly himself had never reported the death and in July Mounted Constable Holland reported that, 'Connelly has left this district some considerable time. His whereabouts at present are unknown'.[203] Connolly may have had good reason to leave – if in fact he did leave. While taking a mob of horses west across the Murranji in October 1908, Samuel Muggleton found the fully clothed skeleton of a white man between the Yellow Waterholes and Murranji.[204] No further information has been found concerning this discovery, but the remains may well have been those of Connolly.

In February 1906, the *Northern Territory Times* reported that A. Muggleton had found the bones of a man named Lewellyn,[205] but a police report in March stated that it was James Fleming who'd found Lewellyn's bleached and scattered remains somewhere between the Yellow Waterholes and the jump-up.[206] Lewellyn was believed to have first come to the Territory from the White Range goldfields in the McDonnell Ranges.[207] He was timber cutting at

Pine Creek in about 1904, and is also said to have engaged in mining with (or for) Paddy Cahill.[208]

According to Hely Hutchinson, Lewellyn was a lunatic who arrived at Newcastle Waters station on foot in 1905, and although advised that it was certain death to try he set out to walk across an eighty mile dry stage to Daly Waters.[209] He only had a small waterbag so after he left a message was telegraphed to Daly Waters. In response a horseman rode from Daly Waters to meet Lewellyn on the track. He found no sign of him along the road and when he reached Newcastle Waters he found that Lewellyn had returned there. Determined to try again, Lewellyn filled all the empty tins he could find (or perhaps a single eight gallon drum[210]), loaded them on a borrowed wheelbarrow and set out once again.[211] He never arrived at Daly Waters and was later found to have changed his mind and headed across the Murranji. When he arrived at Murranji Waterhole it was dry. Seventy kilometres further on he abandoned his barrow and managed to get another thirty-odd kilometres before despair gave way to suicide. Facing death from thirst, Lewellyn ended it all with a bullet[212] and his wheelbarrow was later hung up in a tree as a 'grim reminder' to travellers for many years.[213]

1908 was a bumper year for deaths on the Murranji Track. Apart from the on-again off-again death of Connolly, a man named Jack Scott lost his life there, apparently from fever. Scott had been helping Drover McLean lift a mob of Wave Hill bullocks when he became ill about seventeen kilometres west of Murranji. Reporting Scott's disappearance to Mounted Constable Gordon at Newcastle Waters, McLean said he'd told Scott to go on to the next water and had eventually left him there. Drover Larkin, coming behind McLean's mob, found Scott's hat on the Track. Apparently no trace of Scott or his horse was ever found.[214] This particular event might be the basis of Ernestine Hill's story of 'Murdering Charley', discussed above.

Another man who died on the Murranji in 1908 was a stockman from Powell Creek named William Lenny. According to an entry in the Katherine Mortuary Book dated June 26th, Lenny died of 'malarial fever' at Murranji.[215] This is probably the man 'Billie Leanie' whom Ernestine Hill lists as having died on the Murranji Track. According to Hill, Leanie came from the Orkney Islands and had been 'one of Todd's men' (that is, he'd worked on construction of the overland telegraph line in the early 1870s).[216]

Another who died on the Murranji was 'Mulga Jim' McDonald, but whether this was the same 'Mulga Jim' McDonald who survived the attack described by Linklater is unclear. In any event, according to Frank Lacy, a New Zealander who spent most of his life in the Kimberley, as a young man he and 'Sid Smith' were employed to help Mulga Jim McDonald take a draft of bulls across the Murranji to Wave Hill. On the way over McDonald came down with malaria, 'but kept going as long as he could, fighting off his sickness. Not far east of the Murranji he had to give in; he lay down in the shade and died.'[217] Although the name 'Sid Smith' provided by Lacy is different from the 'Jack Smith' of Norm Whatley's story, it may be that they are one and the same, and that the two stories are different versions of the same event.

While Lacy's story isn't contemporary documentation and doesn't mention a date for McDonald's death, this is provided by prospector, explorer and author Michael Terry who saw McDonald's grave at Murranji Waterhole when he took the first motor vehicle along the Track in 1923. Terry said that 'a slab of bark had been cut off the tree, beneath which he was buried, where these words had been crudely inscribed: "A. McDonald, died May, 1921."'[218] Curiously, in his biography, *The Rivers of Home*, Lacy indicates that, like Terry, he first travelled across the Murranji Track in 1923, two years after McDonald's death,[219] and Terry didn't mention seeing the grave of the other man Whatley said had died with McDonald.

The Murranji Track came close to being the last resting place for a man who'd been one of the closest associates of the bushranger, Ned Kelly. In 1879 Isaiah 'Wild' Wright had been jailed on the well-founded suspicion that he was a close sympathizer of the Kellys, but he was released in time to be present at the famous siege at Glenrowan.[220] After the breakup of the gang Wright drifted north, among other jobs working as a drover in Western Queensland and beyond.[221] In 1911 he was a member of a droving team that was mustering cattle on VRD when he became seriously ill with fever. In the hope that medicines could be obtained for him at Newcastle Waters homestead he was taken across the Murranji in a buggy, but there were no medicines and soon after arriving Wright died.[222] His grave is said to now lie beneath the Newcastle Waters airstrip.

The deaths from thirst of two airmen, Bobby Hitchcock and Keith Anderson, happened in country too far south to be considered part of the Murranji. In 1929 while searching for the missing aviators, Charles Kingsford Smith and Charles Ulm, engine trouble forced Hitchcock and Anderson to land in a place from which they couldn't take off again. Help came too late to save them.[223] Seven years later, three RAAF men flying a Dragon Rapide had a near miss from death close to the Murranji Track. In 1936 on a trip from Charleville to Halls Creek the men overshot Newcastle Waters, ran out of fuel, and were forced down in bulwaddy country about seventeen kilometres north-west of No. 11 Bore. The plane was badly damaged on landing, although the men were uninjured, and they were stranded for nine days before being found safe and well by a search party[224] (plate 17).

The last person to die on the Murranji may have been a lone traveller named 'Brumby' Baker who apparently was found dead near Murranji Waterhole in September 1927. The only record of Baker's death comes from Tom Cole's book, *Hell West and Crooked*, published in 1988.[225] After arriving in Australia from England in 1923, Cole gradually worked his way across Queensland and into the Northern Territory. By December 1927 he was working on Banka Banka station and while there he was offered a job as head stockman on Wave Hill.[226] On his way to Wave Hill he says he called in at Newcastle Waters homestead where he heard about Baker's death, and later saw Baker's grave at Murranji Waterhole.[227] When Cole wrote *Hell West and Crooked* he wasn't concerned to produce an historically accurate work. It may be that 'Baker' was actually the man McDonald who'd died at Murranji in 1923, and that Cole couldn't remember the precise details of the grave he'd seen so he invented new details for his book.

As a matter of interest, Cole crossed the Murranji one other time. In a letter to his mother in March 1943 he told her that he'd gone across to Western Australia to inspect a mob of cattle,[228] but the truth is he was on the run from the law. Tom had obtained a lease for Tandidgee station, a block previously resumed from Newcastle Waters,[229] and early in 1943 he and his partner Jack Guild 'duffed' a mob of Helen Springs and Newcastle Waters cattle and started them on the road to Tennant Creek. The theft was discovered and police and station hands followed their tracks to Phillip Creek Bore.[230] Guild was later arrested but Cole couldn't be found, and while the police searched for him along the telegraph line, across the Barkly Tableland and in the vicinity of Cole's Kapalga station in Arnhem Land, he was fleeing across the Murranji 'like a whirlwind'.[231] When he reached the Western Australian border he sold his horses and gear, and hitched a ride to Wyndham where he caught a plane to Perth.[232]

There's one other person who, technically, may be said to have died on the Murranji Track, and who is certainly buried there. This was Sid Hawks' mother-in-law, Margaret Anderson, who went to live at Top Springs in 1954. Suffering from cancer, she died there in November 1955[233] and was buried somewhere near the end of the Top Springs airstrip. Sid Hawks dug the grave, and he said that someone else had been buried there, but it was before his time and he didn't know who it was.[234]

The foregoing are the deaths on the Murranji that can be verified through the historical record – four definitely at Murranji Waterhole and at least five more elsewhere on the Track – but what of the legend of eleven or twelve dead men at Murranji Waterhole, and twenty or more along the entire Track? In spite of the fact that many people used the track once it was opened, including a great many miners heading for the Kimberley goldfields, there were only two recorded deaths between 1886 and 1900 – those of Thomas Holden and Daniel Sheahan. It's difficult to believe that there weren't more mishaps in that time and it may be that many of the early travellers were more concerned with getting safely to their destination than with notifying authorities hundreds of kilometres away of any deaths on the Track.

It will probably never be known exactly how many people perished along the Murranji and the circumstances of their deaths, but the absence of records doesn't mean that the claims of legend are entirely wrong. Some deaths may have gone unreported or the records may not have survived, and future research may yet show that claims of twelve men dead at Murranji Waterhole and another eight or more elsewhere along the Track are largely correct.

CHAPTER 7

THE BEGINNING OF THE GREAT DROVING ERA

Twenty years after the first stations were established in the Victoria River and East Kimberley country and eighteen years after the track was opened, the first large-scale eastward movement of cattle along the Murranji Track took place.[235] The year was 1904, and several reasons can be suggested as to why it didn't begin earlier, and why it began on a relatively large scale.

First was the appearance of tick-borne 'redwater fever' in the Top End of the Territory where the original outbreaks occurred in the period 1880-82.[236] Fear of the disease spreading to cattle-grazing areas neighbouring the Territory was such that by the end of 1896 laws had been passed to prevent stock from the Victoria River, Gulf country and most of the Barkly Tableland from moving to any Australian market.[237] Banning the interstate movement of cattle from these areas was a case of the shutting the gate after the cattle tick had bolted. Outbreaks of redwater had been reported in both the Kimberley and north Queensland in 1895,[238] and within a few years the disease wiped out a massive number of Queensland cattle.

Second, during the 1890s there was a national depression that kept cattle prices low.[239] Third, before Queensland cattle numbers could be re-established from surviving station stock a series of dry years set in, culminating in the great drought of 1900-1903, a drought that also affected large areas of New South Wales.[240] The combined effects of redwater and drought caused a tremendous reduction in the Queensland cattle population, with individual stations losing from one third to nine tenths of their herds,[241] and cattle numbers statewide falling from over 7,000,000 to less than 2,500,000.[242] The drought also severely reduced cattle numbers in much of New South Wales. The depression had eased by the end of the century and cattle prices in Queensland had already risen before the end of the drought, but when the drought ended there was a huge demand in both Queensland and New South Wales for cattle for re-stocking purposes and for meat, and prices rose significantly.[243] To give an idea of the change in the price of cattle, in 1895 most Northern Territory pastoralists were lucky to get £2 10s per head,[244] but by 1904 prices in Queensland had risen to £5 10s per head for fat bullocks,[245] and by 1907 had reached from £7 15s to £8 10s.[246]

This price rise was the break that Northern Territory cattle producers had been waiting for – an opening in the eastern markets – and two 'cattle barons' who owned stations in the Victoria River and East Kimberley districts were quick to capitalize on the high prices. They were Sidney Kidman (plate 18), a major shareholder in Victoria River Downs and Carlton Hill stations[247] and W.F. Buchanan (plate 19), who owned Wave Hill and Delamere stations,[248] and who was a minor shareholder in VRD[249].

The droving of cattle from the Victoria River district to southern or eastern states was a major undertaking, and a major gamble. Competent drovers had to be found who had or could obtain sufficient plant to handle the job. These drovers had to get to the Victoria River district by the end of the wet season so that on the journey back with the cattle they could take advantage of plentiful water and feed. This meant they had to be hired during the previous dry season to give them time to get organized and to ride the thousands of kilometres to the stations where they were to lift the cattle. If the coming wet season proved poor, it would be difficult or impossible to bring the cattle over. This happened to Drover Walter Rose, 'the prince of cattle drovers'[250], who started out from Lissadell station in July 1905, the driest year on record to that time. He was held up by severe drought conditions for many months, lost nearly 1400 head from disease, starvation and rushes, and didn't arrive at Charleville until October 1906[251] (plates 20 & 21).

Buchanan and Kidman both hired drovers in 1903, and their gamble that conditions on the overland route in 1904 would be favourable for droving paid off. In the Victoria River district the 1903-04 wet season was the best on record[252] and good rains were reported right across the Barkly Tableland and into Queensland.[253] Kidman hired Blake Miller and Flavelle 'Jumbo' Smith to take cows from VRD to restock Austral Downs.[254] Buchanan hired Charlie Phillott, Jack-Dick Skuthorpe and Steve Lewis to take mobs from Wave Hill – Phillott and Skuthorpe to take bullocks to Buchanan's Killarney station near Narrabri in New South Wales and Lewis to take bullocks from Wave Hill to

Hergott Springs (Maree) in South Australia.[255] The drovers taking cattle to New South Wales were paid '1s 6d per head per 100 miles', and this was considered to be a first class rate.[256]

Almost nothing is known about Blake Miller and little more about 'Jumbo' Smith. In 1902-03 Smith overlanded a mob of 250 bulls from Queensland to VRD. On the way he passed through Elsey station and was later immortalised as 'Brown of the Bulls' in Jeannie Gunn's book, *We of the Never Never*.[257] His nickname 'Jumbo' came from the fact that he was a very big man, 'a veritable son of Anak, standing well over six feet and riding 17 stones 5½ lbs'[258] [over 110 kilograms]. In the year he took the cattle from VRD Phillott was described as 'a very old Australian drover, of the Never Mullah, who years ago drove for Cobb & Co., of Devonport Downs, on the Diamentina' (sic).[259]

Steve Lewis was a part-owner of Newcastle Waters station and was manager there from 1894 until 1899.[260] On the 1904 trip he was assisted by his brother Harry who was also a part-owner of Newcastle Waters.[261] Harry had previously handled station business in Adelaide[262] and also had taken cattle from Newcastle Waters to 'southern markets' in 1901.[263]

Drover Phillott put together a plant of 100 horses and a team of twenty-five men to handle the 3000 cattle he was to lift from Wave Hill (plate 22). He paid the men a small wage for the journey out and provided their keep, and promised them £2 per week and their keep on the return journey.[264] Drover Miller paid his men nothing during the journey out and £2-10 per week on the trip in.[265] When Phillott's men got to Wave Hill they almost certainly discovered that Miller's men were to be paid ten shillings more than they were on the return trip, so they went on strike for the extra money. Phillott had no choice but to pay it.[266]

A team of twenty-five men to shift this number of cattle wasn't unusual at the time – the following year Drover Rose hired twenty-five men, 'many being the sons of well-known Queensland pastoralists', to help shift 4000 head from Lissadell station to Queensland, a distance of several thousand kilometres.[267]

These large teams of men had to be fed, but there were very few stores between the East Kimberley-Victoria River district and Queensland, and drovers couldn't expect to obtain more than small amounts of rations, if any, from the stations they passed through. Instead, the drover had to obtain large amounts of stores before the trip began, or arrange to pick up supplies from the towns closest to their route. No information about the rations being carried in the 1904 season is available, but for similar trips the following year Drover Skuthorpe arranged for about seven tons of rations to be delivered to

Katherine,[268] and Drover Rose arranged for three tons of supplies to be shipped from Townsville to Wyndham and delivered from there to Lissadell.[269] These rations were carried on wagons or packhorses. In 1905 Drover Rose used two 'stanch spring drays'[270] while in 1909 it was reported that Drover Albert Williams, who was taking 3000 head from Lissadell to Lake Nash, had decided to 'discard the wagonette style of travelling, and is fitting up his plant with packhorses and leather water bags'.[271] These two methods, or a combination of both, remained in use for another fifty to sixty years (plates 23-27).

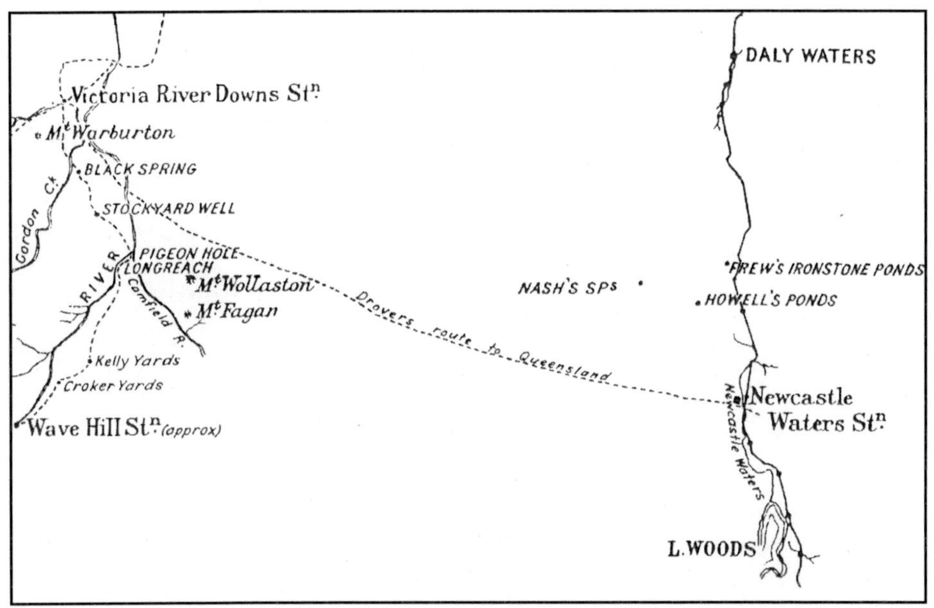

A 1909 map showing the Murranji Track in very general terms. This crude map and verbal information was all the drovers had to go on in the days before the Track was properly surveyed.

The grand scale of these cattle movements created a great deal of interest in the eastern states and South Australia, probably best explained in an article some years later when it was said that, 'There is something peculiarly fascinating about these long slow trips with a great mob of cattle across a whole continent.'[272] This fascination was such that on some occasions when droving teams set out from their home towns large crowds turned out to farewell them (plate 28). When Skuthorpe arrived at Narrabri he was photographed (plate 29), and interviewed by the local press:

> *What is perhaps a record droving feat has been accomplished by Mr. John Skuthorpe, who is bringing 3000 head of cattle from the extreme north of Queensland [Northern Territory], the property of Mr. W. F. Buchanan, of Killarney Station, to Narrabri. After travelling 2,600 miles, 700 of which was through practically an unknown part of the Northern Territory, the*

cattle originally starting from Waste [sic] Hill Station, N.Q., are reported to be in the pink of condition.[273]

This report contained errors that may not have been Skuthorpe's fault, but he was blamed for some of them and accused of trying to glorify himself.[274] Within a year or two a minor but acrimonious controversy developed over who was actually the first drover to begin the great trek across the continent. Claims and counterclaims were published in different papers and journals, and details varied as to which drovers actually made the crossing, the order in which they came, how many cattle they had, how long their dry stages were, where they came from and where they were going to. By examining and comparing accounts of the various participants in the debate it's possible to build up a picture of the 1904 droving season that is reasonably accurate.

It seems that at least six separate mobs made the trek, amounting to something in the order of 8000 to 8500 head. First onto the Murranji Track was Blake Miller with either 1000 or 1500 VRD cows.[275] It was probably his cows that were said to have been 'a very mixed lot ages barying [sic] from less than twelve months to over 12 years and calving all along the track', and that this circumstance would 'spoil the sale of cows in towards Queensland.'[276] Miller camped his cattle for a day at the Yellow Waterholes before continuing east.[277] Next came Steve Lewis and his brother Harry with 1000 Wave Hill bullocks. These men are said to have camped their cattle at the Yellow Waterholes for 'six or seven days', though no reason was given for this delay.[278] 'Jumbo' Smith followed the Lewis brothers with 1000 head of cows, and owing to a bad attack of fever he camped two days at the Yellow Holes. Next came the two mobs of 1500 bullocks, ostensibly in charge of Drover Skuthorpe but actually managed by Dave Warneke[279] and Skuthorpe's nephew, Oswald Skuthorpe.[280] Last of all was Drover Phillott with his 3000 Wave Hill cows.[281] Like Skuthorpe, Phillott probably split his herd in two and had another man in charge of the second lot, but there's nothing in the records to say who this second man might have been.

In one of the newspaper reports about Skuthorpe's trip he must have claimed to have had a dry stage of 192 kilometres (115 miles) across the Murranji, because this became a point of contention between various correspondents. The distance was disputed by Hely Hutchinson who claimed in the Rockhampton *Morning Bulletin* that 'in all truth there was enough water at both Bingacootra [the Yellow Waterholes] and Murranji to float the Japanese navy'.[282] In reply Skuthorpe wrote to the *Morning Bulletin* and enclosed a telegram which he said he'd received 'from the nearest telegraph station to his route' and which said, 'No rain; Murranji dry; very little yellow waterhole'. Unfortunately the

Bulletin didn't reproduce or confirm the telegram and chose instead to ridicule Skuthorpe.[283]

Ben Martin, who'd piloted the various mobs across Illawarra station to the Yellow Waterholes, wrote a letter in support of Skuthorpe. He said that by the time the mobs of Miller, Lewis and Smith had been through, the Yellow Waterholes had been reduced to 'pea-soup', and because of this Skuthorpe's cattle couldn't get a drink until they reached Ikadee (Hickety) Waterhole on Newcastle Waters, 190 kilometres further on.[284]

The answer to the debate may be in a diary kept by one of Skuthorpe's own men and later published in the *Pastoralists' Review*.[285] According to this diary, when Skuthorpe's second mob reached the Yellow Waterholes on June 10th there was 'Good water, and plenty of it.' The mob was kept there for a day and watered again in the evening. The next morning they began a dry stage of eighty kilometres and when they reached Murranji Waterhole three days later they found '12 ft. of water in main hole.' The cattle were kept at Murranji for the next two days, some of them 'wading up to their bellies in water after swamp reeds,' before setting out on the morning of the 17th. Thirty-three kilometres further on they came to Howell's Ponds (just above the Bucket Waterhole) where there was '7 ft. of water in one hole (1/4 mile long); cattle swimming.'[286]

By the time Phillott got to the Yellow Waterholes there wasn't enough water there for his cattle, but luckily for him Ben Martin knew of a waterhole four or five kilometres to the west.[287] Phillott had to pay Martin 'a big price' to be shown the hole. He then 'cut a track for his waggonette, and by so doing conferred a great benefit upon the travelling public, to whom this hole was not generally known before.'[288] This hole, known by the Aboriginal name *Largungen*, was later included on the first surveyor's map of the Murranji Track.[289] Apparently Phillott's cattle were unable to get a drink, or an adequate drink, in any of the other waterholes along the Murranji Track. In a letter Wave Hill manager Tom Cahill wrote to the Government Resident in 1905 he said,

> *The 1904 season in the Victoria River district was the best we have ever had, and the rainfall the highest. Notwithstanding this, the last lots of cattle from Wave Hill, in the early part of June last year (1904), did not get a good drink of water from the head of the Armstrong Creek, until they got to Newcastle Waters.*[290]

It would appear that Skuthorpe's cattle found adequate water at the Yellow Waterholes in early June, but when Phillott's cattle arrived about ten days later they didn't.[291] Skuthorpe's cattle arrived at the Yellow Waterholes in the afternoon, stayed all the next day and left in the morning. After walking all day a bullock will drink at least ten gallons,[292] so when Skuthorpe's mob of 1500 arrived it would've consumed at least 15,000 gallons. The mob spent all the next day drinking at the waterhole, and probably wading in it and 'puddling' it, so by the time they left the cattle had probably consumed more than 30,000 gallons and perhaps rendered what was left undrinkable – the 'pea soup' that Ben Martin said Skuthorpe himself encountered.

The dry stage faced by Phillott was the first of many encountered by Murranji drovers before the Government bores were put down, and they were a feature which contributed significantly to the legendary status of the Track. In fact, before bores were put down the majority of drovers regularly faced dry stages of seventy-five to eighty-five kilometres (45 to 50 miles) between the main waterholes, distances that caused comment when negotiated in later times.

All the mobs that crossed the Murranji in 1904 made it through to their destinations without major drama. The mob Steve Lewis took to Maree was thirty-one weeks on the road,[293] while Skuthorpe's mob took more than thirteen months to reach Narrabri[294] (including a delay of month or two near Charleville),[295] but the prices received made these long droving trips well worth the cost, time and effort. After fattening on Killarney some of the Wave Hill cows fetched an average of £6 16s at the Sydney markets.[296]

A letter published in the *North Queensland Herald* in January 1906 declared that the Murranji Track would become,

> *one of the most important stock routes in Australia, as it will be from the immense herds of cattle west of the O. T. line in the Northern Territory, and in the East and West Kimberley districts of Western Australia that most of the cattle for re-stocking purposes in Queensland will be drawn... Many hundreds of thousands of cattle are destined to cross this track from the west*[297]

Even more cattle were sent east again in 1905,[298] and the next year, and the next, and so on for the next sixty years, even though cattle prices fluctuated and the Murranji Track was sometimes closed before the Government bores were sunk in the early 1920s.

CHAPTER 8

THE HARDEST YEARS: 1904 TO 1924

Romantics might see the years between 1904 and 1924 (when the first lot of Government bores were completed) as the 'Golden Age' of Murranji droving, years when men and cattle had to overcome the most difficult conditions. For the drovers concerned they were probably years of Hell. In this period they had to contend with numerous dangers and difficulties – dry stages, cattle rushes, Aboriginal harassment, 'poison bush', rough tucker, bushfires, dust in the 'dry', bog in the 'wet', 'drummy ground',[299] and lack of feed for their stock.

Rainfall on the Murranji was highly irregular so at the end of the wet the Murranji and Yellow Waterholes could be full or dry, or anything in between. Charlie Schultz remembered hearing a story that after each wet season and before any drovers set out for Queensland, the water supply on the Murranji had to be checked. He was told that one of the Victoria River stations would send a stockman – one who was a good bushman – along the Murranji to see what water was available. Depending on his report the drovers would either head across the Murranji or take the longer route via Katherine.[300]

The 1904-05 wet season failed[301] and the next two years were very dry – too dry to use the Murranji although thousands of head were taken east via Katherine.[302] In 1906 the manager of Wave Hill would've liked to have sent 20,000 bullocks away,[303] but conditions were too dry so only 8000 were overlanded.[304] In 1908 Wave Hill sent 11,000 head on the road[305] and Drover Rose took a mob of Lissadell cattle over the Track early in the season – as it turned out, a bit too early. A day after leaving Lissadell heavy rain began and continued for eighteen days, and Rose later reported that before reaching

Murranji Waterhole 'we crossed two miles of black silt, supposed to be the tail of a traveling lake. Numerous wild myall blacks followed us, and caught the stray fish which were overflowing from the lake's borders.' Further on he discovered the supposed remains of Drover Hussey, as already described.[306]

After 1908 reports of drovers and cattle crossing the Murranji are sporadic and difficult to find, and most are only the shortest of notes. For example, the Sub-Inspector of Stock at Powells Creek reported in 1910 that, 'About 14,150 cattle passed through Newcastle Waters from western districts, mostly all for Queensland'.[307] An exception is William Lavender's story. In 1912 William 'Young Bill' Lavender and a mate travelled to Victoria River Downs in search of adventure. Fifty years afterwards he put his experiences on record, including an account of how he and his mate joined Drover Herb Cuthbert who was taking a mob of 1500 Wave Hill bullocks and spayed cows across the Murranji.[308]

Young Bill remembered the track as being 'exceedingly winding at times, the original trail markers picking the thinnest patches to hack and burn through.'[309] The drovers experienced two minor rushes between the Yellow Waterholes and Murranji, but it was at Murranji Waterhole that the most memorable event occurred. As they were approaching the waterhole rising smoke showed that a mob of 'munjongs' (wild blacks) were camped nearby. The boss went ahead with one of his men to make sure the Aborigine's camp was well away from the water, and Young Bill remarked that,

> *A decade or two earlier the whites would have ordered the myalls off at the point of their guns, providing the munjongs... were bold enough not to clear for their lives immediately the white man was detected, but [the Aborigines knew] it was then too strictly against the law of the all powerful "perleece" to shoot blacks outright for nothing at all.*[310]

Whether or not the munjong's camp had been too close isn't clear, but by the time Young Bill arrived they were nowhere to be seen. However, the drovers feared the Aborigines would try to rush the cattle during the night so that they could pick up stragglers or wounded beasts later on. After the cattle were bedded down at dusk two armed men rode around the mob, but this precaution proved ineffective: 'In the small hours, it came, and the worst happened... A heavy hunting boomerang [was] thrown a comparatively great distance [in amongst the cattle].'[311] The resulting stampede delayed the drovers for several days while they tracked and mustered the scattered stock. Many cattle were injured and 'One great bullock had galloped chest-on to a parallel spiked, hard, dry and bare bulwaddie [sic] limb, and same had penetrated over halfway into the beast's "innards".'[312] When the drovers checked the cattle numbers later they were short by about twenty head, and several bullocks were so badly injured that they had to be destroyed over the next few days. Of the Aborigines, Young Bill remarked that,

> *The tribesmen had certainly done themselves well, if they ever followed their killing up, but from tracks found it was clear they had started something they couldn't handle, became scared and cleared off south deep into the desert. All hands were incensed at the myall's behaviour, and there is no doubt that had any been sighted during the mustering, they would have been fired on with "intent to kill", so high was the indignation against them.*[313]

For years after Young Bill's trip there seem to be no detailed accounts of droving trips across the Murranji although, seasons permitting, the Murranji was being used. For instance, a report from June 1918 stated that 'already 2,500 [head] passed Newcastle Waters en route Queensland... Muranjai [sic] drying rapidly'.[314]

Some time before the Government bores went in two of the three Farquharson brothers of Inverway station – Hughie, Harry and Archie – accomplished what is probably the most famous dry stage in the history of Australian cattle droving. This story has been told many times over the years, but there are no contemporary records and the Farquharsons never wrote their own account of the trip. As a result the details of exactly when they made the trip, how many cattle they had, how many were lost and the distance travelled varies from source to source. Some versions appear to be based on hearsay and some on earlier published accounts. A number are based on conversations with one or the other of the Farquharsons, but even in these accounts the details vary. Rather than trying to determine the 'true' account, in the following the different versions written by people who actually met the Farquharsons are summarised.

According to Gordon Buchanan, a cousin of the Farquharson brothers and closely associated with them for many years,[315] the dry stage occurred in 1919 and covered 184 kilometres (110 miles). He noted that,

> *This achievement may have been approached by smaller and therefore more mobile mobs, or when aided by parakeelia [sic] or other moisture–holding plants, but these cattle had no such advantages, and no adventitious aid except cool and cloudy weather.*[316]

Writing in *Cummins & Campbell's Monthly Magazine* a writer calling him or herself 'Vanguard', who met the Farquharsons in 1933, said that, 'In 1918 the

Farquharsons took one thousand head of cattle from Inverway to Headingly, on the Georgina. There was a dry stage of one hundred miles to negotiate; and it seems almost incredible that only six beasts were lost.'[317]

Ernestine Hill met the brothers a number of times in the 1930s and 1940s, and in 1946 she asked Archie Farquharson when the trip took place. He told her he, 'could not remember the exact year…because he was not in it and they had a good few dry stages across the Murrunjai [sic], but he thinks about 1915.'[318] In spite of Archie's comments on this occasion, when she published *The Territory* in 1951 Hill said the year was 1909 and added that,

> *they traveled a thousand head for a hundred and twenty-five miles without even the smell of water, flogging the poor brutes on all day lest they should break back to perish, and leading them on with hurricane lamps all night. They counted at Newcastle Waters and had lost only five.*[319]

George Farwell provides the only verbatim account of the famous trip:

> *"There was whips of feed," Archie Farquharson, the last surviving brother, told me at Inverway shortly before his death in August 1950. "The big problem, of course, was water. Cattle going without water don't want too much feed. We had to take our plant of horses ahead of the mob to water them. We rode on to the Yellow Hole from the Armstrong, then went back for the cattle. Then we rode right on past the Murranji to the Bucket, watered them again and went back once more. The cattle were pretty quiet all the time, and they travelled well. Mind you, we had to watch them sharply. Double watch all the time. But we made that trip inside five days."*[320]

Farwell says the trek took place in 1909 and the distance, from Top Springs to the Bucket Waterhole, was 210 kilometres (125 miles). They travelled mostly at night, resting their cattle in the heat of the day and stringing them along through the dark with lanterns, and despite the rigours of that journey they reached Newcastle Waters with the loss of only five bullocks.

Drover Mick Coombes took cattle across the Murranji many times – including in 1967 the second last mob to cross the Track.[321] He met the Farquharsons at various times and told the story as he heard it from one of the brothers:

> *they had a blackfella of course, all blacks, and this blackfella knew… where the waters were. See they used that No. 12 soak of course, and they used Nash's Soak... And they didn't camp like ordinary times where you walk, you know, feed your cattle along all day and water 'em and camp at night. They*

> *kept goin'. When the cattle wanted a spell, they'd give 'em a spell. There was no night camps, and they had a blackfellow with a piece of board on his back and a piece of tin nailed onto that, and a hurricane lamp – that was to protect him on the back from gettin' burnt, and he rode along in the lead of the cattle with this hurricane light on of a night time and they followed him. Old Archie Farquharson told me that himself.*[322]

In the 1940s-early 1950s Leone Biltris was the 'missus' at Mistake Creek station, a neighbour of the Farquharson's Inverway station, and she was told about the trip by Archie Farquharson when he was eighty-eight years old. According to her, Archie,

> *told me of the epic trip made by Harry from the Bucket Hole just outside of Newcastle Waters to Top Springs, just on a hundred miles with a mob of cattle, and every mile of it dry. That was before the Government bores were put down on the Murranji, and the waterholes had dried out early. But Harry came through with every head.*[323]

In this account the direction the cattle were taken is incorrect, but it's impossible to say whether this was Biltris' mistake, or Archie's – unlikely to be Archie's, perhaps, but then again he was eighty-eight years old. However, it's interesting to note that Archie said the trip was made by Harry, which confirms Ernestine Hill's version in which Archie said he wasn't there.

Eddie Connellan, who pioneered air services in northern and Central Australia, met the Farquharson brothers at various times and heard the story of their trip. When the brothers told Eddie that the dry stage was 114 miles (190 kilometres) long he found it difficult to believe but,

> *finally one night, when no one else was around, they told me the secret of it. Instead of waiting until nearly daylight to move the cattle off camp, as would be normal practice in a droving camp, they moved them off several hours earlier and travelled during the cool of the night, thereby minimising loss of moisture by the cattle and also giving them the opportunity to feed on grass that had a little dew on it. They had always kept that part of it a secret and asked me to keep it a secret too, but now they are all dead and gone, I do not feel bound by that request any longer.*[324]

One other account is worth retelling, even though it's not clear if it came direct from one of the Farquharsons. In the *Brisbane Courier* in 1938 A. Fleming told how,

What the old timers describe as one of the finest droving feats in the history of the Territory took place on the Murrunji [sic] track. In 1917 three brothers, who still have a station near the border of Western Australia, travelled 1000 head of cattle 120 miles without water. They pushed the beasts on slowly in the sun and continued by moonlight for four days. They lost only four, two of which were killed in the final stampede to a waterhole.[325]

The facts common to these stories, or at least, those that are not contradictory, are as follows: Harry Farquharson was in charge and while it's not clear if Hughie was on the trip, Archie almost certainly had remained at Inverway. The cattle were driven more or less continuously, with only occasional rests, and at night they were led by a horseman who carried a hurricane lamp fixed to a board on his back. It took between four and five days to get through, and very few cattle were lost. Water for the horses and men was obtained from Aboriginal soaks, one known as Nash's Well (near No. 10 Bore) and the other (Kinganut) close to where No. 12 Bore was later put down. As a matter of interest, on some early maps the name of the latter soak is rendered as 'Kismet', a Persian word which translates as 'fate' or 'destiny', and which possibly alludes to discovery of the soak by someone (an Afghan?) who was close to perishing.[326]

From available evidence it's impossible to say exactly what the dry stage was point to point, or when this famous trip occurred, though the weight of opinion seems to favour 1915-1918 rather than 1909. The Murranji Waterhole was dry in 1917[327] and normally cattle would've gone via Katherine, but it's possible that the Farquharsons decided to try the Track anyway. The year 1918 also was dry and it was, 'Doubtful if Murranji track open this season. No cattle water there fourth February. Total rainfall locally [Newcastle Waters] 20 inches, outside country lighter,'[328] but later it was reported that, 'Frog Hollow [Inverway] bullocks are on the road en route to Queensland, and should reach the line via Mursasji [sic] early next month.'[329]

CHAPTER 9

WATERING THE DRY LANDS

From a European perspective the need for improved water supplies along the Murranji was apparent from the beginning. When Stuart failed to get through he wrote,

> *Thus end my hopes of reaching the Victoria in this latitude, which is a very great disappointment. I should have dug wells if my party had been larger, and I had the means of conveying water to those engaged in sinking the wells...I had no idea of meeting with such an impediment as the plains and heavy scrub have proved to be. For a telegraphic communication I should think that three or four wells would overcome this difficulty and the want of water, and the forest could be penetrated by cutting a line through and burning it.*[330]

Once the Murranji Track was established it was of great benefit to travellers – when it was passable. The natural waters on the Murranji weren't permanent so for half the year or more the Track couldn't be used.

As early as 1895 a group of Northern Territory citizens, including two Victoria River pastoralists, recommended to a Royal Commission into the Northern Territory that 'boring operations and well-sinking be continued with increased vigour in localities where water is required and is likely to exist'.[331] It's not known whether the pastoralists had the Murranji Track in mind, although this seems likely. In any case, their recommendations weren't acted upon, or at least, not in the short term.

In November 1899 M.P. Durack wrote to W. Griffiths (MP), offering to sink two wells on the Murranji Track at his own expense, one about 'midway between "Endracooch" – on Newcastle – and "Moorangi" [sic] the other well between "Moorangi" and head of "Armstrong Creek".'[332] His offer was made with the provision that if the wells were successful the Government would provide the troughing and would reimburse costs not to exceed £350. Durack's proposal was viewed favourably by Griffiths who forwarded it on to the Minister for the Northern Territory.[333] It also received qualified support from Government Resident Charles Dashwood,[334] but nothing ever came of it.

When G. Sabine stood as a Northern Territory candidate for election to the South Australian Parliament in 1902, he proposed that 'wells should be sunk where suitable or water conserved on the Overland Telegraph line, and on the main stock route', and he said that he'd been 'advised that it would greatly facilitate traveling stock if two or three wells were sunk on the route between Newcastle Waters and the Western Australian boundary.'[335] Again, nothing was done.

Water problems were highlighted with the first large-scale movement of cattle eastward along the Murranji Track in 1904. Of the six mobs known to have made the crossing, the last two apparently had dry stages of 192 kilometres (115 miles).[336] In 1905 Tom Cahill, the manager of Wave Hill station, wrote to the Government Resident about the problems his drovers had faced the year before on the Murranji and suggested that, 'What this stock route wants, to make it so that cattle can come through, is three bores — one at Indrocooch, one at Murrangi [sic], and one at Bandricoochara or Yellow Water Holes. It will never be any use until something like this is done.'[337] As usual, nothing was done.

1905 was a dry year and the Murranji Track was closed, so large numbers of cattle were sent to Queensland via Katherine. 1906 was an exceptionally dry year because the 1905-06 wet season failed,[338] and there were greatly increased calls for wells or bores to be sunk on the Murranji. Signs of a bad season approaching were evident in March when the *Northern Territory Times* bemoaned the lack of water along the stockroutes, and suggested that, 'the sooner the Government recognises the fact, and makes some serious attempt to open up the routes between Victoria River and Newcastle Waters, and between Powell's Creek and Camooweal, the better will it be for the N.T.'[339] The *Pastoralists' Review* pointed out that if the Murranji route was dry cattle had to travel an extra 400 miles, and if the Barkly route was dry they had to go by the old Coast Track,[340] and the manager of Wave Hill and the Government Resident also called for bores to be sunk along the Murranji.[341]

During a meeting of the North Australian League, held in Darwin in September 1906,[342] one of the participants, Drover Huddlestone, suggested that, 'One of the most pressing points at which water should be conserved is between the Armstrong and Newcastle Waters on the Murranghi [sic] track.' Some members of the League were dubious about whether wells would be any use because they thought cattle wouldn't drink from troughs. This suggestion wasn't as silly as it might seem. Old drovers say that cattle that have only ever used natural waters are accustomed to the smell of wet earth around the waters' edge. Water in a trough has no smell, or at least, has a smell completely different to that in a waterhole, so the cattle do not realise that a trough might contain water. Some drovers overcame this problem by splashing water from the trough onto the ground or allowing the troughs to overflow to create the smell of wet earth, and the cattle would then investigate and discover the water.[343]

In 1907 something at last *seemed* to be happening. In his annual report, Government Resident Herbert wrote that,

> *Mr. Townshend, [the manager] of Victoria River Downs, informs me that he has received plans and specifications from the Engineer-in-Chief for a well or wells to be sunk on the track between Armstrong Creek and Newcastle Waters, and asking him to get contractors to quote a price per foot. Mr. Townshend states that no one will do so unless the sites are pointed out beforehand. He adds that in his opinion, one artesian well at Murranji would be far better for travelling stock than three ordinary wells on the same track.*[344]

Rainfall in 1906-07 was better than during the previous two seasons,[345] but the 12,000 head that left the Victoria River district for Queensland in 1907 still had to travel via the Dry River.[346] A police officer at Timber Creek called for at least one bore to be put down on the Murranji Track,[347] and the *Pastoralist's Review* repeated its suggestion of the previous year, although in this instance the extra distance that cattle had to travel if the Murranji was closed became 1000 kilometres (600 miles), rather than 670 kilometres (400 miles)![348]

Again, nothing happened. In 1908 Government Resident Herbert again called for improvement of water supplies on the Murranji, and again nothing happened.[349] The Murranji Track was reported open throughout the 1909 season, 'owing to the late rains', but no figures were given as to stock movements.[350] In his report on the Northern Territory for 1909, Resident Herbert reported that, 'The Honorable the Minister...approved of a contract being let for sinking a sub-artesian bore' – at Anthony's Lagoon, over 200 kilometres east of the Murranji! This site was chosen on the well-founded logic that Anthony's Lagoon 'is situated at the junction of the central and coastal cattle routes from the west into Queensland. One or the other of these routes is always open as far as Anthony's Lagoon, but when that Lagoon is dry both of necessity are closed.'[351]

Rainfall in 1909-10 was very good in both the Victoria and Barkly districts,[352] and during 1910 over 14,000 cattle were reported to have passed through Newcastle Waters from western stations, most bound for Queensland[353] and most probably via Murranji because, 'if possible they [drovers] prefer going the Murangie track'.[354] During this season a new record was set by Drover Burgess who, 'With a mob of 3000 cattle…and eight or nine stockmen covered 1852 miles in 24 weeks, and only lost 124 beasts by the way'[355] (plate 30).

1911 seems to have been another good year with 15,000 head being driven across the Murranji.[356] It was also the year when control of the Northern Territory was transferred from South Australia to the Commonwealth and therein lay the reason why nothing had been done for so long. The South Australian Government took control of the Northern Territory in 1863, but eventually found it to be a financial liability and in 1901 began negotiations to hand control of the Territory to the newly formed Commonwealth Government.[357] With such a handover in the wind the South Australian Government had no interest in spending money there.

When the Commonwealth Government finally took control of the Territory action was soon taken towards improving the Murranji water supply. In November 1911 Captain H.V. Barclay, a surveyor, explorer and civil engineer, arrived at Newcastle Waters (plate 31). Barclay had just completed an exploration of the central-eastern part of the Northern Territory for the Commonwealth Department of External Affairs[358], and had been instructed to go to the Murranji to select well sites and to recommend sites for stock reserves.[359] Travelling by camel, Barclay selected sites at the Bucket Waterhole, 'Muriangie' Waterhole and at the Yellow Waterholes. He noted that near these sites there was plenty of lancewood that could be used for timbering wells, but because termites were a major pest in the region he strongly recommended bores. He suggested that if a trial bore put down at Murranji Waterhole was successful it would open up a very large area of valuable country suitable for small holdings.[360]

The action in 1911 was followed by inaction the following year, at least in terms of work on the ground, but in 1913 additional work was begun on the Murranji. On May 16th 1913 Surveyor A.B. Scandrett received instructions to carry out a 'Trigonometric and topographical Survey' of the Murranji country, during which 'the principal rivers and creeks must be traversed and all waterholes and springs correctly fixed'! Obviously those instructing him had no idea what the Murranji was like. He was also instructed to determine the best locations for roads and stockroutes, but there was no mention of bore or well sites.[361]

In July Scandrett established his first base camp at the western end of the Murranji, at the site of the abandoned Illawarra homestead where he probably could make use of a yard and perhaps shelter. The project must have been something of a surveyor's nightmare. Extremely dry conditions prevented him from surveying the Murranji for several months.[362] While he waited for rain he carried out survey work in the immediate area. He began at a cairn built at Hawk Knob by Surveyor Larry Wells in about 1905, and followed Armstrong Creek, Illawarra Creek, Fig Tree Creek, and extended his survey to Nelly's Waterhole and Gallery Hill.[363] He built cairns on a number of hills in the area, including Peak Knob and Flat-topped Hill near the Murranji Track.[364] When enough rain fell and the Murranji survey began he was soon to write that,

> *I have found out how difficult it is to trig this country, owing to no remarkable hills – all low lying heavily timbered scrubby rises...the Table lands...are one mass of Hedgewood & Lancewood flat country...I cannot see 20 chs ahead... no such thing as a spring exists in that country.*[365]

Scandrett often had to carry water for his men and horses, but had only a few small canteens and 'the horses had to be continually going back & forward' to get supplies. He had trouble obtaining meat, remarking that being 'out of the Cattle District 80 miles one side and 60 the other…we get no fresh meat at all', and extreme heat made it difficult to keep the meat he did get. He also commented that the 'heavy Hedgewood & Lancewood scrub has & is hampering us a great deal.'[366]

It may have been during this survey that one of Scandrett's men accidentally discovered an Aboriginal well near where No. 10 Bore was later erected (possibly it was the well at Nash's Spring). Told by the surveyor to move over a little, the man carrying a staff walked on top of an Aboriginal well covered with logs and grass. The covering gave way and he instantly disappeared from view. Luckily he was only stunned by the fall and the well proved useful for the surveyors.[367]

Along the Murranji Track there wasn't enough stone to build cairns so Scandrett put in 'substantial posts and mounds',[368] and he marked trees at various locations, one of which survives to this day at Murranji Waterhole (plate 1). He completed his survey early in 1914, but after twenty years of requests, suggestions, offers and surveys, the water supplies on the Murranji had not been improved, nor had any commitment been made by the Commonwealth Government to sink wells or bores.

In April 1916 representatives of Vestey, the powerful English company that had recently acquired cattle stations throughout Australia, added their name to the list of those asking the Government to improve water supplies on the Murranji. They requested, 'that three bores should be put down, between Wave Hill and Victoria River Station and Anthony's Lagoon'. This, they said, would 'enable them to bring their cattle from stations across the dry portion of the Territory and so gain access to Queensland and the stock market'.[369] It's been suggested that Vesteys was influential in convincing the Government to act on the issue of bores,[370] but this doesn't appear to be the case.

Captain Barclay's strong recommendation for bores in preference to wells seems to have been taken seriously because in August 1917 a contract was finally let to a Mr Gorey for the drilling of bores.[371] However, in spite of the fact that for years almost every request for help (including Vestey's) had referred to the Murranji and Barkly stockroutes and none had mentioned the north-south route, all except one of these bores were to be put down between the Roper River headwaters and Newcastle Waters – on the north-south stockroute rather than on the Murranji or Barkly.[372]

Gorey was under written contract to put down six bores and in verbal agreement with the Government to put down four others 'to connect with Eva Downs'. The latter included one at Frew's Ponds and another at Tandyidgee Waterhole (on the Barkly Tableland). By November 1917 Gorey had fulfilled his written contract and had put down, but not equipped, the bore at Frew's Pond. He then withdrew from the agreement.[373]

In spite of Gorey declining to continue with the work it's clear that the Government still intended to have bores put down on the Barkly and Murranji routes. In August 1918 the secretary of the Townsville Chamber of Commerce inquired whether a bore would be put down at Murranji in time for the next droving season. His concern was that 'missing a season means capital tied up, depreciation of the stock, a national loss and serious delay in supplying the Imperial Government and our Armies at the Front with necessary meat.'[374] The Government replied that a bore would be put down at Murranji Waterhole 'when the bores east of Newcastle Waters have been completed.'[375] In fact, a bore wasn't put down at Murranji Waterhole until many years after other bores along the Murranji Track were drilled and equipped.

To expedite the work yet to be done on the stockroutes east and west of the telegraph line, throughout the 1918 dry season the Northern Territory Administration transported equipment to a depot at Newcastle Waters.[376] In October 1918 – twenty-three years after the first recommendation that stockroute waters be improved, nineteen years after Durack's offer to put down wells on the Murranji, and two and a half years after Vestey's request for Government bores – tenders were called for the drilling and equipping of eight bores on the Murranji and Barkly stockroutes.[377] In April 1919 a driller named S.T. 'Territory' Peacock was awarded a contract to put down and equip eight bores across the Barkly Tableland,[378] and plans were being made to put bores across the Murranji. Syd Peacock was a Queenslander, a very religious man who would get down on his knees to pray every night[379] and a man with 'a reputation as being a rather touchy character.'[380] Peacock's contract included construction of six earth tanks, for each of which he was to be paid £450.[381] It appears that he began work near Anthony Lagoon in 1920 (No. 1 Bore), using a rig powered by a suction gas engine which required little water or wood, a clear advantage on the dry and treeless plains of the Barkly Tableland.[382]

In August 1920 the Acting Administrator gazetted a network of stockroutes throughout the Territory, including the Murranji Track.[383] In June of that year, 'an inspection of the stock route to the west of Newcastle Waters was made... and the remaining bore sites necessary to open this stock route selected and marked.'[384] The contract to put down these bores was also awarded to Peacock[385] and he began work on the first of the Murranji bores in 1921[386] (plates 32 & 33).

Putting down the bores wasn't without incident. During 1921 Peacock's drilling team was twice burnt out by bushfires. Much of their transport relied on horse and donkey teams and the fires destroyed essential stock feed; after the second fire they were forced to leave until after the wet season.[387] Work on No. 9 Bore on the Murranji was begun in 1922 and completed the following year.[388] According to Frank Lacy, a New Zealander who was one of Peacock's employees in 1923 and who later pioneered Mount Elizabeth station in the Kimberleys, 'the initial hole was abandoned after the loss of a string of tools in a cave-in of driftsand [sic] deep in the hole'.[389] Then, during the sinking of the second hole, Syd Peacock's son Percy, 'momentarily unthinkingly placed his hand upon the protruding casing, to feel if it was driving. The hammer fell, and his four fingers and part of his thumb were severed at the base instantly.' His two sisters who were in the camp tended him as he was taken over 300 kilometres along the rough overland track for treatment at Katherine.[390]

Peacock completed the last bore (No. 13) in September 1924. Each was equipped with a 7.3 metre [24ft] Comet mill on a 9 metre [40 ft] tower, 61.8 metres [200ft] of troughing, and an earthen tank. Some of the bores were also equipped with 'auxiliary engines',[391] though none had galvanized iron tanks. The Murranji bores were put down as follows:

No. 9: 42 kilometres from Newcastle Waters.

No. 10: 28 kilometres from No. 9 and 27 kilometres southeast of Murranji Waterhole.

No. 11: 30 kilometres northwest of Murranji Waterhole.

No. 12: 26 kilometres west of No. 11.

No. 13: 25 kilometres west of No. 12.

Almost as soon as the first bores were operating, problems arose. One concerned maintenance; it appears that in the case of bores on Crown Land the Administration had made no provision for their upkeep, and where it had done so it found it difficult to force those responsible – leaseholders upon whose land some of the bores were located – to meet their maintenance obligations.[392] In 1921 Peacock found one of the mills in need of oil. He rectified this and then put it to the Government: 'the next question is of the upkeep of the Mills, who is to do that, and who is now responsible...are the Mills to be allowed to be spoilt for the want of attention, and our work to be blamed[?].'[393] Peacock's own suggestion was that the police should be given responsibility for the bores, with assistance from the local leaseholders.

Maintenance problems continued for at least several more years[394]; moving parts were often not lubricated, troughs weren't cleaned and re-tarred for rust-proofing, and worn-out or broken parts were neglected for long periods.[395] In one instance a faulty ball valve resulted in all the water in an earthen tank draining away.[396] Problems persisted even after two men from the newly established Department of Works Depot at Newcastle Waters were assigned to this task as part of their overall duties. Apparently they were expected to spend only a few weeks a year maintaining all the bores in question.[397] Eventually two men were assigned to this task fulltime (on a seasonal basis) and the problem was considerably reduced, though certainly not eliminated.

Other problems included the earthen tanks at No. 12 and No. 13 Bores, both of which leaked. In 1924 Vestey's Manager G. Edwards wrote to the Department of Home and Territories citing a letter from one of their drovers who'd recently travelled a mob across the Murranji: 'The bores between here (Newcastle Waters) and the Jump Up are of no use to cattle. In my opinion the tanks all have a large leakage. Their holding capacity when I passed was only enough to give about 500 bullocks a drink.'[398]

In 1925 Peacock commented that,

Nos 12 and 13 Tanks are built on sites chosed [sic] by the Director [of Works], and all the money spent on them, or likely to be spent, will not make them to hold water.

Verbally I protested against No. 12 being built over a "Soak"... [while] At No. 13 I suggested to the Works Director that Iron should be provided to build a 30,000 [gallon] Tank.[399]

Peacock was right. By 1926 the Works Director had recommended that two Comet-type corrugated iron tanks be installed at each bore.[400] Tenders eventually were called for the supply of six 20,000 gallon galvanised iron tanks[401] to be placed at three bores and these were installed by Andy Rindberg in time for the 1927 droving season.[402] Rindberg also won the tender for putting troughs on tanks along the Murranji and he hired Eric Erlinson to assist him, on the promise of plenty of fresh meat. After two weeks on tinned food, Erlinson asked where the fresh meat was, so Rindberg went out and shot galahs – that was the promised fresh meat![403]

Apart from maintenance troubles or ill-considered methods of water storage, there was the problem of vandalism of bore facilities. The practice during wet seasons was to prevent the mechanical action of the mills by chaining the tails back against the fan. During the 1920-21 wet season someone allowed the mills to start work again by undoing the chains. The Director of Mines reported that,

The consequence was that one mill had the crank pin worn off, and the slide arm ruined, owing to its working without lubrication. In another mill the rods were broken, owing no doubt to the mill having been working during the cyclonic weather.[404]

He added that, 'Many other ways of interfering with the proper working of the mills and with the equipment are practiced by travellers and others'.

In 1920 'two Mills had about a bucket of stone thrown down into the pump casing,'[405] and in 1924 someone 'interfered with the troughing' at No. 10 Bore on the Murranji. On the Barkly, No. 1 Bore was almost wrecked when someone stole some bolts and loosened others. 'Territory' Peacock reported that, 'Every bolt above the platform had been loosened, and most of the bolts below the platform, while it would rock to and fro with the wind, and had worn two bolts partially through, the last remaining of six holding two legs together.'[406]

It was virtually impossible to do anything about such sabotage. Apparently none of the culprits were ever apprehended, nor was a reason for this vandalism forthcoming. Fortunately instances of serious vandalism seem to have disappeared after the mid-1920s though minor vandalism or damage through carelessness continued throughout the life of the stockroute.

Plate 1: Murranji Waterhole. The tree in the foreground was marked by Surveyor Scandrett in 1914 (Lewis Collection).

Plate 2: Murranji Waterhole full to overflowing, c1950 (Syd Jones Collection).

Plate 3: A bulwaddy thicket – 'Scrub as thick as a hedge' (Lewis Collection).

Plate 4: A typical bulwaddy tree, with many trunks sprouting from ground level, and dead and living limbs tangled together (Lewis Collection).

Plate 5: Bedford bullocks stringing across the Sturt Plain at the eastern end of the Murranji Track in 1950 (Jessop Collection).

Plate 6: Bedford bullocks climbing the Murranji jump-up in 1950. This cutting was probably made by Colson in 1943. The original and much steeper jump-up was about one kilometre to the north-east (Jessop Collection).

Plate 7: 'A crude but effective way of timbering them'. One of 'Territory' Peacock's men in an Aboriginal well on the Murranji between No. 9 and No. 10 Bores, c1923 (Stockman's Hall of Fame Collection, 8627).

Plate 8: 'Murranjo Natives' (Adelaide Observer, May 11 1912).

Plate 9: Aborigines from Newcastle Waters Station. It was warriors like these who defended the Murranji country (Adelaide Observer, November 13 1920).

Plate 10: Mudburra elder Nugget Kiriyalangungu cutting a boomerang from a bulwaddy limb, 1991 (Lewis Collection).

Plate 11: Nat 'Bluey' Buchanan, 1881 (The Bulletin, July 9 1881).

Plate 12: Michael Terry in the car in which he made the first motor vehicle crossing of the Murranji Track in 1923 (M. Terry, Through a Land of Promise. Herbert Jenkins, London, 1927: 89).

Plate 13: A car passing through a narrow laneway in a lancewood thicket on the Murranji Track, c1930 (Australian Investment Agency Collection).

Plate 14: Drover Mork (mounted), who had a hard time on the Murranji in 1899, photographed in 1933 (NT Pastoral Leases Investigation Committee Collection).

Plate 15: The Farquharson brothers and a neighbour in 1934. L-R: Archie, Harry, Charlie Young and Hughie. Young had a block near Tanami and perished there in 1939 (Fraser Collection).

Plate 16: A coolibah tree at Murranji Waterhole with the date 1926 and three sets of initials carved on it, possibly marking the grave of three men (Pankhurst Collection).

Plate 17: Airmen planning the days' search for the aviators who crash-landed near No. 11 Bore on the Murranji in 1936 (Roden Collection).

Plate 18: Sidney Kidman, whose drover Blake Miller took the first cattle east across the Murranji Track in 1904 (Pastoralist Review, January 16, 1911: 1224).

Plate 19: W.F. Buchanan, whose herds followed those of Kidman across the Murranji Track in 1904 (The Pastoralists' Review, January 15 1907).

Plate 20: Drover Walter Rose (lower left) and his men, 1906 (Adelaide Advertiser, December 1 1906).

Plate 21: A drover's idyll – Drover Rose's plant horses and packs (Adelaide Advertiser, December 1, 1906).

Plate 22: Charlie Phillott's men and plant photographed in western Queensland on their way out to Wave Hill in 1903 (courtesy Charlie Phillott's daughter, Betty Burrowes).

Plate 23: Drover Burgess' plant leaving Charleville for Wave Hill, 1909 (North Queensland Register, February 15 1909).

Plate 24: A mustering plant en route to Victoria River, 1920 (Adelaide Observer April 16 1921).

Plate 25: Humbert River wagonette and packs, and cattle wading in Murranji Waterhole, 1935 (Charlie Schultz Collection).

Plate 26: Drover Wason Byers' plant – pack and riding horses – on the Dry River stock route, c1940 (Walkabout, January 1 1942:20).

Plate 27: Drover's cook Frank Kearney loading a mule with canteens on the Barkly stock route, 1951 (Hoofs & Horns, August 1951: 30-31).

Plate 28: Drover Jack Burgess being farewelled by townspeople at Charleville as he sets out for Wave Hill, 1909 (Adelaide Observer, May 1 1909).

Plate 29: Jack-Dick Skuthorpe and his team photographed on Killarney Station (Narrabri) at the end of their trip from Wave Hill in 1904. Skuthorpe is probably the man standing (Pastoralists' Review, May 15, 1905: 182).

Plate 30: Drover Burgess who took cattle off Wave Hill in 1908, 1909 and 1910 (Adelaide Observer, October 25 1909).

Plate 31: Members of 'The Barclay Exploring Expedition,' taken before setting out for the Northern Territory. L-R: R. McPherson, G. Hill, Captain H.V. Barclay and W. Waldron sitting (Adelaide Observer, November 2 1911).

Plate 32: Peacock's suction gas plant & engine putting down No. 10 Bore on the Murranji in 1924 (E Schultz Collection, NTRS 1017).

Plate 33: Peacock's boring plant on the Murranji, 1924 (E. Schultz Collection, NT Archives, 1017/P1).

Plate 34: Dead dingoes in a water tank on the Murranji Track. In spite of such problems drovers had no choice but to drink the water, after a good boiling (Charlie Schultz Collection).

Plate 35: Charlie Swan (front), one of the old time Murranji drovers (Hoofs & Horns, October 1949).

Plate 36: Murranji Bore in the 1940s. The smooth sides of the water tanks became the 'pages' of the 'Bagman's Gazette', a notice board for drovers and other travellers (Walkabout Collection).

Plate 37: Drover Bill Cussens in his dinner camp, 1951 (Mahood Collection).

Plate 38: The notice of deviation of the stock route near Newcastle Waters in 1948 (Harney/ McCaffery Collection, NT Library).

Plate 39: Drover Wason Byers (left) and Jim Martin counting the bullocks near Dashwood Yard before Byers took delivery (Walkabout, March 1 1942).

Plate 40: Drovers Dick Morton and Dick Smith with Inverway cattle on the way to Brunchilly in 1951. During the big drought of 1952 Smith was the only drover to take cattle across the Murranji Track (Mettam Collection).

Plate 41: Drover Claude Prendergast on the Murranji Track with the 'galloping Newrys' in 1955 (Mettam Collection).

Plate 42: The government experimental road train near Montejinni in the late 1930s, a forerunner to the road trains that eventually replaced the drovers (Roden Collection).

Plate 43: The death knell of the drovers. A road train loading VRD cattle at Dashwood Yard in 1961 (Rayner collection).

Plate 44: Dick Scobie, his wife Kath (nee Zigenbine) and their son Len, c1950 (Scobie Collection).

Plate 45: Hidden Valley Station homestead as it was in 1955. No nails were used in its construction, everything being held together with wire (Scobie Collection).

Plate 46: Dick Scobie and Scotty Watson installing a pump at Scobie's Rockhole, c1952. Water was taken from this hole for domestic use (Scobie Collection).

Plate 47: Charlie Schultz at Humbert River in 1928. Charlie took cattle across the Murranji to Queensland in 1935, 1937, 1939 and 1941 (Charlie Schultz Collection).

Plate 48: Humbert River cattle watering at No. 12 Bore in 1935 (Charlie Schultz Collection).

Plate 49: Charlie Schultz overseeing the trucking of his cattle at Dajarra, western Queensland, at the end of a trip from Humbert River Station (Charlie Schultz Collection).

Plate 50: Drover's graffiti No. 11 Bore. TVH is the brand for Wave Hill Station (Lewis Collection).

Plate 51: A Hollywood-style cowboy on the side of a water tank at Murranji Bore, 1998 (Lewis Collection).

Plate 52: Drover Sid Biondi on the Murranji Track with VRD bullocks in 1955 (Mettam Collection).

Plate 53: 'Wirrawarra' Mick Cussens (brother of Bill Cussens), regarded by some who knew him as one of the best drovers(Scotty Watson Collection).

Plate 54: Drover 'Slippery' Prendergast on the Murranji, 1955 (Mettam Collection).

Plate 55: Jack Beasley, one of the early setters in the Victoria River district. He was variously a cattle duffer, ringer and drover (Lilly Collection)

Plate 56: 'Puddlin" Paddy Conway, old-time drover and 'travelling drovers' manager for Vesteys (Hoofs & Horns, July 1950: 45).

Plate 57: Harry Zigenbine resting at Bedford station in the Kimberley while taking delivery of bullocks in 1950 (Jessop Collection).

Plate 58: Sisters Kath and Edna Zigenbine surrounded by military admirers at Newcastle Waters during their first droving trip from the Kimberley to Queensland in 1942 (Argus Newspaper Collection, State Library of Victoria).

Plate 59: Elmore Lewis, 'the perfect seat on a horse', and Ken Hammer, in front of the Newcastle Waters hotel, 1951 (Mahood Collection).

Plate 60: One of the Murranji Track windmills, torn off and wrecked by a storm (Lewis Collection).

Plate 61: A water tank from McColls (Pandanus) Bore, at the western end of the Murranji Track, destroyed by a flash flood (Lewis Collection).

Plate 62: The drovers' memorial at Newcastle Waters, erected in 1988 (Lewis Collection).

Plate 63: Ex-Drover Dave Allworth's protest at the state of the Murranji Track in 2000. Murranji Bore (Lewis Collection).

CHAPTER 10

DROVING WASN'T MEANT TO BE EASY

The provision of bores and tanks across the Murranji and Barkly vastly improved the situation for drovers. They eliminated the old problem of the stockroutes being closed during dry periods and probably were a major factor in the almost total elimination of travellers dying along the track, but lack of water could still create difficulties for drovers and travellers. Indeed, water remained one of the greatest concerns for many years to come. One problem was the distance between the bores. On their completion, water points on the Murranji were an average of thirty-five kilometres (twenty-one miles) apart. Peacock's contract had not provided for a bore at Murranji Waterhole so if this hole went dry – as it did at some time every year – there would be a dry stage of seventy kilometres (forty-two miles) from No. 11 Bore to No. 10 Bore.

Likewise, there was no bore put in between No. 13 and Top Springs, so if the intervening natural waters dried up, drovers had a ninety kilometre (fifty-five mile) dry stage to negotiate. Dry stages of roughly eighty kilometres were also necessary if for some reason there was insufficient water at a bore. This could happen through lack of wind to turn the mill, failure of the mill through lack of maintenance or mechanical breakdown, wastage of water by careless drovers or travellers, or the outright selfishness of some drovers who would allow their cattle to drink two or three times at the expense of other drovers following behind.

In addition to these shortcomings with the water supply, other problems remained virtually unchanged since the Track was first opened. In many places it was still only a narrow laneway cut through the scrub, making it difficult to control the cattle, and there were still no officially declared stock reserves where the men and cattle could be rested. Almost every year a number of cattle died from eating an unknown poisonous plant. The dense scrub and the drummy limestone ground made the cattle nervous and rushes were a constant threat; if a rush occurred the scrub hindered the drover's efforts to regain control and posed a serious danger to both man and beast.

In October 1927, the Northern Territory's Chief Stock Inspector, Captain Frank Bishop, addressed many of the ongoing problems with the Murranji Track. In a letter he wrote to the Government Resident he described the track as being so narrow that the cattle would string out for up to three kilometres (two miles) and there was no chance for a horseman to head them if they rushed.[407] He added that the grazing and water were poor which meant that cattle had to be pushed through quickly, and a trip which should take twelve days had to be done in seven or eight, weakening the cattle and contributing to outbreaks of disease. Bishop stressed the urgent need for reserves along the Track, especially at No. 9 Bore where the country changed to grassland because 'cattle traveling from all western areas require to be rested after the severe ordeal which they pass…Continuous droving of stock over long stages without rest and water is one of the causes why cattle depreciate in value so quickly.' He pointed out that with the numbers of cattle passing along the track the windmills were barely able to provide sufficient water and suggested that engines with pumps should be installed at Bores 9, 11 and 13. He also noted that the section of track between Top Springs and the jump-up was 'practically impassable for motor traffic, owing to the bad state of the track and numerous deep creeks which have to be crossed,' and this should be 'made negotiable for motor traffic, if for no other reason than that of controlling outbreaks of disease in stock, as was the case in eight outbreaks of Pleuro-Pneumonia which occurred this year.'

The problems addressed by Bishop may be summarised as the need for improved water supply, stock reserves, scrub clearance and road works, and to this list could have been added 'removal of poison bush' and 'increased responsibility on the part of the drovers themselves'. At least two of his points were addressed within the next decade: a pathway was cleared through the bulwaddy and lancewood 'jungle' and engine pumps were installed at Bores 11, 12 and 13. With respect to the engine pumps, a third man was employed to do the pumping during the droving season because otherwise two men were expected to maintain twenty-one windmill pumps and three engine pumps along the Murranji and Barkly routes, with the result that many were out of order when the cattle season commenced.[408] Establishing reserves and improving the road took somewhat longer.

Occasionally other situations arose that were more an inconvenience for the drovers than a major problem for them or their cattle. In 1927 there were plans to cover the tanks with wire netting,[409] but if this was ever done it didn't last long and as a result the open nature of the tanks sometimes led to problems. Charlie Schultz said that sometimes there were so many dead birds in the tanks that you could hardly put your billy into the water. To try and stop this, drovers would throw big branches in so that the birds could get to the water safely or get out if they happened to fall in. On one occasion Charlie arrived at No. 12 Bore and found two dead dingoes in one of the tanks (plate 34). Apparently there was no water in the troughs and the dingoes, perishing for a drink, had walked along a large horizontal overflow pipe extending from the top of the tank. They had eventually fallen or jumped into the water, but the tank was only half full, so they couldn't touch the bottom or get out again, and slowly drowned.[410] Of course, unless a drover had sufficient water to take him on to the next bore he had no choice but to drink this contaminated water. In Charlie's case he used the water 'after boiling it up for a good while'.[411]

In spite of constant calls from drovers, station owners and Government employees for these problems to be rectified, from the time that the original Murranji bores were put down until the outbreak of the Second World War in 1939, very little progress was made. Without doubt this lassitude was in large measure due to the Great Depression, but Government inefficiency and indifference also played a part. It wasn't until the advent of the Second World War that serious consideration was given to these problems, and even then change was slow.

Establishing Reserves

Within seven years of the first eastward movement of cattle along the Murranji Track it was evident that stock reserves were needed so that cattle and horses could legally be rested or held to recuperate from disease outbreaks. When the Commonwealth Government sent Captain Barclay along the Track in 1911 to choose sites for wells, he was instructed to reserve ten square miles at each site.[412] In his report on this trip, Barclay wrote,

> *I consider a reserve of 10 sq. m. at each site would be sufficient for travelling stock, it would be better, however, to reserve 100 sq. m. at each since in such country an area like this could be leased with the well or bore for maintenance, moreover in the event of the surrounding country being taken up it would be difficult to enlarge the areas whilst they can always be reduced.*[413]

Barclay's well sites at Howell's Ponds and the Yellow Waterholes were determined to lie within the Newcastle Waters and Victoria River Downs pastoral leases, respectively.[414] A Department of External Affairs memo of October 1911 suggested that, 'Provision [had been] made for resumption and rent reduced proportionately',[415] but there's no evidence that this actually was done or that any reserves were declared at this time.

Eighteen years later the issue of travelling stock reserves was raised again. In February 1927 the North Australian Commission (NAC) was 'of the opinion that it is desirable that there should be reserves for travelling stock, at intervals along the Stock Routes'. The Commission recommended that an area of nine square miles in the form of a square and with the bore as the central point be declared at Bores 10, 11, 12, and 13, and that twenty-five square miles be reserved around Murranji Waterhole.[416]

Captain Bishop's letter of October 1927, cited above, added support to the NAC's recommendations and in June the following year C.W.L. Conacher, the Managing Director of Vesteys, wrote to the NAC suggesting among other things the establishment of travelling stock reserves. Conacher recommended a nine square mile reserve around each Government bore, a twenty-five square mile reserve at No. 9 Bore, and a twenty-five or fifty square mile reserve at Murranji Waterhole. The larger reserve at No. 9 was suggested because,

> *However good the water supply on the route, the 120 miles to this bore from Top Springs is always going to try cattle severely. Most of the way is along a narrow lane cut through the bulwaddy scrub and lancewood forest with practically no feed. It should be possible to rest the cattle here for a day or two to recover. In the case of sickness developing, it would be better to treat it here than to take the cattle right on to Newcastle Waters run.*[417]

The Murranji reserve was suggested because, 'people who wish to make a nuisance of themselves might take it up for a short period if it is not a reserve.'[418] Echoing Barclay's earlier warning, Conacher added that,

> *The time to make reserves for the future is now, before the country is fully developed. It is better to make such reserves too large than too small, they can be reduced if necessary later, but it would be almost impossible to increase without great expense later an area that was found to be too small.*[419]

The NAC acknowledged Vestey's letter, finding their suggestions 'reasonable and necessary', and recommended (again) to the Assistant Secretary of the Home and Territories Department that a reserve of fifty square miles be declared around Murranji Waterhole and that reserves of nine square miles be declared around the Government bores, including No. 9 Bore.[420]

It appears that the recommendations of Captain Bishop, the NAC and Vesteys resulted in the establishment of at least one stock reserve in practice, but not in law. In February 1941, in reply to a letter from the Australian Investment Agency (Vesteys) as to the status of the reserve at No. 10 Bore, the Northern Territory Administrator stated that,

> *no formal proclamation under any ordinance has been effected. However, you may take it that administratively that area is reserved for travelling stock... The Chief Inspector of Stock has very wide powers and...it is not necessary for any area to be proclaimed a reserve when he exercised his powers in quarantining travelling stock found to be infected with a disease... I am having an inspection made of the 16 square miles reserve and also of the 50 square miles reserve adjoining Pastoral Lease 208N, with a view to determining which of the two is the more suitable for quarantine purposes, having regard to all factors and in particular that of water supplies.*[421]

No action had been taken by June 1941 when Captain Bishop recommended that a quarantine reserve be created at No. 10 Bore,[422] or by August when J.W. Allen recommended a reserve at No. 10 Bore of at least ten square miles.[423]

It's not clear whether travelling stock reserves had been formally declared by 1942, but in September that year A.S. Bingle, the Managing Director of Vesteys, agreed with Administrator Abbott that areas of five square miles should be enclosed at 'certain important bores', including No. 9 Bore. He suggested that these be known as 'camping reserves'.[424] Whether this proposal came to anything is unknown.

According to the Chief Veterinary Officer, A.L. Rose, a fifty square mile reserve existed at Murranji Waterhole by 1947 and reserves of either ten, nine or five square miles had been established elsewhere.[425] Apparently there was a sixteen square mile reserve around No. 10 Bore before 1948 when a further 200 square miles of surrounding country was resumed from pastoral lease 208N (held by Vesteys) for a stock and quarantine reserve.[426]

In 1948 plans 'evolved' to establish a quarantine reserve at Top Springs because,

> *in a normal season something like 40,000 head of cattle are cleared from there onwards to Elliot [sic]. We have always considered that to adequately cater for this traffic, we must have a quarantine and holding reserve in this area, a bore additional to the Top Springs hole and eventually also a depot. We hope also to ultimately establish a dip there and if possible*

accommodation for one or two officers.[427]

During 1949 the area around Top Springs was inspected and the Lands Department was asked to earmark the necessary land, but in 1952 the entire area was included in the Montejinni block resumed from VRD, put up for ballot and won by Bill Crowson and Bill Tapp.[428] The need for a reserve at Top Springs was highlighted in 1954 when some weak cattle from a Vesteys mob were caught by rain near Pussycat Bore. The stock inspector told the drover to rest the cattle for a few days, but Bill Crowson, 'arrived the following day and hunted them off.'[429]

The proposal for a reserve dragged on for two more years and was complicated by the fact that the owners of Montejinni station had carried out improvements in the area, and that some land at Top Springs had previously been leased for the establishing of a store.[430] These problems were eventually resolved and in July 1956 an area of eighty-four square miles was declared as the Top Springs Quarantine Reserve.[431]

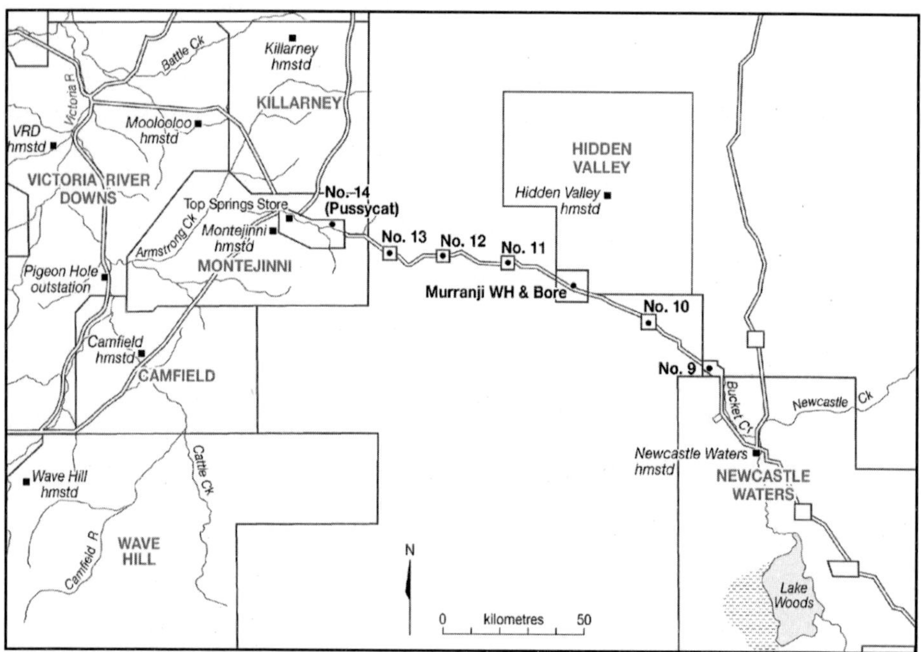

The Murranji Track showing bores and reserves, c1960

Clearing the Track

The difficulties that dense scrub on parts of the Murranji created for drovers and other travellers have already been described. According to Ernestine Hill, 'The path was burnt out in the early years, and hacked with axes'.[432] In 1904 Drover Phillott had to cut a track from the Yellow Waterholes into Largungen Waterhole for his waggonette,[433] so it seems likely that those who brought the first wagons and drays across the Murranji also had to cut a track in various places. In any case, where it passed through the bulwaddy and lancewood thickets the track was a winding narrow pathway for nearly fifty years (plate 13).

The first formal mention of the need to clear the Track to assist cattle droving is in the letter Captain Bishop wrote to the Administrator in 1927. In this report Bishop described the Track as being,

> *so narrow that cattle get a lead on of at least two miles, due to the thick scrub growing on either side of the track which a horse-man has no chance of getting through.*
>
> *The tail end of the cattle spread out and become, at times, lost in the scrub; very often the lead rush with the result some of the cattle are lost, and the galloping of the individual bullocks depreciates their value'.*[434]

Drover O'Keefe undoubtedly would've heartily endorsed Bishop's call. Apparently he was a large man with a high opinion of himself; carved on a boab tree on Auvergne station is the statement, 'The Fallop O'Keefe the Big I Am'.[435] In certain Irish and Scottish dialects a 'fallop' (or falloch) is a word for a large lump of something unpleasant. In a Cumberland dialect 'fallop' is a word for something tattered, and in east Yorkshire 'fallap' refers to something like a sail or a sheet blowing and flapping about.[436] After taking 1300 Wave Hill bullocks across the Murranji in 1927 O'Keefe certainly fitted the bill. The *Northern Territory Times* reported that,

> *O'Keefe being of extra large statue [sic] could not negotiate the Bullwaddy [sic] scrub on the Murrangi [sic] track successfully although his bullocks did so. When seen O'Keefe was tattered and torn and would have won a special prize at any fancy dress ball.*[437]

The *Times* went on to describe the Murranji Track as, 'the worst in Australia' and to note that 'vast improvements are required to bring this route up to a normal one.'

Bishop's call to widen the Track through the lancewood and bulwaddy was repeated in a letter from C. Conacher (Vesteys) to the NAC in 1928:

> *Most of the way is along a narrow lane cut through the bullwaddy [sic] scrub and lancewood forest... We would like you to seriously consider doing something to widen the narrow lane above referred to. In similar situations in Queensland, a road one or two chains wide has been cleared right through the scrub.*[438]

In 1931 VRD manager Alf Martin wrote to J.W. Allen (NTPLA), highlighting the difficulties of droving cattle along the narrow laneway through the Murranji scrub:

> *The cattle out this way get very touchy in timber. One of our drovers lost the whole mob of One thousand head at No. 13 Bore.*[439] *The scrub was that thick that the cattle just trotted away and the men could not head them. Another drover lost Ninety head in daylight going through this scrub.*[440]

Martin pointed out that the Track, 'could be one of the best roads in the North as there is not a creek or a stone on it but the stumps and anthills make it one of the most dangerous roads out this way,' and he suggested that 'a track say twenty chains wide [400 metres], cut through this scrub would overcome the difficulty'. He said 'it would only be necessary to cut the biggest timber so that the drover can see his cattle and the cattle can get a little daylight.'[441]

The NTPLA took up Martin's concerns with the Director of the Works Department, suggesting that a track twenty chains wide would be best but 100 yards would do to begin with, and that the timber should be cut down and burnt. It proposed that the work be done by genuine local unemployed at the end of the droving season.[442]

By December 1932, £300 had been allocated, 'to be utilised for widening the stock route in question.'[443] A contract was let to Fred Colson in 1933 to clear a path twenty-one metres wide through the worst patches of scrub between No. 13 Bore and No. 9 Bore, this apparently amounting to 'approximately two miles of scrub more or less.'[444] Colson completed his contract in May 1934,[445] and while his work undoubtedly eased the scrub problem for drovers, there was room for vast improvement. However, the next attack on the Murranji scrub didn't take place for another decade, for reasons that the Resident Engineer explained to the Director of Allied Forces in 1944:

> *The matter of clearing and widening the Murranji Stock Route is one which has been dragging on for many years due to the fact that there was no*

> *mechanical equipment in this Territory prior to the reconstruction of the North-South Road, and the small amount made available from year to year was quite insufficient to even make a showing on this route.*[446]

In October 1943 Colson was again employed to clear scrub from the stockroute, this time a strip 109 metres [330 feet] wide over a distance amounting to about twenty-five kilometres. He was also to clear areas of 50 acres around Bores 11, 12, and 13, make thirteen creek crossings and grade and widen part of the road,[447] all this to be done before the start of the 1944 droving season[448] at a cost of £15,000.[449] It appears that Colson managed to do the work on schedule. A journalist driving across the Murranji some time in 1944 reported that,

> *Great work has been done on the Murranji stock route this year. Where the lancewoods, bauhinias and bulwaddy forests had in the past made droving so difficult, there are now wide majestic boulevards, all cleared by men of the Territory who have made use of the bulldozer...this mighty modern machinery has bashed ways through, and the heaps of trees and roots and creepers that were strewn about have been burnt.*[450]

Without doubt this additional clearing made the work of the drovers much easier, but within a few years a heavy growth of lancewood suckers on the cleared areas became a matter of concern.[451] As a result, in September 1950 £3826 was allocated for re-clearing the Track and areas around the bores.[452]

While the wide laneway through the scrub certainly improved the situation for drovers, the Murranji Track was still dangerous and feared by many, and the drummy ground and the dense bush bordering the cleared corridor still made the cattle nervous. Rushes were frequent and if the cattle scattered into the scrub drovers still had to risk their lives chasing them through the 'jungle'. For example, some years after the initial clearing work in 1933-34, Drover Swan (plate 35) lost 700 head after a rush on the Murranji,[453] and in 1941 a VRD drover lost 500 near No. 10 Bore.[454] Likewise, reports of rushes continued after the last major clearing work was completed in 1944.[455]

'Poison Bush'

Instances of European livestock falling ill or dying in mysterious circumstances began from the time that Europeans first entered the Murranji region. Explorer Stuart had one horse die and another fall ill during his retreat from the 'dark and dismal forest', northwest of Nash Spring.[456] Stuart speculated that the problem was due to, 'the days being so extremely hot and the feed so dry that there is little nourishment in it', but it's just as likely that 'poison bush' was involved.

During his crossing of the Murranji in 1886 Bluey Buchanan had several horses die at Frew's Pond and two more at the Yellow Waterholes, 'apparently from the same cause, probably poisoned.'[457] This is the first clear-cut instance of what was to be a persistent problem for Murranji travellers.

Camels were particularly susceptible to something in the Murranji flora. In 1908 Surveyor L.A. Wells lost three camels in one night at 'Murrunjai',[458] and when Captain Barclay was choosing locations for wells on the Murranji in 1911 his camels,

> *had a bad time, one of them (my riding camel) eating nothing for eight days and also refusing water, they are now recovering – No doubt they ate some poisonous plant of which we know nothing, since they certainly did not get at any known to us.*[459]

Barclay was lucky that none of his camels died. Sarli Mahommet, one of the early Afghan camel-drivers in the Victoria River country, lost all twenty-six of his team while travelling across the Murranji.[460]

While it seems likely that there were many instances of cattle losses from 'poison bush' during the early decades of Murranji droving, the earliest documentation appears to be a report by Captain Bishop in 1932. By this time suspicion was focused on two plant species – ironwood (*Erythophylem chlorostachys*) and caustic vine (*Sarcostemma australe*):

> *The reported cases of poisoning of travelling stock were investigated during the year and specimens of 'caustic vine' and 'ironwood leaves' were collected in the vicinity of No. 13 Bore. Similar specimens had already been investigated by the Council for Scientific and Industrial Research, and were found to be toxic... A notice board was erected warning drovers not to camp cattle in the vicinity of No. 13 Bore.*[461]

The signboard and the subsequent clearing of the Track by Colson in 1934 apparently made no difference as reports of cattle poisoning continued. In April 1934 D.D. Smith, the Resident Engineer, expressed the view that concern about poison bush was out of proportion to the actual problem. He pointed out, first, 'that Ironwood trees are growing practically the full length of the Stockroute [and] Caustic Vine grows in isolated patches also along this route', and second, 'From personal observation...very few cattle are being poisoned...

Last year approximately 30,000 cattle travelled this route and only ten dead beasts were counted between No. 13 Bore and Newcastle Waters.'[462]

What amounted in Smith's view to a 'few cattle' being poisoned, was apparently a few too many to other Government officials and to the Northern Territory Pastoral Lessees Association. Reports of poisoning continued, and repeated suggestions were made to remedy the situation. For example, in 1935 Captain Bishop wrote that,

> *Mortality in stock travelling this route, due to poison plants, was again reported...continuous attention to the new growth of ironwood shoots and caustic vine, which are the plants suspected of causing the mortality, appears the only solution.*[463]

This same solution was suggested by J.W. Allen when he wrote to the Department of Interior in April 1936 and reported that,

> *it is not advisable for a drover to hang up at No. 13 Bore after giving cattle the first drink...owing to the presence of poison bush in the vicinity... Every year a few head of travelling stock are lost through eating the poison bush, and it is asked that arrangements should be made for the bush to be grubbed out each year as soon as the wet season is over.*[464]

Later that year Allen suggested that the stockroute be changed to run, 'from Yellow Waterhole to the head of the Townshend River thence to Winari Springs and on to No. 45 Bore. Such a route would cut out a very great deal of rough travelling over hard limestone and bad creek crossings,'[465] and 'would [also] have the effect of avoiding a tract of poison plant country around No. 13 Bore.'[466] Allen's concerns about poison bush and his suggestion for changing the position of the stockroute were supported by Vesteys who claimed that Drover Johnstone lost eighteen head near No. 13 Bore in 1936[467] and that Drover Swan lost twenty head in 1937.[468] With respect to Johnstone's losses, Captain Bishop cast doubt on many of them being caused by poison bush. He expressed the opinion that Johnstone was 'a poor man on the road in charge of cattle', and suggested the losses were as much to do with cattle being debilitated due to drought in the western areas. He added that if Johnstone had taken notice of the sign at No. 13 Bore he probably wouldn't have had any trouble.[469]

In April 1938 the Department of Interior allocated £250, 'for investigations in the vicinity of Yellow Water Hole, Mt. Townsend and No. 49 Bore' (Red Rock) for a stockroute deviation to avoid the poison bush. The Department also determined that the cause of death of cattle should be thoroughly investigated because, 'For some years past the ironwood suckers in the immediate vicinity of Bore No. 13 have been cut down each year', and, 'This route has been used for many years and unless definitely proved that cattle are being poisoned in this locality the expenditure necessary to deviate the stock route does not appear to be justified.'[470]

In May 1938 Captain Bishop was sent to inspect cattle passing by No. 13 Bore and to examine any dead beasts to determine the cause of death. After talking with Drovers Swan and Winters and examining their mobs, Bishop concluded that,

> *all the evidence obtained from past boss drovers who travelled many thousands of bullocks from Wave Hill across Murranji Stock Route without losses, and some present day drovers namely Regan and Crouch who have had no losses in the area, conclusively proves that the poison theory can be set aside, and there is another more prevalent cause namely, Delivering [sic] weak and debilitated young steers to drovers to be driven a distance of 650 miles from Wave Hill to Morestone.*[471]

The cause, according to Bishop, was due primarily to two factors: weak and debilitated cattle incapable of walking long distances being delivered to drovers, and drovers being short of man-power which required cattle to be huddled up and rounded up too much, causing them stress. Both factors led to cattle becoming lame or diseased, and drovers put the resulting shortages down to poison bush.

When he read Captain Bishop's report, A.S. Bingle wrote to the Department of Interior expressing doubts about Bishop's assessment.[472] The Department replied in support of Bishop, citing his inspection of Drover Regan's cattle near Newcastle Waters made shortly after his inspection of Swan's and Winters' cattle at No. 13 Bore. Regan told Bishop he'd lost eight bullocks after they ate poison bush and that one bullock in his mob was still suffering from poison. Bishop examined the bullock and diagnosed it as a case of pleuro-pneumonia. The bullock was killed and the diagnosis confirmed by post-mortem examination.[473]

The following year Bishop confirmed his 1938 assessment when he inspected seven mobs; he diagnosed cases of pleuro', 'three-day sickness' and redwater fever, but none due to poison bush.[474] However, in November 1942 D.J. Walker, the then Acting Chief Inspector of Stock, reported that, 'there is little doubt that some poisonous plant is growing in the vicinity of No. 13 bore. Losses occurred in about two mobs out of every three.' He then went on to describe in some detail the post-mortem features of poison victims and also the symptoms which included a cough exactly like that of cattle with pleuro-pneumonia, and he concluded that,

> *The sudden onset of the condition affecting a considerable number of stock and the absence of fresh cases when clear of the area, together with the linear appearance of the inflammation point very strongly to the effect of a highly irritant poisonous plant.*[475]

Walker recommended a scientific investigation to identify the species involved including, in particular, 'feeding tests at suitable locations.'

During the war the question of 'poison bush' appears to have been dropped, but in 1947 feeding trials with cattle and horses were conducted.[476] These apparently confirmed the opinion of many drovers that ironwood was involved,[477] but didn't implicate caustic bush. Release of these results led to requests for the authorities to grub out ironwood suckers along the Murranji Track,[478] but the authorities were reluctant to remove them. They thought 'these trees are a bit too numerous to warrant complete scrubbing out' and they believed incidents of poisoning were caused by 'the absence of water between Top Springs and No. 13 Bore which caused the cattle to pick at anything green along that portion of the track.' It was decided to wait and see if the newly installed No. 14 (Pussycat) Bore would make a difference to the problem.[479]

Pussycat Bore made no difference. Losses continued throughout the following decade, but there's no record that any action was taken until 1959 when Aborigines were employed to clear ironwood suckers along the western part of the stockroute.[480] In 1960-61 the old idea of a stockroute deviation south of the affected area was considered again, but again nothing eventuated. Trial spraying of suckers was carried out in 1965, but was considered impractical, and cases of poisoning or suspected poisoning continued to be reported until road transport replaced droving across the Murranji in 1967.[481]

Improving the Water Supply

In 1927 Captain Bishop described the water supply on the Murranji – the number of water sources, mill equipment and storage capacity – as, 'inadequate to meet the requirements of travelling stock, during the months of April, May and June', when demand was heaviest,[482] and by 1928 calls for extra bores had begun.[483]

Inadequate maintenance added to the problem well into the 1930s. The bores weren't maintained at all during the wet summer months when no droving took place. Instead, the tanks were filled at the end of the droving season and the mills turned off.[484] This policy almost had dire consequences for Vestey's General Manager, Alex Moray, who suffered an attack of fever while travelling across the Murranji on horseback in March 1933. At best he found the water supplies very low. The mill at No. 9 Bore wasn't working and at No. 12 Bore, 'there was not a drop of water for ourselves or our horses'. He decided to push on and, 'was very lucky in getting water at the Yellow Waterholes'.[485]

In 1935 Bishop listed various troubles with the water supply and blamed the situation on under-staffing and the administration of the Murranji stockroute from Alice Springs. He recommended that an extra man be hired for the maintenance crew and that control of the stockroutes be centred at Newcastle Waters.[486] Bishop's criticisms weren't substantiated in a field investigation by J. Flemming, the Chief Mechanical Engineer, and his recommendations were rejected.[487]

Justified or not, complaints about the water supply continued.[488] In April 1936 J.W. Allen reported the Murranji Waterhole dry for the third successive year, the Yellow Waterholes dry, and water supplies at No. 9 and No. 10 low.[489] He repeated an earlier suggestion that a bore be put down at Murranji and water pumped into the waterhole. A few months later Drover Saltmer reported water along the Murranji as 'the best I have ever seen it. Bore and surface water in abundance.'[490]

Allen's suggestion that a bore be put down at Murranji Waterhole was favourably received, but his proposal that water from the bore be pumped into the waterhole was regarded as impractical.[491] Extra bores for the Murranji stockroute may already have been on the Government's agenda because by July plans were being made to sink a bore at the Yellow Waterholes and another at Murranji Waterhole, and if successful to equip them in time for the 1937 droving season.[492]

It doesn't appear that a Government bore was ever put down at the Yellow Waterholes[493] (although eventually the hole itself was cleaned out by bulldozer in 1948[494]), but work on the bore at Murranji Waterhole was in progress by August 11 1936.[495] J. Gorey was the contractor[496] and apparently it was an extremely difficult hole to drill.[497] However, a good yield of water (72,000 gallons per day)[498] was struck at about 600 feet and a mill, four 25,000 gallon tanks and 200 feet of troughing was erected in 1937[499] (plate 36). New 25,000 gallon tanks and 400 feet of troughing were installed at other bores along the track in 1936-37, including at least three tanks at No. 10 Bore.[500]

Construction of the Murranji Bore largely eliminated the possibility of a dry stage between No. 11 Bore and No. 10, but water problems due to malfunction of equipment continued. In some instances problems were caused by the drovers themselves. For example, in October 1937 D.D. Smith described a long-standing problem:

> *During the droving season thousands of gallons of water are allowed to go to waste by irresponsible drovers employed by Vesteys... In many instances I have received complaints from the Management of Vesteys to the effect that tanks on this section of the Stockroute are dry or not sufficient water to water their oncoming cattle.*[501]

Before 1936 the troughs had been fitted with self-acting float valves. These were 'invariably abused' by drovers, leading to 'considerable waste of water which created bogs around the troughs.'[502] Drovers brought their cattle in to water in lots of about 200 and would take off the float valve to allow a full flow of water until the cattle had had enough to drink. While the first lot of cattle was drinking the drovers would return to the main herd to bring in another 200. If the drovers were short-handed or for some reason they were slow to return, hundreds of gallons might overflow from the troughs, a problem said to be particularly common at No. 13 Bore.[503]

In an effort to prevent wastage the float valves were replaced with hand-operated stopcocks. These were supposed to 'not occasion any difficulties to the drovers and [were] definitely to be preferred from the viewpoint of wastage and maintenance'.[504] In fact, they appear to have made little difference as reports of bogs around troughs continued long after stopcocks were installed. For example, in 1941 at least 50,000 gallons ran to waste at No. 10 Bore,[505] and at No. 9 Bore there was a bog two feet deep.[506] In July 1950 D.D. Smith reported water had been let run out of tanks at least ten times that year.[507]

Auxiliary pumps were provided at many bore sites to be used if the windmill failed to provide adequate water, but they were expensive to run. In an effort to reduce annual pumping costs, in May 1939 the 24 foot mill and auxiliary engine pump at No. 11 Bore was replaced with a 27 foot mill. Government officials believed the 27 foot mill performed satisfactorily, so similar changes were made at No. 12 and No. 13 Bores with a total saving to the Government of between £500 and £600 per year.[508] This change wasn't greeted favourably by the cattlemen and drovers,[509] especially with the increase in numbers of cattle using the Track after the outbreak of the Second World War.

CHAPTER 11

THE DROVERS' WAR

During the droving season immediately preceding the outbreak of the Second World War in September 1939, 33,288 cattle travelled across the Murranji.[510] With the coming of war one would reasonably expect an increase in cattle numbers the following year, but instead of rising, the number of cattle appears to have dropped. Vesteys sent 21,000 head to Queensland, but only 14,000 were sent via Murranji[511] and it seems unlikely that cattle from other stations would've boosted the total number of cattle to anything like the 1939 figure.

In 1941 Constable Morey at Newcastle Waters reported that approximately 33,000 cattle had crossed the Murranji between May and September, and with the exception of three mobs from VRD, all were Vestey's cattle.[512] Morey believed this number to be a record, but more than 33,000 had passed over the Murranji in 1939.[513] Drover Elliott (senior) in charge of one of these mobs experienced a rush in which he lost about five hundred bullocks. He stopped for two days at Murranji Bore and recovered many of them, but had to leave about 160 head behind.[514]

Just as cattle numbers didn't rise markedly after the outbreak of the war, conditions on the stockroute remained little changed from the pre-war period, although a few works were undertaken. For example, in September 1941 a new bore was put down at No. 10 to replace the old bore that had collapsed and filled with sand.[515] Unfortunately it did little to improve the supply.[516] In other ways conditions on the stockroute deteriorated. An example is the installation of larger windmills at No. 12 Bore and No. 13 Bore to save engine pumping costs.[517] It appears that the auxiliary engine pumps at these bores were left in use until about 1939, after which they were given to the Army and removed.[518]

The decision to do away with the engines and to depend upon windmills came as a surprise to A.S. Bingle who informed the Administrator that,

> *during the last two seasons...the engine had to be used to pump up the tanks before the beginning of the season and the pumper from Newcastle Waters was continually backwards and forwards keeping up sufficient water for the numbers of cattle which were travelling....I think with increased numbers the position will become precarious and there is a likelihood of a bad smash.*[519]

Bingle pointed out that over 14,000 cattle had crossed the Murranji in 1940, with greater numbers expected in 1941, and suggested that a portable engine should be purchased, mounted on a truck and used as an emergency pumping unit. Apparently there were plans to install extra tanks at this time because Bingle's final comment was to express his hope that 'the additional tanks are erected before the start of the next cattle season.'[520]

Bingle's concerns about the engines were shared by Field Officer McInnes who warned of the consequences of an outbreak of 'pleuro', as had happened in a number of mobs in 1940:

> *One has only to contemplate on the serious position which would arise should a mob of 1,250 cattle be held up at a bore equipped with a windmill and storage of 100,000 gallons, and supplying the quarantine stock with 10,000 gallons per day for 14 days. Even assuming the mill was in perfect running condition it still could not pump nearly 10,000 gallons per day.*[521]

The NTPLA and others voiced similar concerns[522] so late in 1940 the Administrator moved to have the engines put back on the bores. This had not happened up to July 1941, causing severe problems as VRD manager Alf Martin explained:

> *Across the Murrenji [sic] route the P.W. Department have taken the engine pumps away and replaced them by Mills and these do not pump enough water to water the cattle at the rate Vesteys are sending them in – only a day or two days between mobs of 1,250 head. When the writer was passing No. 10 it was dry last week, from there it is about 16 miles on to the Murrenji Bore. This tank only had enough water for one mob and unless there was a big wind the mob that was back at No. 12 bore would not get a drink until they reached No. 9 Bore. ...Have never seen the bores in such a bad way as*

they are now. The number of cattle on the stockroute now is Vesteys 27,000 and 3,700 of our cattle[523]

In May 1941 Captain Bishop wrote to the Government Secretary urging the installation of an engine pump at No. 10 Bore:

Please expedite action for installing an engine at No. 10 Bore Murranji stock route which is the most important centre of all on N.T. stock routes.

The area in the vicinity of No. 10 bore is the first place to rest and hold cattle after a severe treck [sic] across Murranji Jungle and timbered country.

The present watering arrangements at this site has been long inadequate...[524]

It appears that in this instance the shortage of water at No. 10 Bore was caused by Captain Bishop quarantining several mobs in the vicinity because of sickness. For this he was reprimanded by the Administrator who alleged that there wasn't enough sickness to warrant holding up the herds and also that this should've been done much further west. He alleged that the real reason Bishop held up the mobs was to please Newcastle Waters, and that he had an unprofessional relationship with the station because he stayed at the Newcastle Waters homestead rather than in the cottage provided for him. The Administrator advised the Department of Interior that he believed 'Bishop's actions this regard so irresponsible it may be necessary to recall him to Darwin' and that 'under circumstances may be necessary Minister appoint temporarily field-officer McInnes as Deputy Chief Inspector Stock[525] It appears that Bishop was removed or resigned shortly afterwards because there are no further reports by or about him, and the following year Bingle advised Abbott that, 'We seem to be getting along very well with the new Chief Inspector of Stock.'[526]

As there's no further correspondence in Government files relevant to the issue of engine pumps it appears that they were replaced late in the year or early in 1942, but complaints about water supplies and also the dense Murranji scrub (and no doubt about poison bush) continued throughout the rest of the 1940s,[527] and Government action was as slow as ever – until the entry of Japan into the war. Then everything changed, and maintaining the Murranji Track took on great importance.

In 1942 over 47,000 cattle passed along the Murranji stockroute.[528] A number of factors combined to cause this dramatic increase, the most important being the Japanese bombing of Darwin and other north Australian centres in

February 1942. One effect of these attacks was the closing of the Wyndham meatworks so that cattle which would otherwise have been sent to Wyndham now had to be sent across the Murranji; Vesteys alone made plans to send 30,000 head by that route.[529] In addition, the tremendous influx of Allied troops to the eastern states created a rapidly increasing demand for beef.

The movement of cattle in such huge numbers intensified all of the problems encountered in previous years, and the price was paid for years of neglect. The most critical problem continued to be the unreliable and inadequate water supply. The facilities along the Murranji, long neglected and inadequate for the numbers of cattle using the route, were stretched to breaking point.

At the beginning of 1942, Bingle was well aware of this potential problem. He wrote to the Government Secretary in Alice Springs in March, asking him to ensure that the bores on the Murranji were kept in working order during the coming season:

> *it is very necessary that proper attention should be given to the supplies of water at the bores en route. Last year several of these bores were not working, others that were equipped with only windmills and no supplementary pumping power were fortunate in that they were in an area where good surface water remained until late in the year...Last year auxiliary pumping power was supposed to be available on the Murranji track. We consider this is very necessary as mills are liable to become becalmed in the winter months and cannot possibly pump sufficient water for the big numbers of cattle which are travelling close together.*[530]

In addition, new problems were being encountered because top priority for resources was given to the military. In another letter in March, Bingle wrote to the Administrator asking his help:

> *You are no doubt well aware of the difficulties we are experiencing... particularly in regard to the lack of communication. The aerial services between stations have suspended and, of course, supplies of benzine are limited and consequently motor trucks belonging to the stations have to be used very sparingly until such time as we can get gas producer units to these stations...We recently sent forward several of these units by ship from the west, but unfortunately they did not reach the port of destination. Now we are anxious to try and get some preferential freight through to Alice Springs.*[531]

Labour shortages were also apparent on the stations,[532] although whether this problem affected the drovers is unclear.

Another effect of the bombing of northern centres was to raise the fear of a Japanese invasion to fever pitch. To deny any invading force access to a readily available food supply, plans were immediately drawn up to move huge numbers of cattle from the Kimberleys and the Victoria River district to Queensland, via the Murranji Track. The invasion fear only lasted for a short time – less than a year[533] – but by the time it had diminished, contracts had been signed and the cattle movement was under way.

The only organisation believed capable of handling a project of this size was Vesteys, so in April 1942 the Commonwealth Government gave Vesteys responsibility for the supply of cattle to the armed forces and for the removal of cattle from the Kimberley and Victoria River districts.[534] This was in spite of the fact that Bovril (VRD) already had signed a contract to deliver 10,000 head to the Army at Adelaide River.[535] Bovril protested and claimed that the military in Darwin and a 'big part of the military in Melbourne' were opposed to Vesteys receiving this contract, which had been drawn up 'by a few in Melbourne in the Food Control Department'.[536] They were almost certainly justified in their belief that something underhand had gone on, but their protests came to nothing.

Vesteys gained a virtual monopoly over the supply of meat to the army and other producers, including Bovril, had little option but to sell their cattle to Vesteys. This caused considerable resentment because it was believed that Vesteys could name the price they'd pay, and some pastoralists thought they weren't paying enough.[537] When the contract came up for renewal in 1943 it was decided that 'the prices being paid for cattle under Vestey's contract constituted a matter which, in the absence of competition, should be determined by the Prices Commissioner.'[538] However, Vesteys appears to have had its contract renewed each year for the duration of the war.

The job of organizing and controlling the evacuation of an additional 20,000 to 30,000 cattle fell to Bingle, making his earlier concerns all the more pressing. It was one thing to be given the contract to move this huge number of cattle, but another to get them across the Murranji and beyond. Large numbers of drovers had to be hired, many of whom were new to the Territory and which Bingle noted 'did not know their routes and distances'.[539] This assessment was shared by Drover Bill Cussens (plate 37) who said that, 'During the war like they brought out drovers'd, you know, never seen a mob of cattle before. And there were cattle run away and left 'em and walked off and left 'em. They didn't know what they were doing, of course.'[540]

The movement of so many mobs had to be controlled to prevent 'traffic jams', and Vestey's contract included a guarantee from the Government that adequate water would be provided. On April 10th 1942 Bingle wrote again to the Government Secretary and said that,

> *we have now agreed to undertake the contract on behalf of the Commonwealth Government to remove from the East Kimberleys as many fattening age bullocks as possible into Queensland or on to other suitable areas where they will be marketable...*
>
> *It is necessary that the greatest co-operation shall be given in the maintenance of the watering facilities on the stock routes concerned...We expect this year to move an additional 20/30,000 cattle over the route, that is in addition to the number of our own that I gave you in my previous letter.*
>
> *I suggest that you should make a survey of the existing conditions of the various water improvements and see that they are put in order for there must be no chance of a mishap, through lack of attention, which will cause any undue losses among the travelling cattle.*[541]

With this guarantee the ball was firmly in the Government's court and the relevant departments focused greater attention on the problem. One response was to equip two trucks with portable pumps to be on hand as required during the 1942 season.[542]

On April 17th Field Officer Clough inspected the Murranji stockroute and reported all tanks full, but that at No. 9, 'cattle are watering out of the [earthen] tank itself, and making a terrible pollution of the water. This fence will have to be rebuilt to at least 2 ft higher.'[543]

The Newcastle Waters police were also asked to make regular patrols and report on the Murranji bores.[544] Apparently there were no problems until June 1942 when Constable Littlejohn reported that 'the water in the tanks at No. 11 was dangerously low and that No. 12's tanks were dry.'[545] Problems were also encountered in June by Drover McIndoe who reported that,

> *Generally I had a bad trip from Wyalong Bore to Newcastle there being no water for cattle at bores No. 48, 49, 12 and 9.... Bores No. 9 and 10 are situated on favourable sites for wind, while Murranji 11, 12 and 13 bores are in densely timbered country with no wind tracks cut to these bores and only benefit by a very strong wind.*[546]

McIndoe went on to suggest that,

> *four and half inch pumps be put on these bores so they may utilise the full power of the pumping plant, most of the pumps are three and quarter inch which are definitely too small. Also I would like to mention that the present staff engaged in this matter worry too much about union hours and overtime and not the welfare of travelling stock.*

In July 1942 Administrator Abbott reported that, 'There have been so many complaints regarding alleged shortages of water along this route that I decided to give it my close personal attention.' What he found was that since they were first put down the bores and bore facilities had deteriorated and that,

> *Many of these bores were put down at least 20 years ago and their flow has diminished, apparently, in some instances, from corroded bore casings.*
>
> *The majority of windmills pump into earth tanks and in most cases the holding capacity of these earth tanks has been greatly diminished by a profuse growth of rushes and weeds in the tanks.*[547]

Such problems were compounded by the ever-increasing numbers of cattle crossing the Murranji.

In September 1942 Bingle wrote to the Administrator and suggested that to improve efficiency of cattle movements a stockroute be established running northeast from Nelly's Waterhole (north of Top Springs), along Western Creek and on to Mataranka. The cattle could then be trucked from there which would ease congestion at the trucking yard at Katherine.[548]

Alternative stockroutes out of the Victoria River district had been proposed as early as January 1896,[549] not only to avoid the Murranji Track, but to shorten the distance to Central Australia by many hundreds of kilometres. Bluey Buchanan tried to find such a track later in 1896,[550] and Charles Chewings tried once again in 1909,[551] but both failed. In the first half of the twentieth century various cattle and horse thieves (including the famous bushman Joe Brown) lifted mobs from Wave Hill and other stations on the desert's northern fringe and took them south to Alice Springs,[552] but these were ad hoc wet season routes that never came into general use. In 1929 Harry Farquharson requested that a stockroute be opened from Inverway to Alice Springs via Tanami which would save over 800 kilometres (500 miles) on the Murranji route,[553] and though his proposal was supported by other cattlemen[554] nothing came of it at the time.

The Administrator didn't address Bingle's proposal but revealed plans to establish a more direct road to the south-east from the Victoria River district, a road that might also serve as a stockroute:

> *We have been endeavouring to find a new road to Wave Hill for our Inland Transport Service and the engineers have now located one which comes off at no. 9 bore, Wave Hill, on the Murranji and runs south easterly direct to Muckety.*
>
> *This saves over 100 miles...It has been suggested that this form part of a new stock route from Wave Hill to the Rankine but I am doubtful about this*[555]

The Administrator told Bingle he'd been advised that most of the proposed route was sand and spinifex and he sought Bingle's views on its potential as a stockroute. Bingle replied saying that,

> *I cannot see that the alteration would be at all beneficial as a stock route...If it had been at all possible to put a road across from Muckety in a Westerly direction to No. 11 bore just on the Eastern portion of Wave Hill, then undoubtedly there would be a big saving in the stock route distance going into Queensland, also the type of country through which such a road would traverse is much better class of desert country than that on the Murranji.*[556]

He suggested that a better route would be 'a line from about No. 47 bore across to No. 9 bore. This would be fairly open country and would not be passing through any great amount of Bulliwaddy [sic] timber.'[557] Apparently the plan got as far as a fireplough cutline being made along the proposed route by 'Grader Jack',[558] but nothing more eventuated.

On September 8th 1942 Bingle reported to the Administrator that,

> *We are having some trouble with the Commonwealth cattle as they appear to be particularly touchy and were slow to settle down...I think it was probably due to the fact that most of them were from open country and had not been worked very much in yards or paddocks.*[559]

Ten days later Bingle reported that there'd been unfortunate losses with the 'Commonwealth cattle', that is, the cattle evacuated from the East Kimberley.[560] These 'unfortunate losses' increased until the last cattle were delivered at the end of an exceptionally long droving season. In December Bingle reported to the Secretary of the Chamber of Commerce in Canberra that,

> *six of the seven mobs have been delivered into Queensland. Details of four of*

> *these...show their losses as approximately 1360 head or 26 percent, but it is estimated that 75 percent of these are recoverable.*
>
> *From each of these four mobs considerable numbers of cattle are missing through stampeding or "rushing" on or near the runs from where they were lifted...*
>
> *Undoubtedly the lateness of the year and the health of the cattle also the condition of the last section of the route, was responsible for these losses and the poor condition of those delivered.*[561]

On figures to hand at least 260 cattle had died, 736 were missing and 725 had been left behind. Bingle wrote about these losses to the Administrator on December 8th, explaining that,

> *Those cattle which were travelling under the Government Scheme were all on their toes at the beginning of the journey, knocked themselves about badly, suffered from both Redwater and Pleuro and generally knocked their constitution about to the extent that they were in poor condition when they had only negotiated half the journey and the poor unfortunate drovers had a troublesome time in getting them to their destination without leaving big numbers at nearly all the bores...As it was, nearly all mobs collapsed over the last hundred miles*[562]

Early in 1943 Administrator Abbott drew up a list of 'Essential Requirements' for improving Northern Territory stockroutes. For the Murranji he suggested the clearing of the scrub around No. 12 Bore, No. 13 Bore and Murranji Bore, and the sinking of two new bores – one twenty-five kilometres east of Top Springs and another halfway between No. 9 Bore and Newcastle Waters.[563]

In response to these suggestions Bingle advised the Administrator that, while he didn't anticipate as many stock using the Track in 1943 as had done so in 1942, he nevertheless strongly supported the proposals[564] which included fenced 'camping areas' around some of the bores and new stockroutes designed to shorten distances between key points.[565] None of these new routes ever eventuated.

It appears that after the threat of Japanese invasion faded and as organisation of wartime services improved, greater attention was given to civilian needs. A Government conference held in February 1943 to discuss supply of essential goods to civilians gave high priority to the cattle industry, including the provision of materials for improving stockroutes.[566] In the months that followed facilities on the Murranji were improved, the most important of which were the widening of the laneway through the dense Murranji scrub (and straightening the route between No. 13 and No. 9 in the process),[567] the clearing of 50 acre camping areas around No. 11, 12 and 13 Bores,[568] and construction of a new Works Depot building at Newcastle Waters.[569]

Only one reference has been found to cattle numbers on the Murranji in 1943. This is in a report on the stockroutes by Field Officer Clough in October where he said that,

> *No complaint has been received this year regarding the capacity [of the tanks], but only a small number of cattle came through – some 17,000 – and the distance between the mobs was sufficient to enable the mill to fill the tanks.*[570]

In the same report Clough mentioned that there would be a big demand for cattle by the Army in the eastern states in the coming year, and he recommended a general overhaul of the old equipment and installation of some new equipment at the Murranji bores. This work was carried out by May 1944.[571]

Clough's prediction of a big demand was correct. At a conference held in Brisbane early in 1944 it was reported that,

> *The General [sic] position of meat supplies is so critical at the present time that it is imperative that all available stock should reach the markets. Steps must be taken to ensure that all cattle from the East Kimberleys and outlying areas may be brought in to market – an impossibility under existing conditions.*[572]

The conference recommended that the Federal Government allocate £5000 to cover the costs of improvements on Northern Territory stockroutes. The statement about meat supplies made at the conference probably led to a report in the *Weekly Times* on March 8th 1944 which claimed that, 'Federal authorities hope that 140,000 cattle will arrive at Queensland coastal markets from the Northern Territory this year. A big proportion will come from the Kimberleys.'[573] Unfortunately many Government records on the period 1944 and 1945 appear to be missing and there's very little information from other sources, so it's unknown whether the stated figure of 140,000 head travelling in to Queensland was achieved.

In April 1944 it was reported that the road across the Murranji was badly washed out with one traveller taking five days to drive from Wave Hill to Newcastle Waters.[574] By May the road had been repaired to a standard sufficient to take trucks loaded with eighteen tons, and in addition all the bores had been overhauled and the tanks were full.[575] The only information on cattle numbers crossing the Murranji in 1944 is a list of Vestey's drovers who were on the road by June with 9,962 head bound for Queensland.[576]

The only reference to the 1945 droving season suggests that a very large number of cattle crossed the Murranji. An Animal Industry Division 'circular letter' of 1946 mentions that Works and Housing, responsible for maintaining the stockroute, found it 'very difficult for this service to be effective when the route is stampeded with stock as was done last year.'[577]

CHAPTER 12

THE POST-WAR DROVING BOOM

With the end of the war in August 1945 the allied servicemen in Australia soon returned home, taking their hunger for beef with them. Nevertheless (and fortunately for Territory cattle producers), demand for meat remained high during the post-war period. Five and a half years of war had brought major changes to the stockroute – the clearing of a wide corridor through the bulwaddy and lancewood scrub, the clearing of large camping areas around several of the bores, the declaration of a number of travelling stock reserves and the upgrading of many bore facilities. However, there was still room for improvement and problems still beset the drovers.

Nothing could ever be done about the dust or the drummy ground and dense bush that made the cattle nervous, so rushes of 'touchy' cattle continued as of old. 'Poison bush' remained an aggravation, and in spite of improved facilities water supply problems still afflicted drovers and Government officials alike. In addition, the sheer number of cattle being taken across the Murranji created problems of its own.

Complete records are not available but drought years aside, cattle numbers crossing the Murranji appear to have remained high throughout the 1950s and into the early 1960s. In 1953 over 30,000 head crossed the Murranji;[578] 31,850 were taken in 1957, 25,200 in 1961 and 24,550 in 1962.[579] As long as the Murranji continued to be 'stampeded with stock' competition for feed and water was intense, and if for some reason a mob was delayed there was the risk of it becoming mixed with others coming behind.

The need to regulate cattle movements across the Murranji as a means of keeping the mobs apart and ensuring water for them had been forecast by Vesteys as early as 1928,[580] and was raised again by them in 1933.[581] Their calls were echoed in 1936 by Government Engineer A.C. Fleetwood, who wanted regulations introduced to assist the bore maintenance crew in supplying water for each mob.[582] Nothing was done. By at least 1942 Vesteys was providing the Northern Territory Administration with a list of their proposed stock movements to Queensland, the only company to do so.[583] A.S. Bingle said that in 1942 the company planned to send twenty-six mobs of 1250 or more to Queensland, and he pointed out that,

> *Even allowing that these mobs can be started off with three days duration between each mob, it means that between the start of the first mob and the last mob is 2½ months so, supposing that the first mob can start from Wave Hill about the 15th April, the last mob is leaving about the first week in July. However, I am afraid three days is really too close between mobs and I would suggest five days.*[584]

Bingle pointed out that with other stations also sending cattle the gap between mobs was often less than three days.

With the number of cattle using the Track remaining high after the war, in June 1946 the topic of regulating cattle movements was raised again. The Chief Veterinary Officer, A.L. Rose, discussed the problem with Field Officer Clough and suggested that,

> *the Administration should do something to control the cattle on the stock route and the distance they are apart.*
>
> *The only organisation we get any co-operation from is Vesteys who never put a mob on any of the stock routes without first notifying us...unless something very definite is done the way is open for serious water shortage...and possible catastrophe*[585]

Late in 1946 another Government official addressed the issue:

> *During the 1946 season, and also in previous seasons, the main West to East Stock Route has been very grossly overloaded with stock at certain periods in the season. This has occurred because of a lack of liaison between the principal users of the route as to when large mobs are being started and also because there has been no official effort to regulate the movement. The inevitable result has been a ruthless competition between drovers for water and for feed.*[586]

Finally, there was action. A scheme to regulate cattle movements was introduced by 1947, and a drover's schedule printed and distributed.[587]

TELEPHONE No. 54
TELEGRAPHIC CODE — CHIEFVETOFF

ANIMAL INDUSTRY DIVISION
BOX 12. P.O..
ALICE SPRINGS, N.T.

NORTHERN TERRITORY ADMINISTRATION

1948 DROVING SEASON — TENTATIVE DROVING PROGRAMME FOR MURRANJI-BARKLY STOCK ROUTE

Serial No.	No. in Mob	Drover	From	Top Springs	Newcastle Waters	Anthony Lagoon	Rankine River	Lake Nash	Camooweal	Destination
(a)	(b)	(c)	(d)	(e)	(f)	(g)	(h)	(i)	(j)	(k)
1	1,250	C. J. Williams	BRUNETTE, 22/2/48	-	-	-	9/3/48	23/3/48	-	Djarra
2	1,250	W. Williams	BRUNETTE, 28/2/48	-	-	-	11/3/48	25/3/48	-	Djarra
3	1,250	D. Booth	BRUNETTE, 1/3/48	-	-	-	13/3/48	27/3/48	-	Sth Q'land.
4	1,250	?	BRUNETTE, 3/3/48	-	-	-	15/3/48	29/3/48	-	Sth Q'land.
5	1,250	Swan	ALROY, 18/4/48	-	-	-	-	10/5/48	-	Charleville
6	1,250	Forster	ALROY, 12/5/48	-	-	-	-	3/6/48	-	Windorah
7	1,300	Neville	ROCKHAMPTON, 8/5/48	-	-	-	-	4/6/48	-	Sth. Galway
8	1,240	Brown	CRESWELL, 12/4/48	-	-	18/5/48	5/6/48	20/6/48	-	Q'land.
9	1,250	Booth	ALROY, (?)	-	-	-	-	?	-	Wyandra
10	1,250	Lidster	CRESWELL, 10/5/48	-	-	16/5/48	3/6/48	18/6/48	-	?
11	1,250	Howard	CRESWELL, 11/5/48	-	-	17/5/48	4/6/48	19/6/48	-	?
12	1,250	?	ALROY, 31/5/48	-	-	-	-	22/6/48	-	?
13	1,100	Conway	HELEN SPRINGS, 7/5/48	-	-	21/5/48	10/6/48	26/6/48	-	Djarra
14	1,400	O'Keefe	HELEN SPRINGS, 11/5/48	-	-	25/5/48	14/6/48	-	26/6/48	Morstone
15	1,250	Byers	V.R.D., 25/4/48	28/4/48	14/5/48	3/6/48	21/6/48	6/7/48	-	Walgra
16	1,250	Byers	V.R.D., 27/4/48	30/4/48	16/5/48	5/6/48	23/6/48	8/7/48	-	Walgra
17	1,100	Huggins	HELEN SPRINGS, 20/5/48	-	-	7/6/48	28/6/48	12/7/48	-	Djarra
18	1,250	Byers	V.R.D., 1/5/48	4/5/48	20/5/48	9/6/48	29/6/48	13/7/48	-	Walgra
19	1,100	Bohning	HELEN SPRINGS, 3/6/48	-	-	17/6/48	8/7/48	26/7/48	-	Djarra
20	1,350	Charlton	WAVE HILL, 7/5/48	16/5/48	1/6/48	21/6/48	8/7/48	-	18/7/48	Morstone
21	1,350	R. Smith	INVERWAY, 1/5/48	21/5/48	4/6/48	-	-	-	-	Alcoota
22	600	?	COOLIBAH, 4/5/48	22/5/48	6/6/48	-	-	-	-	Tennant Ck.
23	1,250	Byers	V.R.D., 20/5/48	23/5/48	8/6/48	28/6/48	16/7/48	1/8/48	-	Walgra
24	1,350	Pankhurst	WAVE HILL, 14/5/48	23/5/48	8/6/48	28/6/48	16/7/48	-	26/7/48	Morstone
25	1,250	Byers	V.R.D., 22/5/48	25/5/48	10/6/48	30/6/48	18/7/48	3/8/48	-	Walgra
26	?	Skeen	MISTAKE CK., 30/4/48	28/5/48	13/6/48	-	-	-	-	Helen Springs
27	1,250	Burns	V.R.D., 26/5/48	29/5/48	14/6/48	4/7/48	22/7/48	7/8/48	-	Walgra
28	1,000	?	COOLIBAH, 15/5/48	31/5/48	16/6/48	-	-	-	-	Ti Tree
29	1,250	C. McKenzie	V.R.D., 3/6/48	6/6/48	22/6/48	12/7/48	30/7/48	14/8/48	-	Walgra
30	1,250	Byers	V.R.D., 5/6/48	8/6/48	24/6/48	14/7/48	1/8/48	16/8/48	-	Walgra
31	1,350	Nipps	WAVE HILL, 31/5/48	9/6/48	25/6/48	15/7/48	2/8/48	-	12/8/48	Morstone
32	1,250	?	ELSEY, 7/6/48	-	27/6/48	17/7/48	4/8/48	19/8/48	-	?
33	?	?	WILLEROO, 31/5/48	-	30/6/48	-	-	-	-	Helen Springs
34	1,350	McKenzie	WAVE HILL, 7/6/48	16/6/48	2/7/48	22/7/48	9/8/48	-	19/8/48	Morstone
35	?	?	NUTWOOD, 15/6/48	-	2/7/48	-	-	-	-	Helen Springs
36	?	Zigenbine	MISTAKE CK., 25/5/48	21/6/48	7/7/48	-	-	-	-	Helen Springs
37	1,350	Coombes	WILLEROO, 15/6/48	-	15/7/48	4/8/48	22/8/48	-	1/9/48	Morstone
38	1,400	Conway	HELEN SPRINGS, 14/8/48	-	-	28/8/48	17/9/48	-	28/9/48	Morstone
39	1,400	Huggins	HELEN SPRINGS, 21/8/48	-	-	3/9/48	24/9/48	-	1/10/48	Morstone
40	1,400	Bohning	HELEN SPRINGS, 28/8/48	-	-	10/9/48	1/10/48	-	11/10/48	Morstone
41	?	?	WILLEROO, 30/6/48	-	31/7/48	-	-	-	-	Helen Springs
42	1,350	Brett	NICHOLSON, 10/7/48	9/8/48	25/8/48	14/9/48	2/10/48	-	12/10/48	Morstone
43	?	Zigenbine	WAVE HILL, 31/7/48	9/8/48	25/8/48	-	-	-	-	Helen Springs
44	?	?	NICHOLSON, 21/7/48	20/8/48	5/9/48	-	-	-	-	Helen Springs
45	?	?	WATERLOO-LIMBUNYA-WAVE HILL, 7/9/48	16/9/48	2/10/48	-	-	-	-	Helen Springs

NOTE: The first mob from ALEXANDRIA was approaching Camooweal on 3/5/48. This station hopes to send off four additional mobs, but has not yet been able to make the necessary arrangements. All the NEWCASTLE WATERS turn-off is going to Darwin in seven small mobs commencing 30/3/48 and finishing 10/11/48. SHANDON DOWNS has one mob of two hundred to move if a sale is effected.

Part of the Drover's Schedule for 1948. For reasons of space a small section concerning droving to Wyndham has been omitted. Reproduced here is the section of the schedule for the Murranji-Barkly stock route. A schedule was compiled for 1947 but doesn't appear to have been produced as a large poster as this and subsequent schedules were, so this may be the first officially-printed drover's schedule.

Meanwhile, in 1946 moves were afoot to put down two bores between No. 13 Bore and Top Springs.[588] Until this time drovers had to rely on natural waters on this leg, and if these waters dried up (as they often did) they had to negotiate a dry stage of about fifty kilometres.[589] This shortcoming had been noted by Michael Terry in 1926 when he suggested that, 'To make this route safe for stockmen at all times of the year, another bore or maybe a catchment dam is apparently needed half-way between No. 13 and Top Springs.'[590]

The need for water on this leg was raised again in 1943 when Administrator Abbott suggested a bore, '15 miles east of Top Springs',[591] but as usual there was a long delay. Four years later the problem was taken up by Chief Veterinary Officer A. Rose, who pointed out that,

> *The waterless interval between No. 13 bore and Top Springs is twenty-eight miles. I have been reliably informed that all attempts to provide bores on this section have failed. It is therefore recommended that the amount of the vote, £3000, be allotted for the provision of stock water by the most suitable means. This will allow the Department of Works and Housing to employ dam sinking if boring is not indicated. One dam could be sunk and equipped for the money provided for two bores and this would be quite adequate if sited within a mile or two, or half-way between No. 13 bore and Top Springs.*[592]

Rose's recommendation eventually bore fruit. Pussycat Bore (No. 14) was put down in 1948 and was fully equipped (including an earth tank) in time for the 1949 droving season.[593]

Government action in July 1946 to solve a problem for Newcastle Waters station led to a new problem for drovers.[594] Apparently Newcastle Waters had requested that the stockroute be moved away from the homestead because it passed through a small paddock adjoining the station.[595] In response, the Government decided to change the stockroute so that instead of going from No. 9 Bore direct to No. 8 Bore at Newcastle Waters, it would run from No. 9 to a new bore at the causeway on the North-South route. From there it would follow the North-South route down to No. 8 Bore.[596] Once the deviation had been proclaimed, signs were erected to warn drovers of the change and to advise them that they risked prosecution if they travelled the old way (plate 38).

The change wasn't welcomed by the drovers who tore the sign down and continued to use the old route. This led Newcastle Waters to charge several of them with trespass, though the charges were later dropped. Early in the 1947 season drovers Althans and Byers (plate 39) wrote letters of complaint to A.

McAlister Blain, MHR.[597] Among other things they alleged that the new route passed through a thick bulwaddy scrub, across 'dry bog' and swamp country, that it was twelve kilometres longer, and that it by-passed the Newcastle Waters store by thirteen kilometres. While their complaints about the bulwaddy and the bog were undoubtedly correct, it may have been the latter point which was of greatest concern, and it was this point that was taken up by Chief Veterinary Officer Rose:

> *For many years past, drovers have looked forward to terminating their difficult negotiations of the Murranji route by a re-stocking and obtaining alcoholic beverages at the Newcastle Waters hotel. The new route means that they miss this point by some eight miles...In my opinion, it would be a real hardship for the drovers were they not permitted the opportunity of re-stocking, etc., at Newcastle Waters. This is the strongest argument against the new route, and is probably the one that hurts the drovers most.*[598]

Rose later made a field investigation of the situation and discovered a major problem where the new route crossed *above* the causeway on Newcastle Creek:

> *By virtue of the fact that the causeway itself blocks the free running of this creek, its intersection with the new stock route is a boggy morass for a distance of half a mile. In my opinion this factor alone is sufficient to negative the value of the new deviation... It will be a severe obstacle for horses, and particularly pack horses, and will bog any cattle that are weak.*[599]

In time-honoured tradition, investigation of the drover's complaints dragged on for several years while the drovers themselves continued to use the old route. In 1949 the Chief Veterinary Officer recommended that the new route be revoked and the old reinstated.[600] As far as the drovers and others were concerned the old stockroute *was* reinstated in 1949. Moves had been made to do this by early 1951,[601] but in fact it wasn't done until 1959.[602]

Generally speaking, facilities on the stockroute improved throughout the 1950s, but other problems had to be dealt with. In successive years, fire, drought and flood caused problems on the Murranji. Bushfires from 'carelessness in camp fires' were a problem in the early 1950s;[603] a motorist boiling his billy was believed to have started a particularly bad fire that burnt about 5,200 square kilometres (2,000 square miles) of Newcastle Waters and Murranji country in 1951.[604] This fire burnt the Murranji Track in patches from Pussycat Bore to No. 10 Bore,[605] creating difficulties for drovers:

Mr. Dick Smith, a drover, [had] to move his mob off the stock route. Previous fires on the Murranji stock route...has made it necessary for cattle to go for three days without grass... The stock water, provided by the Government bores, is in the burnt-out area. Cattle can go without feed, but cannot safely go for three days without water.[606]

In 1951-52 the wet season failed. The Murranji Track remained open to vehicles right through the summer which was 'unprecedented in the "wet"',[607] and the 1952 dry season was one of the worst droughts on record in the Kimberley, Victoria River, Murranji and Barkly regions.[608] There was no feed along the Murranji and Barkly stockroutes so droving came to a virtual standstill and no droving schedule was issued by the Animal Industry Division. During the year it was estimated that, 'there was only one tenth the usual movement of cattle from the northern part of the country',[609] and not one mob travelled right through to Queensland. Drover Dick Smith took the only cattle across the Murranji Track, a mob of 1300 bullocks from Inverway to Brunchilly station, on the Barkly Tableland (plate 40). He made it across the Murranji with the loss of only four head and though somewhere he had a three days stage without water and his cattle rushed at No. 22 Bore, he got them all safely to their destination.[610]

The following wet season was heavy and motor vehicles struck problems on the Murranji. Early in the year, 'Stan Martin and Charlie Hoskins tried to get a loading out to Monteginni [sic], but the Murranji Plain was a lake and they had to turn back to Newcastle',[611] and trucks were bogging along the Murranji in early May.[612] The 1953 droving season was particularly busy as cattle that couldn't be shifted during the 1952 drought boosted overall numbers. By June ninety-one mobs were listed to leave the Territory and at least 30,000 head passed along the Murranji Track.[613]

Cattle rushes were reported several times throughout the 1950s. Drover Prendergast had an exceptionally hard time in 1955:

When I saw Claude Prendergast at No. 10 Bore he was heaving a sigh of relief at leaving the Bullwaddy [sic] and Lancewood behind him. Claude started out with 1,250 head of bullocks from Newry Station bound for Queensland. His mob was very touchy and had jumped or rushed every night that he had had them.[617]

Prendergast, or someone on his team, recorded his troubles on the side of a water tank at No. 11 Bore: 'C Prendergast Past Here with 1082 Head of Galloping Newrys 22/6/55' (plate 41). In another incident 1,460 head from

Montejinni rushed after Pussycat Bore and again between No. 10 and Murranji Bore. Over 110 were lost and a few sustained broken legs.[615] In 1957 a drover from Camfield lost ninety head between Top Springs and Murranji Bore,[614] and in 1958 Drover Scotty Watson 'bringing the Moolabulla cattle over the Murranji Stock route ran into a series of sleepless nights with rushing cattle and thunderstorms.'[616]

When the Top Springs quarantine reserve was declared in 1956 it appears that No. 15 Bore (McColl's or Pandanus Bore) was put down and equipped at the same time. Within two years a house for a resident stock inspector was built at Top Springs, and a cattle dip and steel yards were constructed at Pussycat Bore.[618] While necessary for disease control, dipping wasn't helpful for the drovers because it was stressful for livestock and would make cattle nervous and horses 'half psycho'.[619] When the dip first began operations someone suggested that being dipped at Pussycat would 'fairly put the Bullshead stags on their toes before they hit the scrub.'[620]

The establishment of the quarantine reserve and construction of the dip yards at Pussycat Bore were the last major improvements on the Murranji Track. From this time on the drovers had only bore-maintenance problems, 'touchy' cattle, and the vagaries of nature to contend with. Ironically, with these final touches the stockroute reached a peak of efficiency, but within a decade the droving era would end.

CHAPTER 13

THE END OF DROVING

The Commonwealth Government began experiments with road trains for transporting goods in the Northern Territory in 1934[621] (plate 42), and the first movement of cattle by truck began in the mid-1940s.[622] In 1954 Kurt Johannsen's road train delivered stud bulls to Wave Hill from Helen Springs; on the return trip it broke down and was stranded for ten days on the Murranji.[623] By 1957 the increase in use of trucks to shift cattle was such that the Animal Industry Branch (AIB) reported, 'Developments in regard to road transport will be closely watched to ascertain if this will materially affect the number of cattle moving on the hoof'.[624]

By the early 1960s trucks were rapidly taking over the transport of cattle (plate 43). As well, abattoirs were opened in Darwin and Katherine in 1963 and 1964 respectively, and these received many of the cattle that would otherwise have been sent across the Murranji. The decline in Murranji droving was dramatic. From 24,550 head in 1962,[625] only 14,350 crossed the Murranji in 1963[626] and a mere 2,653 in the final year, 1967.[627]

Shortly after the passing of the last mob, maintenance at most of the bores ceased and scrub began to grow on the Track, but the yard at Pussycat Bore remained in use until at least 1974 to dip cattle being transported by truck.[628] In 1978, the Top Springs and Murranji Reserves were claimed by Mudbura Aborigines under the *Aboriginal Land Rights Act (NT) 1976*. In response to these claims, stock inspector Cliff Rideout reported on the current condition of the stockroute. He found that two of the mills were in bad repair and that tanks and troughing at a number of bores were rusted. He remarked that the stockroute itself was overgrown and that he didn't think that cattle would be driven along the Murranji stockroute again because of the scrub and the poison bush. He suggested that if 'freight costs became exorbitant, then owners would drove to Top springs, transport to Elliott and drove across the Barkly Tableland', and he suggested that, 'This would be a last resort.' However, he believed that Pussycat Bore was 'a strategically sited reserve for stock entering and leaving the district' so with respect to the land claim he recommended a compromise in which the Department of Primary Industry offered to surrender the western 50 square miles and retained the eastern thirty-four square miles as a stock reserve.[629] Whether or not this offer was ever made, the claim over the entire reserve proceeded.

By 1981 it appears that the A.I.B. had given away any lingering thoughts that the stockroute might ever be used again and begun to divest itself of the remaining stockroute facilities. The reserve at No. 9 Bore was relinquished for inclusion in the adjoining pastoral lease[630] and the section of stockroute that passed through Dungowan station, including No. 12 Bore and No. 13 Bore, was also relinquished.[631] Documentation about the remaining sections of stockroute hasn't been found, but it seems likely that these too were given back to the adjoining pastoral leases.

The Aboriginal claims to the Top Springs and Murranji Reserves were eventually successful and in 1982 and 1990, respectively, both areas became Aboriginal freehold land. By 1982, therefore, the Murranji stockroute, nearly one hundred years in the making, had ceased to exist.

PART TWO

Tales from the Old Murranji

CHAPTER 14

PODDY-DODGERS AND OTHERS ON THE MURRANJI

Illawarra Downs

Shortly before the great droving era began in 1904, brothers Michael and James Fleming established a station at the western end of the Track. Only Mick Fleming's name appears on the lease documents,[632] but various sources state that he was in partnership with his brother Jim, and apparently at times with two other men, Jim Campbell and Ben Martin.[633] All these men were part of a wave of small settlers who took up leases and grazing licences on the edge of old established stations in various places in the Territory in the early 1900s. They moved in to take advantage of the large numbers of cleanskin cattle on these properties and also a substantial rise in the price of cattle. Although only short-lived, Illawarra Downs played an important role in the first eastward movement of cattle along the Murranji Track.

The Flemings had come to the Territory years before. Jim is said to have been in charge of fifty Chinese brought to McArthur River station in the 1880s to build yards, fences and huts,[634] and for a period he was proprietor of the Macarthur River Hotel at Borroloola.[635] Mick had been in the great Kimberley gold rush of 1886,[636] acted as a guide for the first sheep taken to VRD in 1891,[637] and was one of the drovers who regularly took VRD cattle to Darwin in the 1890s.[638] By June 1899 he probably was working for Wave Hill as he had a camp about thirty-three kilometres west of the station,[639] and in May 1902 he took 2000 cattle from Wave Hill to stock W.F. Buchanan's 'New Delamere' station on Gregory Creek.[640] He built a homestead there and stayed on for some time as manager,[641] probably leaving Illawarra to be run by Jim.

With his extensive experience of the district, Mick clearly had ample opportunity to see the potential for a small station on the margins of VRD and Wave Hill. The first of four leases of what was to become Illawarra was taken up in October 1901[642] and stocked with cattle early in 1902.[643] These leases formed a north-south strip along the VRD boundary and incorporated the only worthwhile waters at the western end of the Track – Top Springs and the Yellow Waterholes.[644] Presumably the name Illawarra (Illawarra Downs or Illawarra Springs) was a reference to the Flemings' place of origin in New South Wales, and they built their homestead on a creek that still bears this name. A traveller passing in 1905 described Illawarra as 'rather a small place as runs go out here…owned by the Flemings, whose brand is 72F. At the present time the herd consists of 700 or 800 head of cattle and some horses.'[645] The fact is that Illawarra didn't need to be big. Its purpose was to provide a legitimate base from which to harvest the unlimited cleanskin cattle roaming on VRD, Delamere and Wave Hill stations.

Ben Martin had come into the district in about 1902,[646] intending to find work with his friend Jim Ronan, the manager of VRD. On the way out he met the Fleming brothers who apparently made him a better offer, and instead of a new stockman, Ronan found himself with 'yet another hard-riding individualist on his eastern boundary.'[647] Martin was later to act as pilot for the first herds moving eastward along the Murranji Track.

'Diamond' Jim Campbell had been in the district since at least early 1902. At that time he obtained a brand for Retreat station,[648] a block within present-day Killarney station, and he was later reported to have a mustering camp on Coolibah Creek (running through present-day Killarney) on a block rented from a man named Kirby.[649] After working in partnership with the Flemings for some years, in 1905 Campbell appears to have struck out on his own, obtaining a block to the north of Illawarra which he called May Vale.[650] Campbell wasn't content with branding cleanskins – he is historically famed for inventing the diamond 88 brand (◊88) which could cover the G10 brand of VRD and those of many other Territory stations.[651]

At about the same time that Campbell left, the Flemings and Martin also dissolved their partnership and Martin left the district with his share of the cattle, 950 head.[652] He made his move just in time because late in 1905 disaster struck the Flemings and Campbell. During 1905 L.A. Wells, the South Australian Government Surveyor, had been working on the first survey of the Victoria River district. Wells' survey provided the first accurate positioning of station boundaries and the effect of his work on a number of landholders was noted by the *Northern Territory Times*:

> *The readjustment of their boundaries – or what they have hitherto looked upon as their boundaries – has come as a great and not too pleasant surprise to a few. It is found, for instance, that the Victoria River Downs boundary runs 25 miles further to the southward and 10 miles further to the eastward than was supposed by some of the settlers, and as one result of this scientific demonstration of correct distances the owner of the adjoining Illawarra Downs Station now discovers that all his principal sources of water supply are located on the [other] territory. As a consequence of this unpleasant discovery I hear that Mr. M. Flemming is now removing the whole of his herd to country on the Daly River. I fear that in that case he will not have so good a time as he has had on the Illawarra Downs country; the country on the Daly River is certainly not so good for cattle, and they will not thrive or breed so quickly there as on the rich pastoral lands around the Victoria Downs. I hear that Mr. Campbell is also beating a retreat from Maryvale [sic]. He is said to be removing his cattle on to Bradshaw's (Fred) Creek, situated between the Daly River and the head of the Fitzmaurice River.*[653]

The results of Wells' survey showed that for more than twenty years Wave Hill had been using something in the order of 6,500 square kilometres (2,500 square miles) of prime Mitchell grass downs country that really belonged to VRD! Wells later claimed that because of this change 'one station [undoubtedly VRD] increased its carrying capacity by 20,000 head.[654]

In spite of the boundary changes depriving Campbell of his waters and forcing him to shift operations, he remained in the district. He was able to make use of a number of different blocks until 1909 when VRD stockmen caught him red-handed with over 400 head of VRD cattle on the Dry River.[655] An intense police manhunt ensued for Campbell, but he was never apprehended. He got away into unsettled country in Arnhem Land where he lived until murdered by 'wild blacks' in 1913.[656]

The Fleming's shift to the Daly River was permanent and apparently was the end of Illawarra station; Jim obtained a grazing licence for a block that formed the basis of what later became Ooloo station, while Mick gained a licence for a block that eventually became Douglas station.[657] It may be that for a while VRD decided to preempt any other cattle duffers from moving in by taking over the particular Illawarra lease that covered the Yellow Waterholes, because in 1911 this hole was determined to be on VRD land.[658]

Paschendaele Station

Around the time that Peacock began the first bore on the Murranji (1919), a returned soldier, William 'Billy' Braitling,[659] successfully applied for a grazing licence (GL316) for 1300 square kilometres (500 square miles) of land east of the point where the north-east corner of Wave Hill and the south-east corner of VRD meet.[660] Braitling had been in the Territory since about 1904, working as a horse-breaker and drover, and joining the goldrush to Tanami in 1909. In 1914-15 he brought 500 bulls from Queensland to Wave Hill and VRD, and afterwards went to Queensland to join the AIF.[661] He served in France and Egypt with the 14th Field Artillery Brigade.[662]

In 1922 he applied for and obtained another 780 square kilometres immediately north of GL316,[663] a block (GL336) that extended across the Murranji stockroute and included the headwaters of Armstrong Creek and the Yellow Waterholes.[664] He built a hut on a creek a short distance below the Murranji 'jump-up'[665] – for a time this was referred to as 'Braitling's jump-up' [666] – and he made a cutting on the jump-up to make it more accessible for wagons and cars.[667] He also undoubtedly took up branding the numerous VRD cleanskins where the Flemings, Martin and Campbell had left off, sixteen years before. He named his combined blocks 'Paschendaele', after a battle in which he'd fought.

Braitling was licensed to run 300 head of livestock on this block,[668] but appears to have stocked it with 825 head.[669] Braitling's herd certainly prospered on this arid fringe of the Murranji. He supplied meat to Peacock's team[670] and it may be that these were the only cattle to go off the place, but four years after he settled below the jump-up his herd had grown to 3,500 head.[671] In 1926 he went into partnership with F.M. Patterson on 6,500 square kilometres of country north-west of Alice Springs and the following year began transferring his stock there.[672] This new block, 'about 200 miles west of Woodford Well, O.T. Line',[673] was eventually named Mt. Doreen station.[674] Towards the end of 1928 Braitling sold his grazing licence to Bovril Estates, and Paschendaele became part of VRD.[675]

Hidden Valley Station

A year after the Second World War ended a station was established in the Murranji country. This was Hidden Valley, pioneered by Dick Scobie in 1946 (plate 44). Dick was born in 1917 and grew up on a cattle station along another great stockroute, the Birdsville Track. Before taking up Hidden Valley he worked as a stockman and drover, and eventually acquired his own droving plant, taking cattle from Queensland to South Australia or New South Wales. He lifted his first mob of Territory cattle in 1944, taking them from Tandyidgee station to Dalhousie,[676] and the following year he went out to Ord River to pick up 1500 bullocks.[677]

At this time most of the Murranji country was still Crown Land, and available for lease. The main reason no one had taken it up before was the lack of surface water in the dry season, but this wasn't a big concern for a man accustomed to the extremely arid Birdsville country. In 1994 he recalled, 'I reckon, well, [I] looked [at] that country, [and it] looked all right to me, goin' out through the Murranji. I said nobody here much, be a good place for me, near VRD.'[678] He applied for a grazing licence for 624 square kilometres (240 square miles) in the north-east of the region in 1945, and this was approved in February 1946.[679]

With only £26, a droving plant and a truck, Dick set up a base camp at Murranji Waterhole and went looking for a place to build a homestead. When he found a suitable spot,

> *I come back then, and me and me wife…and me brother Monty... She drove the truck with two forty-four gallon drums of water on, and me and Monty had a horse each and we used to ride ahead and cut the lancewood down to get through. The truck went right through like that, and I picked that hill where the house is, I said, 'It'll be out of the water here.'*[680]

Lack of water made it impossible to stay long at the homestead site so he stayed at Murranji Waterhole until it rained. Dick's first move was to buy an old army hut at Elliott to use as a homestead (plate 45). He only paid for one hut, but took two, and he also fenced in an area for a horse paddock.[681] Lack of money was another problem. His £26 didn't last long and Dick said that, 'I had to go each year droving to get money, to make a start. I was droving right up until ah, oh when'd I take the last mob? The last mob of cattle I took was me own. It was 1960.'[682]

Hidden Valley station was typical Murranji country – lancewood and bulwaddy scrubs 'that bloody thick it'd break a snake's back',[683] small grassy areas and scant water supplies. 624 square kilometres apparently proved inadequate because in August 1948 Dick obtained two adjoining blocks and these were combined to form a single grazing licence (GL 1724) in 1958.[684]

In 1959 the Hidden Valley block and various grazing licences he held were converted to a single pastoral lease which was described as,

Generally inferior country growing Kangaroo, Blady and Spear grasses and timbered with Bloodwood and Gum with significant areas of spinifex desert. It has an area of 1,578 square miles... It is estimated that the block can carry 4,800 head of cattle.

Improvements consist of buildings, 58 miles of fencing, nine yards and one dam'.[685]

In spite of the fact that Dick had held the country for fourteen years and made many improvements, he was worried that he might not be the successful applicant because there seemed to be something underhand going on. However, he was able to prove that he'd spent more than £10,000 on improvements and this gave him first rights to the new lease.[686]

To eke out an existence Dick made use of water supplies and large areas of land outside the Hidden Valley block. In October 1952 an Animal Industry Branch officer reported that he (Scobie) was obtaining water for himself and his cattle from a 'blow-hole' about halfway between Hidden Valley homestead and Murranji Bore. The officer gave this water source the name 'Scobies' Rockhole'[687] (plate 46).

Aborigines who once worked for Dick showed me Scobie's Rockhole which they call *Panjak*, a site related to the Storm Bird and Black-Headed Python Dreamings.[688] The hole has a small opening, just large enough for someone to climb down about two metres to where it opens out into a chamber. On one side of the entrance there are a number of vertical grooves. Aborigines and Dick Scobie both say that these grooves were worn into the rock through the rubbing of hair belts used to lower wooden coolamons down to the water.[689] However, if the grooves had been created in this manner they'd be of varying widths and depths, and would be angled or curved rather than vertical because the greatest friction would occur at the lip of the hole where the cords were dragged against it. Instead, they are completely vertical, straight-sided and parallel. In addition, the curvature of each groove is perfectly semi-circular and of the same diameter as its neighbours, features which suggest that they were formed at the one time by a rock drill, and the outer side broken away to enlarge the hole.

Late in 1948 Dick was given permission to water his cattle at No. 9 Bore[690] and in 1958 Pastoral Inspector Egan stated that Scobie, 'has constructed a small dam and turkey nest at the homestead. In normal years this lasts fairly well but it is usually necessary to lease the Murranji Bore from the Animal Industry Branch after the droving season'.[691] He is on record as leasing Murranji Bore for one month in October-November 1957 and five months from September 1958 to January 1959,[692] but it's likely that his cattle used it far more often, either with permission or without.

For Dick, being 'near VRD' had the same attractions for him as it had for the Fleming brothers and Billy Braitling in earlier years – unlimited cleanskin cattle – and in his later years he happily acknowledged his raids on VRD. He always made his cattle stealing forays at the beginning of the wet season when early storms had filled the billabongs and gilgais, and there was a bit of green feed about. This meant he could take his cattle 150 kilometres back to Hidden Valley through the bush, well away from bores, roads and prying eyes. On one occasion with six Aboriginal stockmen and a mob of coachers[693] he went right into the area that later became Camfield station. They'd picked up a good number of cattle when Dick went on ahead to the river to see if he could get more, and he ran into the Pigeon Hole plant:

> *I rode down through the scrub, and as I looked into the river a cloud of dust come out. And about 500 bullocks, and about ten blackfellas chasin' 'em. 'Gawd, it's the stockcamp! What a hell of a mess', and they're comin' straight for me. I was in a hell of a pickle here now. 'I'll have to wait and see what happens now. If they come through this scrub they'll find my plant there.' So, anyhow, I raced out and met 'em when they got about a hundred yards or so from the scrub, and I pulled a pistol straight out and I shot a bull and dropped him, but he got up again. [Nevertheless] I turned the mob, and I turned 'em round and they went back.*[694]

Dick watched as the Aborigines pointed towards him and told the head stockmen, Jack McDonald, what had happened, and he expected a confrontation, but McDonald just turned the cattle in the direction of Pigeon Hole and left. As soon as he was gone Dick took his own mob and cleared out back to Hidden Valley, picking up more cleanskins on the way and later branding 700 head. Some years later McDonald told Dick he'd seen him and knew what he was up to, but didn't do anything because, 'you done a good job, you turned them bullocks back at Camfield there. [Otherwise] I wouldn't a got any.'[695] He also had every reason to avoid a man with a gun who clearly was up to no good.

These days Aborigines who knew Dick jokingly refer to him as 'Old Munba', a name associated with sorcery and applied to Dick because of his reputed ability to muster VRD cleanskins and run them back to Hidden Valley undetected.[696] In earlier times they held him in awe. Dick recalled that when Jack McDonald told him he'd saved him from losing the Camfield bullocks, he also told him,

> *The blacks are dead frightened of you. They reckon you're a ghost. They can't talk about yer in the night or you'll appear along side of 'em, on a grey horse, dressed in white clothes, with a revolver.' And he said [they say], 'You'll shoot 'em'. He said, 'They can't talk about yer.*[697]

It was on one of his 'dodging expeditions' that Dick had a bad accident north of Top Springs. In October 1954 he was thrown from his horse while mustering near Nelly's Hole, on the Dry River stockroute. According to a newspaper report Dick broke his leg and was knocked unconscious. Unconscious he certainly was, but as well as a broken leg he had three broken ribs and a broken neck. Fortunately he made a full recovery. As Dick tells the story,

> *this particular time, I was over there getting' a few cleanskins, and I'm moonlightin' [on] a waterhole…and as they're comin' in I'm gittin' 'em. I had the coachers hangin' out about half a mile… I had 500 cleanskins in hand. And I said, 'Oh well, this is the last mob I'll run in… I've got a blackfella on the tail and it's dust and dark night, and I'm on the wing, and a big bull broke out. I jammed me horse onto him and put 'im back, and as I put 'im back in…he come out again. My horse wouldn't go on him next time, and the bull whipped round and drove his horn through me leg, broke it, and through the saddle flap into the horse, turned him over, broke three of me ribs and broke me neck! And I never woke up for fourteen days.*[698]

By some miracle Dick recovered, but while driving on the Stuart Highway in 1968 he swerved to miss a kangaroo, crashed his vehicle and broke his neck again. This accident left him almost completely paralysed, but he ran the station from a wheelchair for another fifteen years before selling out and moving to Charters Towers in 1982.[699]

The Top Springs Store

One of the welcome post-war improvements for drovers was the building of the Top Springs Store in 1952. This was established by Sid Hawks who'd been working in the Victoria River country as a hawker since about 1950. According to a Native Affairs officer, Hawks' visits gave the Aborigines an 'opportunity to spend their credits. I inspected his stocks, they are all of good quality and he claims to be able to sell 10% cheaper than the Station'.[700] During an interview in 1998 Hawks he said had been planning to buy Max Schober's store at Newcastle Waters, but Colonel Rose told him about a big waterhole (Top

Springs) at the junction of the Wave Hill, Auvergne, Dry River and Murranji stockroutes, and suggested that he should establish a store there. Rose also told Hawks that 'they were going to build a railway, and there was a spur line which [was to] come in to Top Springs…and then VRD'd build a yard there, a mustering yard'.[701]

In 1951 there was talk of extending the Darwin line down to Newcastle Waters[702] so undoubtedly this was the basis of what Rose told Sid Hawks. In the 1920s there'd been plans to build a line across the Barkly Tableland to connect with the existing line at Larrimah. Survey work was carried out to determine the best route, including a spur-line south-west from Frew's Ponds and across to the Western Australian border. This crossed the Murranji Track near the present Murranji station homestead (between No. 9 Bore and No. 10 Bore). The surveyors cut through the bulwaddy thickets and marked trees along the line[703] and this marked line was used by a number of parties to access the southern Murranji-northern Tanami country, including the expedition sent out to retrieve the remains of the pilots, Hitchcock and Anderson.[704]

As soon as Hawks built his store he got hold of a 'special American six-wheel truck, driving on all six wheels' (a GMC), and while his wife Thelma ran the store he continued to work as a hawker. The earliest written reference I've found to the Top Springs store is in the newspaper item about the accident suffered by Dick Scobie near Nelly's Hole. This article states that his mate, Alex McNamara, 'did what he could for him, but had to leave him, still unconscious, to go the thirty mile ride for help to Top Springs where Sid Hawkes has a general store to supply the needs of drovers on the lonely Murranji Track.'[705] A few months after Scobie's accident the following advertisement appeared in the *North Australian Monthly*:[706]

The store was described in *Hoofs and Horns* in September 1955 as,

> *a bush timber and paper bark shelter. In its cool shade the traveller can find practically anything he might require. At the present time a new store building is in the course of erection and when it is completed electric petrol lamps [pumps] will be installed.*

Shortly after Sid and Thelma built their store the Animal Industry Branch established a Quarantine Reserve at Top Springs, but when this was declared an area was excised, 'for the requirements of Mr. C J Hawks to carry on his storekeeping business and also for the purposes of constructing an air strip should such be required.'[707]

Apart from running a store and hawking goods around the district, Hawks obtained a grazing licence for an area extending from the Murranji jump-up to halfway between No. 12 and No. 11 Bores.[708] This covered a lot of the country formerly held by Billy Braitling and taken over by VRD in 1928,[709] but relinquished by them in 1952.[710] He obtained the block in 1955 and retained it until at least 1961 when it expired by decree of H.C. Barclay, Department of Interior, 'due to proposals for a change in land tenure in the general area'.[711]

In 1960 Sid and Thelma had a major falling out over money matters and split up, with Sid taking the road train and Thelma taking over the store.[712] Thelma remained at Top Springs until she died in May 1981.[713] As a publican she had to deal with all manner of people – drovers and ringers, rough road-workers, Aborigines, tourists, Government officials and others, and her reputation for toughness led to nicknames such as the 'Armstrong Vampire' and the 'Victoria River Vulture'. However, one former drover who knew her well said that, 'Regardless of what they called her she was a good friend to all drovers. She would stick by you. I had good respect for her.'[714]

Shortly before she was due to retire she died and when the Wave Hill police were called to investigate one of them discovered a stash of nearly $80,000. He handed in $52,000 and a quantity of expensive jewellery, but stole over $28,500 and buried it in the garden of his house beside the Wave Hill police station. Unfortunately for him the police dog dug up the money and it was then discovered by the Aboriginal tracker/gardener. Charges were laid against the policeman and he was eventually sentenced to two years jail, to be released after six months and placed on a bond for the remaining time.[715]

CHAPTER 15

THE LOST MURRANJI GOLDMINES

No good story is complete without a lost goldmine or two, and there are reputed to be a couple in the Murranji country. One is the supposed 'Freegardt's Gold Reef', described in F.G. Brown's book on lost mines in northern Australia.[716] According to the author, Freegardt was a stockman with Bluey Buchanan when Buchanan took cattle across the Murranji in 1883. This is factually wrong as Buchanan didn't open the Murranji Track until 1886. However, the story has it that on the way across Freegardt discovered a gold reef 'studded with cherry-sized lumps of gold'. Of course, he never told Bluey or the other stockmen about the reef and for some reason he never worked it either, but instead drifted around the outback living on stockman's wages and the telling of his story.

Dick Scobie heard about another 'lost goldmine', this one found by a 'Chinaman' way back in the early days. As Dick heard it, the Chinaman had come in to Daly Waters with a packhorse and died there, and when the police examined his packbags they found stone which assayed six ounces to the ton. They also found information that the stone came from a shaft nine feet deep. No one knew where the shaft was, but the story doesn't end there. The same Jack McDonald who'd ignored Dick's poddy-dodging activities on Camfield later told him that his (Jack's) father, who'd worked on the overland telegraph line, had followed some straying camels far to the west from Newcastle Waters. When he found them six days later they were near a gold reef. Jack showed Dick his father's map and told him how his father had described the location:

> *he went down over a little ironstone ridge, and down on the flat there was*

a little billabong there, right on a rockhole.' He said, 'That's where he found the camels. And from there he come straight back to Newcastle, black soil all the way.' I knew where it was then. And he said, 'there was gold there stickin' out the stone. He seen it.' So I went out and had a look, and I found that shaft that Chinaman dug. I didn't find the gold stickin' out [of] the stones.[717]

So, could there be any truth to either story? There might not be any quartz reefs 'studded with cherry-sized lumps of gold', but there *is* gold under the Murranji Track. In 1974 James Weir applied for a mineral exploration license over the eastern part of the Top Springs Reserve. Apparently when the drillers Gorey and Cole put down No. 14 Bore their drill passed through a gold-bearing layer, and Weir's intention was to obtain mineral rights to the area and then interest a company in further exploration.[718] Unfortunately for him it wasn't legally possible for a licence to be issued on a stock reserve, and the idea lapsed.[719]

If a lost goldmine isn't enough, there's also a 'lost oil well'. When the bore was put down at Murranji Waterhole in 1936 one of the drillers, J. Kaczinski, noticed that stone chips from the 460 foot level were sticky and had a peculiar smell. He thought the smell might indicate oil and later showed the samples to N.C. Bell, the Director of Mines, and asked him how to secure oil exploration rights to the area. Bell told him how and immediately Kaczinski and four other men paid £10 each to obtain the rights to 5000 square miles around and north of Murranji Waterhole.[720] They wasted their money. A geological report by Dr Woolnough conceded a 'bare possibility' of oil being found, but stated that 'the probability of success in the search for commercial supplies of oil in this environment is so remote as to be negligible.'[721] No further drilling was ever carried out and of course, the Murranji isn't renowned as an oil field today.

Finally, in 1955 a party went out into the Murranji to look for uranium, gold or whatever else they might find. *Hoofs and Horns* magazine reported that,

Out from No. 10 Bore on the Murranji, Sid Tennyson and Wason Byers were prospecting the country with Geiger Counters. Sid was in Newcastle Waters getting some mail out when I saw him, and he said they were giving the country a thorough survey.[722]

The men involved in this search are said to have followed the line cut by the surveyors during the Trial Railway Survey in 1928.[723] Needless to say, they didn't find uranium or any other commercial mineral deposits in the Murranji country.

CHAPTER 16

THE 'BAGMAN'S GAZETTE'

Droving across the Murranji began in earnest a century ago and over the next sixty-odd years hundreds of drovers faced the Track, but very few of them ever wrote about their experiences and the majority of them have long since died, most taking their stories with them.[724] However, it's still possible to read something of the 'Bagman's Gazette' – the writings on the sides of the stockroute water tanks – and there are still Murranji drovers alive who can tell their stories. The legend lives on.

Construction of the galvanised iron tanks at the Murranji bores brought relative security of water supplies to the drovers and it also provided a medium upon which passing drovers, stockmen and other travellers could leave messages, poems, drawings, and social comments. Writing in *Walkabout* magazine in 1944, Haliden Hartt remarked that,

> *On the walls of the tanks are many drawings—girls' heads with lovely curls, dancers in wide ballet skirts, and charcoaled legends of "Big Boss Drovers" and bitter rivalry of men in from Queensland are all exploited here by the jealous old Territorians.'*[725]

In 1957 Bill Harney made similar though more detailed observations:

> *On the big black iron sheets of the squatters' tanks one could read the "Bagman's Gazette", which is the escape channel for the grievances of the travellers as they go by.*
>
> *All manner of poems and tales are written on these with a white clay, and*

pictures by crude artists portrayed many a warning against, or praise for, the hospitality of the station cooks and their bosses.

One chap who signed himself "Desert-rat" tells all to "shie clear of station ... the cook's a gin-burglar".

Another says that "Drover ... starves his 'Jackies' and pays everybody with a stiff cheque".

Another tells all "Beware, for bulls and bosses mate, beyond the next big boundary gate".

A verse on one of the big tanks was a parody on "Home, home on the range", which was in great demand as a song at "night watch" when the drovers rode around the herd:

Oft times at night, when the stars shining bright
I can hear the old didgeridu.
And my foot-steps will stray, for I can't keep away
from the 'Girls' that are easy to woo.

Chorus:
Home, home on the range,
Where the gins as young heifers will play,
And a 'ringer's' supplied with a 'girl' for a bride,
And wages at ten bob a day."

Each tank we passed had its "news", and only when a boss passed by and saw his name in a headline would he get the tank re-tarred, and the "slate" would then be clean for another issue of the local "News".[726]

Charlie Schultz took four mobs of cattle across the Murranji to Queensland in the 1930s and early 1940s (plates 47, 48 & 49), and until his death in 1997 he could still recite a bush poem from one of the tanks at No. 11 Bore, a poem concerning the wastage of the water at the various bores and the death from thirst of Hitchcock and Anderson in 1929:

For this Metters Patent Steel Squatters Tank,
You have the North Australian Commission to thank.
Someone else's job to fill it,
Yours the privilege to spill it.
The Kookaburra stands without a cover
Fifty miles from where this trough flows over
Of the water you've wasted just a gallon or so,
Would have saved the lives of Hitchcock, Anderson and Co.[727]

Most of what was ever written or drawn on the tanks has long since disappeared, and many of the tanks themselves are gone, but on those that survive it's still possible to make out some of the messages, insults, poems, laments and drawings of the Murranji Drovers, a final distillation of the many 'editions' of the famous 'Bagman's Gazette'. These writings and drawings date from the late 1930s to the 1960s and constitute a unique documentation of the last twenty-five years or so of Murranji droving, detailing the movements of different mobs, rivalry between Queensland and Territory drovers, frictions between stockmen and boss drovers or station managers, dissatisfaction with the droving life, condemnation of the actions of particular individuals, and longings for alcohol or sex.

A few of the inscriptions show up quite well in photographs (eg plates 50 & 51), but most are partly faded and have little contrast with the galvanized metal background, and therefore do not photograph well at all. To make a good record of them for posterity and one that can more easily be seen or read, I've spent weeks tracing many of them onto plastic sheets. I've then had these sheets photocopied and photographed the resulting paper copies. A selection of these writings and drawings is reproduced here. Readers who are offended by swear words should skip past them and go straight to chapter 17.

If this tank could only
talk many's the tale
it would tell of mad
men & mongrel horses &
fucked out bullocks

Murranji Bore.

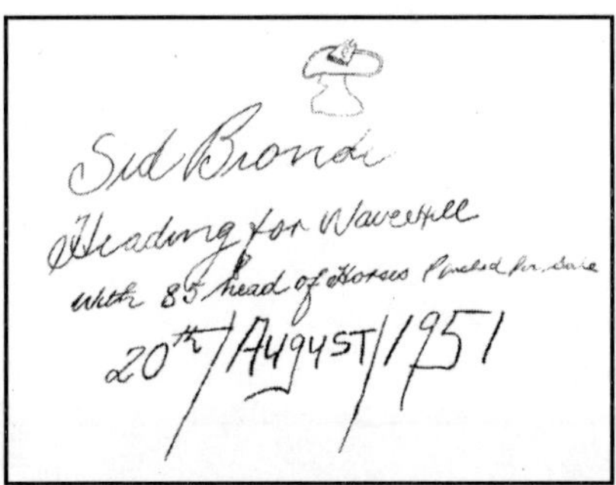

Sid Biondi was a son of reputed Italian Count, Mario Carlos Perefrerrio Biondi, and an Aboriginal woman (see plate 52). No. 13 Bore.

W Caomme de Mt Isa.
Passed here on the 8th June
going home

Murranji Bore.

BPHILLIPS
MT ISA
QLD
PASSED HERE
WITH C GILL 2/9/55
BURRUNDOODA
COWS+CALVES

No. 13 Bore.

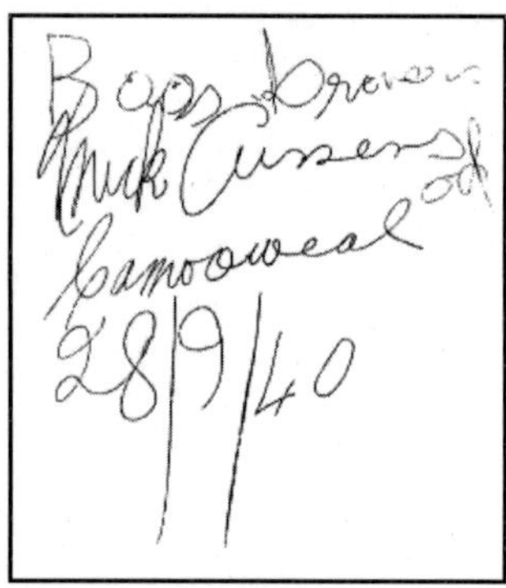

Mick Cussens was given high praise by some as 'a very smart man'. His nickname was 'Wirrawarra' which some interpret as 'mad bugger' (see plate 53).
Murranji Bore.

Jack Costello L Power
Mt Isa 25/11/48
Looking for droving plant
VRD A61
Ian McBean

Ian McBean was a drover in the Territory in the 1950s and early 60s, and later owned Innesvale, Coolibah and Bradshaw stations.
Murranji Bore.

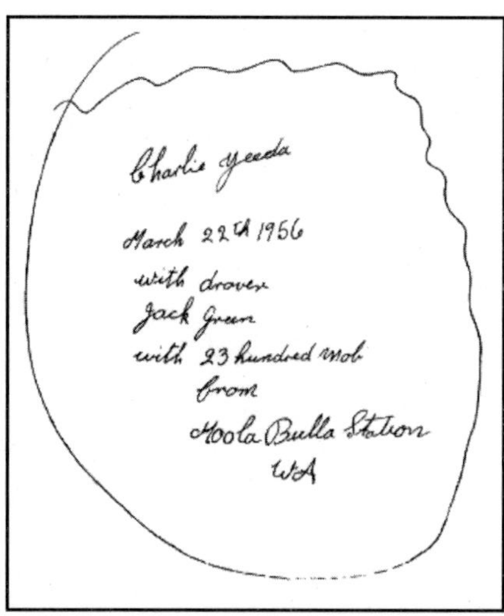

Charlie Yeeda is an Aboriginal former stockman and drover now living near Halls Creek.
Murranji Bore.

The Rushing 1300 hundred
camped here 11th Aug
Curranfilla in charge

The identity of 'Curranfilla' is unknown.
Murranji Bore.

Murranji Bore.

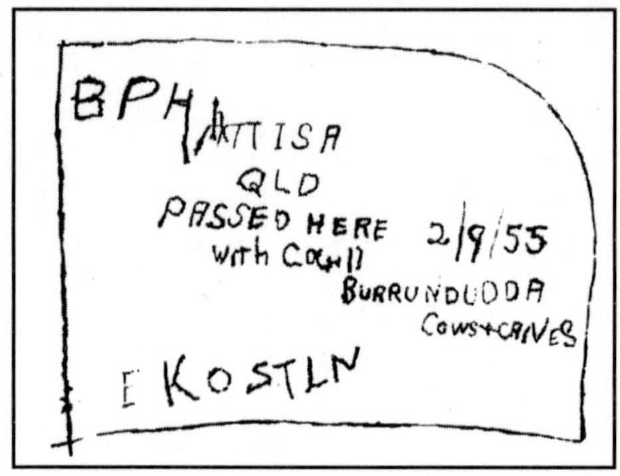

'E. [Eugene] Kostin' is still alive and living at Brunette Downs, one of the last of the Murranji drovers.
No. 13 Bore.

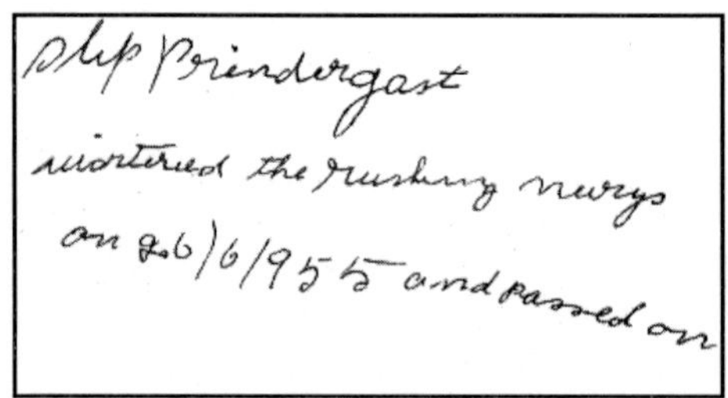

Slippery Prendergast was one of three droving brothers, the other two being Claude and Splinter (see plate 54).
Murranji Bore.

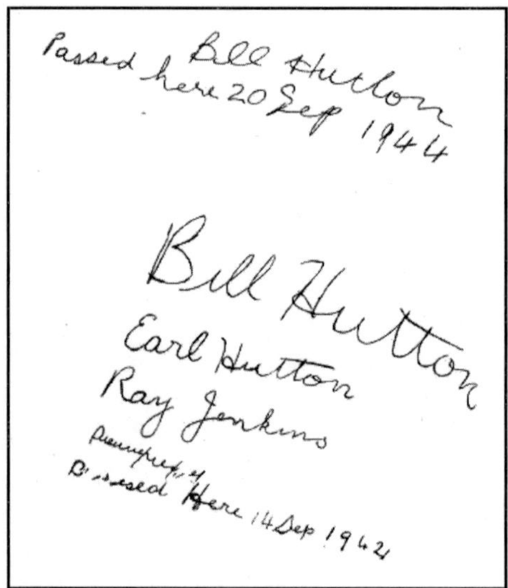

Murranji Bore.

Murranji Bore.

Murranji Bore.

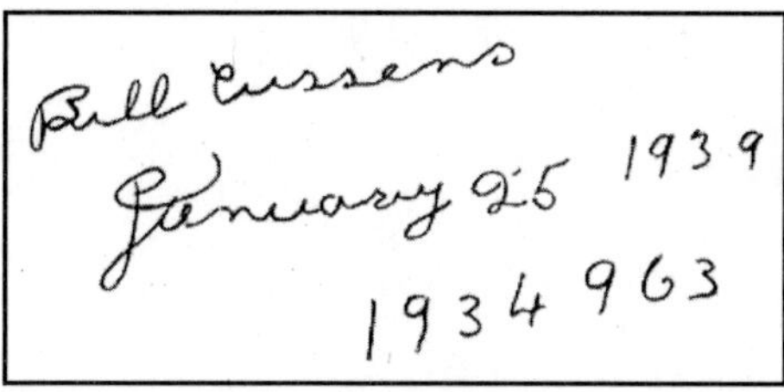

Bill Cussens' father was a drover, and Bill and his brother Mick both followed the droving game all their lives (see plate 37).
Murranji Bore.

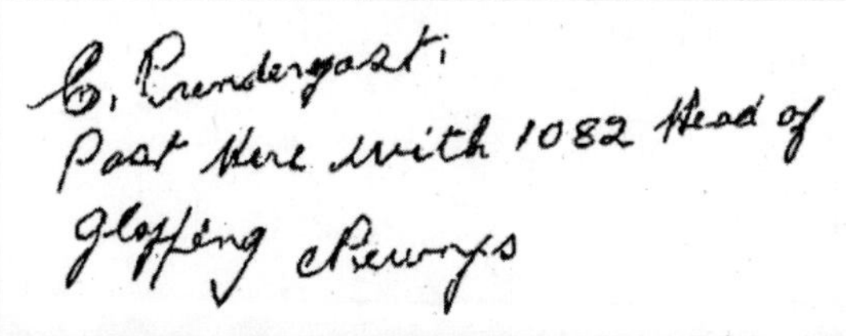

In 1955 Claude Prendergast had Newry cattle and up to Number 10 Bore they rushed every night (see plate 41).
No. 11 Bore.

No. 13 Bore.

Owen Cummins was reputedly 'The Man from Snowy River', and spent many years in charge of the horse stud on Wave Hill station.
Murranji Bore.

Poems

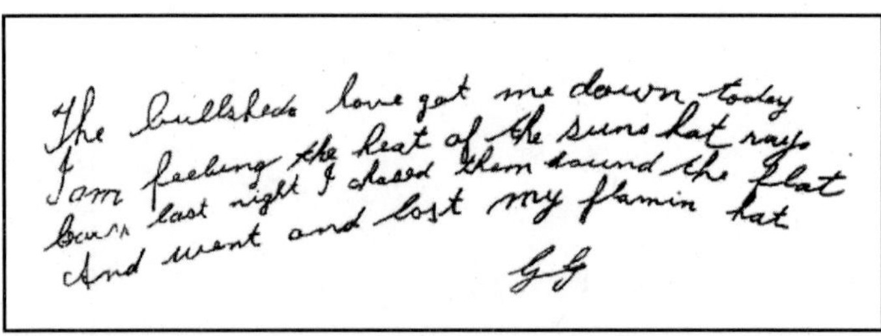

Old drovers have suggested that the initials 'G G' may be those of Murranji drover Gene Green.
No. 11 Bore

Come Drovers mourn and shed a tear
For I am just a bald face steer
And now at last my bones youve seen
For I was just a flamin queen

Im sorry boys youve come to late
Splinter Prendegast shot me with his 38
Alough I knew my end was near
For I hot a cancer on the near side ear.

A poem written from a bullocks' point of view.
No. 11 Bore.

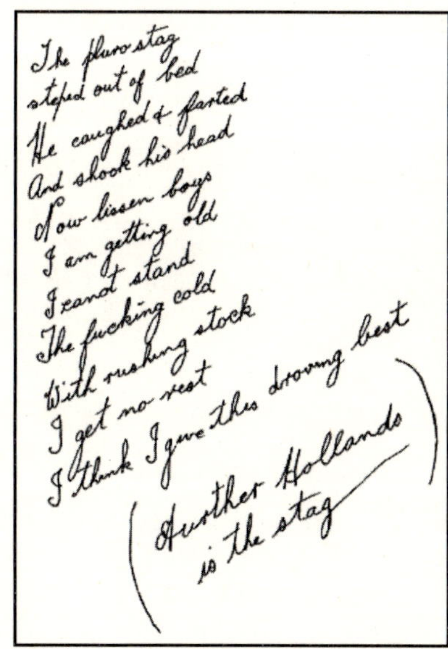

The fluro stag
steped out of bed
He caughed & farted
And shook his head
Now lissen boys
I am getting old
I canot stand
The fucking cold
With rushing stock
I get no rest
I think I give this droving best

(Aurther Hollands
is the stag)

No. 11 Bore.

Pictures and Portraits

The drover as a bit of a galoot?
Murranji Bore.

The drover as clean-cut and handsome?
No. 13 Bore.

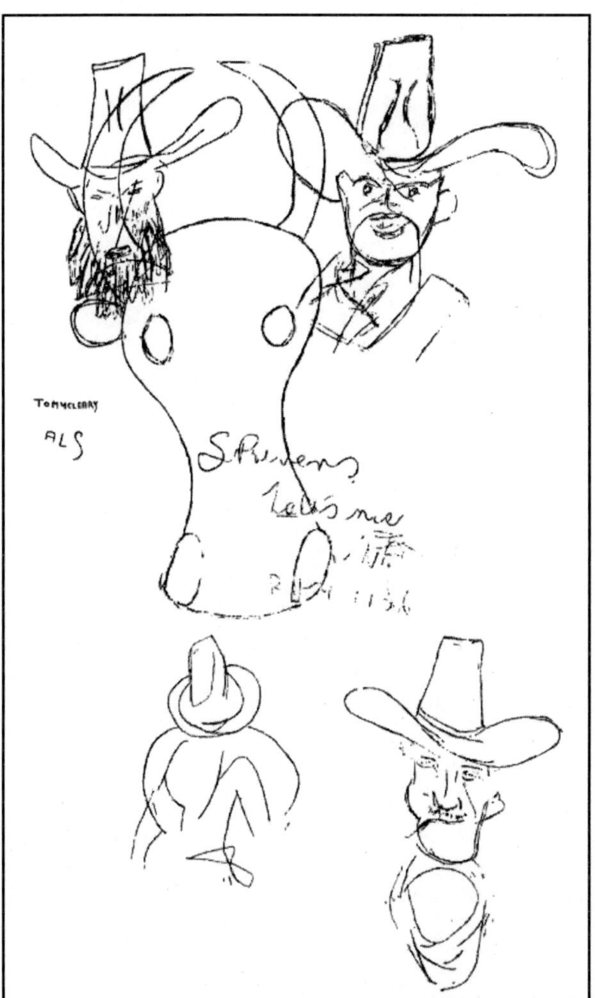

Murranji Bore.

Murranji Bore.

No information is available as to who 'Myndy Bookin' was, but apparently she was one of the few woman drovers on the Murranji.
Murranji Bore.

The tie and square pockets suggest that this represents a Northern Territory policeman.
Murranji Bore.

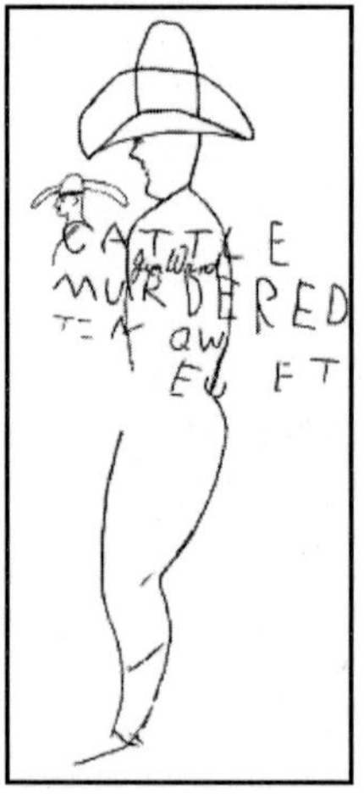

Drovers, and part of a message about the mismanagement of cattle.
Murranji Bore

The drover as Hollywood-style cowboy?
Murranji Bore.

A 'mongrel horse'.
Murranji Bore.

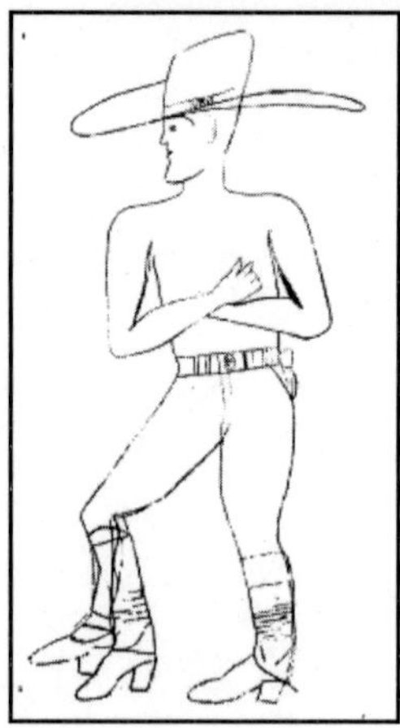

A drover in concertina leggings, with his front leg corrected by being redrawn.
Murranji Bore.

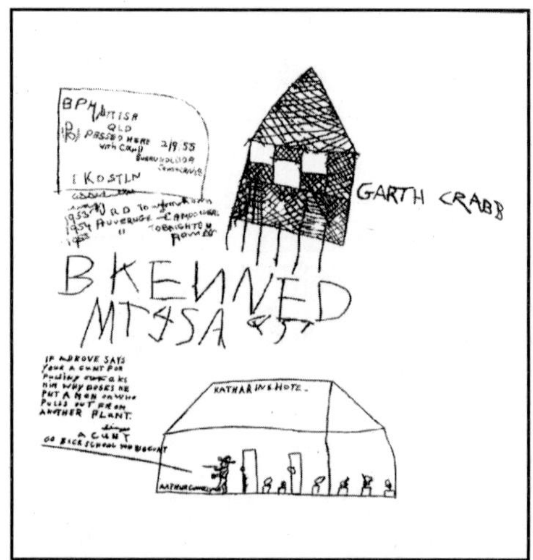

Messages and buildings, including the Katherine Hotel, complete with pot plants.
No. 13 Bore.

Horse branded ◊ZG.
No. 13 Bore.

Some of the early transport vehicles in the Territory were improvised from army surplus Diamond T trucks.
Murranji Bore.

Aboriginal stockman.
Murranji Bore.

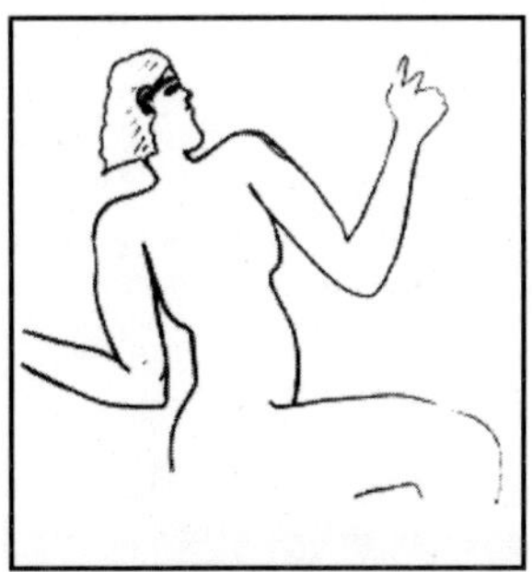

A drover's dream?
Murranji Bore..

Ned Kelly meets a Murranji drover.
Murranji Bore.

Elvis rides the Murranji Track
No. 11 Bore.

A hard day on the Track?
Murranji Bore.

Drover Biondi contemplating his cattle but dreaming of a beer.
Murranji Bore (see plate 52).

A ringer contemplates a Murranji rarity – a white woman, this one labelled 'not a bad sort'.
Murranji Bore.

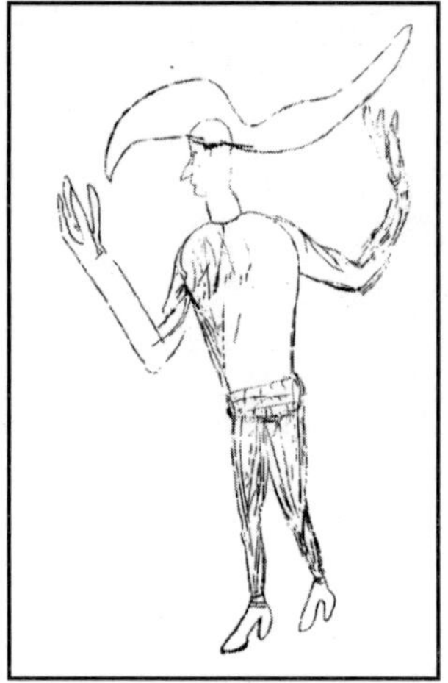

A spoof on the image of the manly drover in sombrero?
Murranji Bore.

Someone liked women, but another didn't like Ted Quinn.
Murranji Bore.

Caricatures of Aborigines. It shouldn't be assumed that these were drawn by a white man as old drovers say many pictures were created by Aboriginal stockmen.
Murranji Bore.

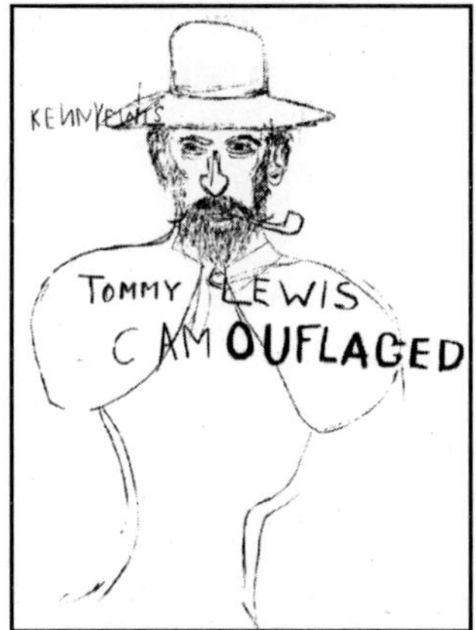

Drover Tommy Lewis.
Murranji Bore.

Various portraits and a slur against Edgar Saunders.
Murranji Bore.

A stockman's elastic-sided boot and a Dragon Rapide Aircraft of the type that delivered mail to stations in the 1930s-1950s.
Murranji Bore.

Disparaging Remarks against Queensland Drovers

THE Drovers from QLD Knowes HOW to undo
His swage when He comes to Station
Where the gins are —

A case of the pot calling the kettle black?: 'The Drovers from QLD Knowes how to undo his swage when he comes to stations where the gins are'.
Murranji Bore.

ther are Some
Queensland Bastards
who comes out here
and runs the N.T. People
down, But the Scabey
Barsteds got to come
out here to get
a fever the cut
the wages down
every time they
come out here

Accusation that Queensland drovers lowered working conditions for Territory drovers. Murranji Bore.

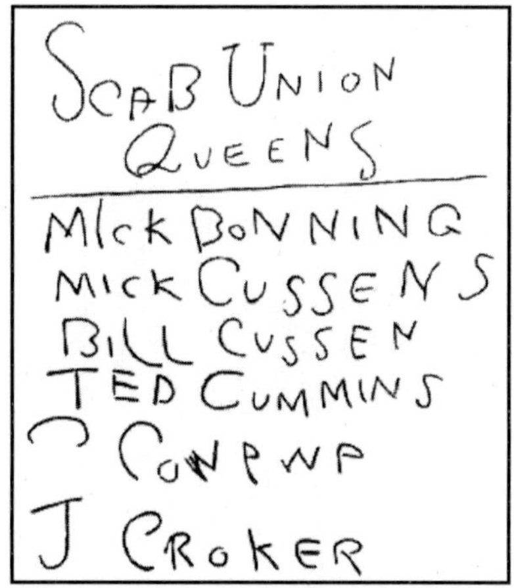
SCAB UNION
QUEENS
MICK BONNING
MICK CUSSENS
BILL CUSSEN
TED CUMMINS
C COWPWP
J CROKER

This message names the drovers who allegedly broke a drover's strike against Vesteys in 1954-55. Murranji Bore.

Against Boss Drovers

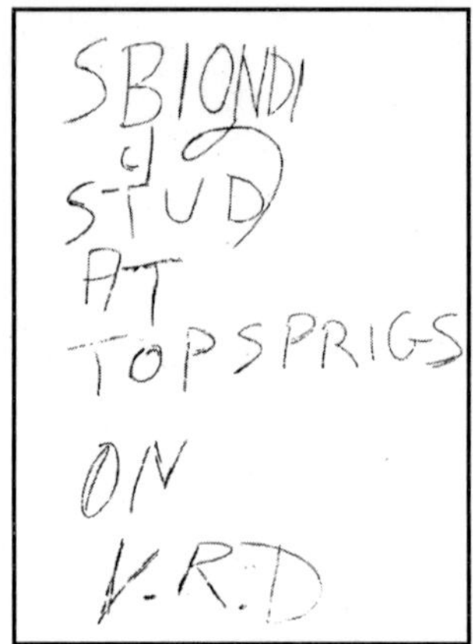

Murranji Bore.

No. 12 Bore.

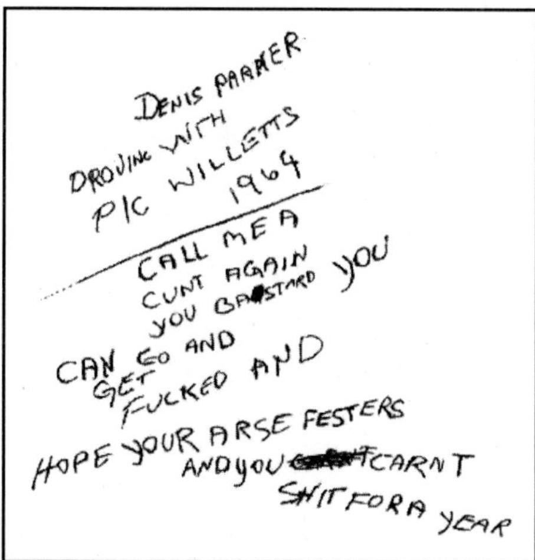

No. 12 Bore.

Murranji Bore (see plate 35).

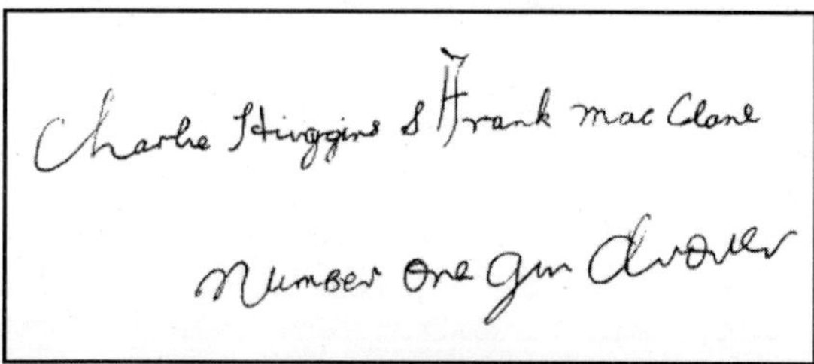

A slur against Higgins and Maclane.
Murranji Bore.

A slur against Drover Mick Cussens.
Murranji Bore.

A bizarre slur against (Drover?) Horrocks.
No. 12 Bore.

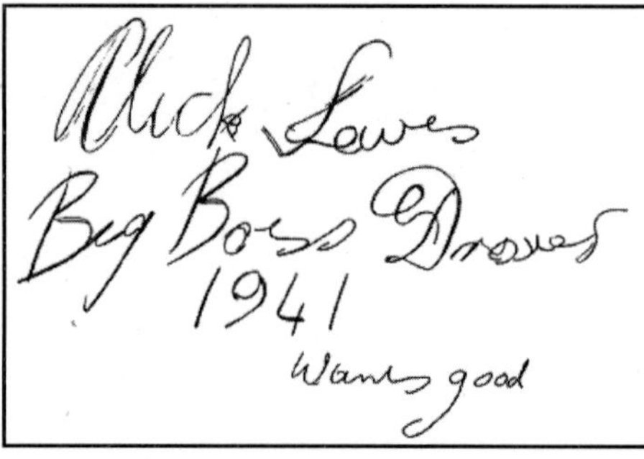

Murranji Bore.

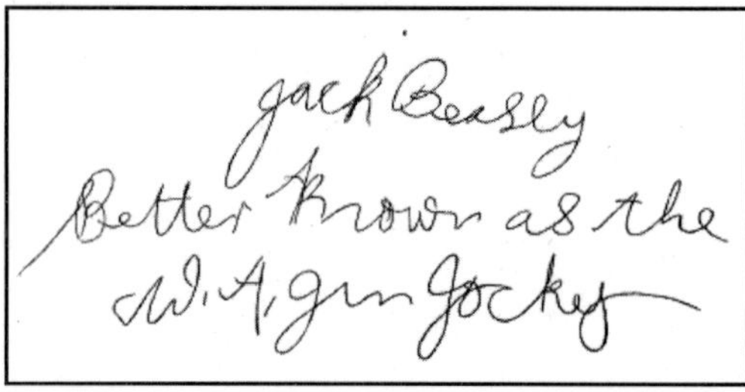

A slur against Jack Beasley who was a drover and stockman, and one of the early settlers in the Victoria River district (plate 55).
Murranji Bore.

Against Station Managers

Hartley Magnussen was manager of VRD from 1945 to 1953, and widely disliked.
Murranji Bore.

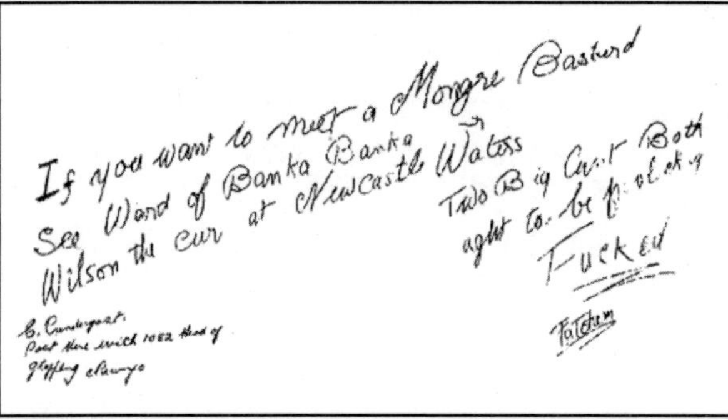

Arthur Wilson was manager of Newcastle Waters, 1942-1952.
No. 11 Bore.

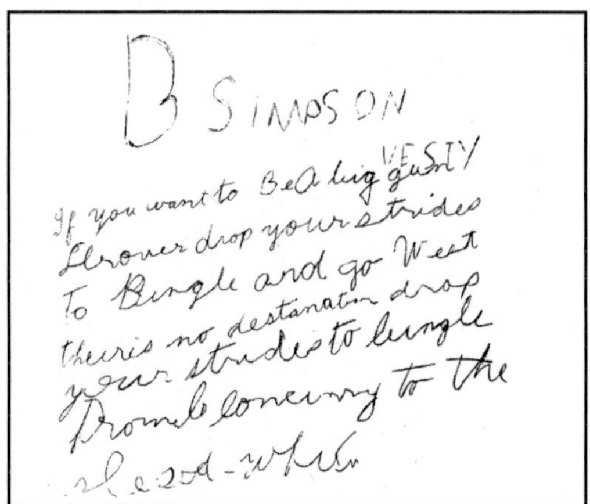

B. Simpson is a former drover who is now a well-known author. Bingle was general manager of Vesteys in the 1940s, '50s and '60s.
Murranji Bore.

Odds and Ends

L. Russell, Sergeant, Royal Australian Engineers 13 Oct 1940.
Murranji Bore.

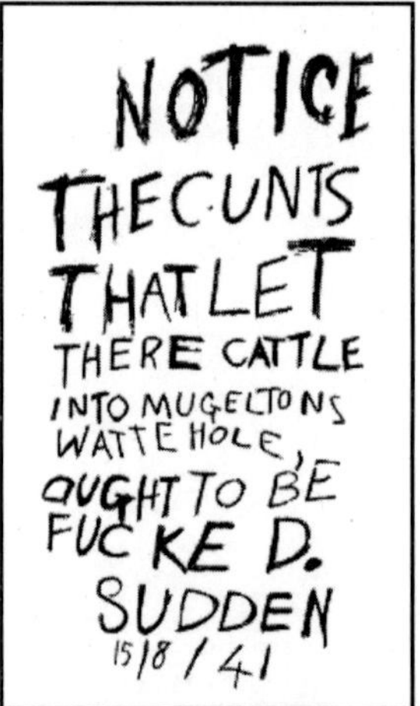

A large message written in red-lead paint, otherwise used to seal the joints in water pipes. Two men blamed for fouling waterholes were 'Puddlin' Paddy' Conway (see plate 56) and 'Whispering' Fred Marton.
Murranji Bore.

ERIC RANKINE PAT
& 2 KIDS Bullwaddy
& Rohnda were with
them in 1959
DROVING CATTLE
FROM V.R.D
TO QLD

No. 12 Bore.

Brand	
TVF	Probably Wave Hill (TVH)
TLP	Limbunya
LTP	
PTL	Waterloo
006	} Western Australian brand
0Q0	} " " "
060	} " " "
LOT	Ord River
NY	
DOX	Western Australian brand
DJT	Kirkimbie
BTA	Helen Springs
MY2	Morestone/Manbulloo
NBT	Stirling Station
3Q7	

A list of brands, most from Vestey Company stations.
No. 13 Bore

HEADLINE
Wason Byers
astor the
Star ting [illegible]
[illegible]
had many [illegible]
all precaution do not
Camp in their old camps
or swim in water that has
been contaminated by them
use Lysol and [illegible]
freely as it is well known
that this m as both
scabby & crabby
[illegible] Border
N T [illegible] Board

A slur against Wason Byers, an infamous character in the Victoria River district from the 1920s to the 1950s, and while managing Coolibah station was one of the actors in the film Jedda. Murranji Bore.

Olive Coomes
Newcastle Water
Buckjumper black
anyone stick to this filly
get £1

No. 11 Bore

CHAPTER 17

OF 'MAD MEN AND MONGREL HORSES'

It's not only the Murranji tanks that can 'talk'. Although the last cattle were walked over the Murranji forty years ago, some of the Murranji drovers are still alive to tell their stories, or have told their stories and passed on within the last decade. Some thought the Murranji was a great stockroute, others hated it – most have vivid memories of cattle rushing through the bulwaddy, or other significant events. A selection of their stories is reproduced here. It will be noted that in one or two instances there are discrepancies between what some remember of their time on the Murranji and the documentation from these times, and no doubt one old-timer will remember things differently from another. These differences are of little relevance. They serve to show the different attitudes they held, their different story-telling styles, or perhaps the frailties of human memory.

Charlie Schultz came to the Territory with his father in 1927 to help him get Humbert River station ready for sale. At that time Humbert River was a 579 square mile block of mostly rough sandstone and limestone country bordering the western side of the 12,000 square mile Victoria River Downs. The Great depression was in its early stages and no buyer could be found, and Charlie ended up managing the place for forty-four years.[727] He sent bullocks off the station in 1931 and 1932, but the drovers who took these mobs both lost over 200 head, so he decided to go with the next lot as far as Newcastle Waters to help get the cattle across the Murranji and settled in to the road. This was in 1935, and it proved a memorable trip:

> *going across the Murranji Track....we got up there at No. 13 Bore and had our first rush... God strewth! That's the first rush I knew of, you know...*

> *you got no idea what a mob of rushin' cattle are like there! They're all layin' down sleepin', chewin' their cud, you know, and that first one that jumps, inside of a fraction of a second, before that bloke can take two steps, the whole lot are on their feet and they're gallopin'. And they're gallopin' the opposite way they hear the noise, and it's like thunder, you know...and they kept on fallin' over logs – there's a lot of logs and that – and of course, they kept on takin' fright at each other. Well anyway, they rushed from there right across to Newcastle Waters... And every night they'd go we'd lose about twenty or thirty, and we'd get out after 'em again next day and we'd track 'em up and we'd pick 'em up. The only trouble was that it was holding up your main mob...you had other blokes comin' behind yer and you're using their water, more or less. Or more than what you're supposed to use.*[728]

Charlie blamed the rushes on the thick scrub making the cattle nervous, and remarked that 'you can't get a run at 'em there on account of the scrubs', but he took cattle over the Track on four other occasions and never had a rush. He said,

> *I generally worked it I went across the Murranji and I had the moon behind me. Full moon. At least if they're gallopin' then you can see where you're goin'. Otherwise you'd be likely to gallop into a tree or somethin' or a overhangin' [branch] – that's what I was afraid of a hangin' branch you see...it'd knock you clean out of the saddle, you know. But when I took off after a beast I'd hold me hand like this so I wouldn't be hit in the head. At least I got it in the hand and I...rode loose in the saddle and it'd throw me back onto his haunches, something like that. But I was very lucky. I hit a couple of branches but I managed to evade 'em, more by good luck than good management I'd say.*[729]

Reg Hart was born in western Queensland in 1915 to parents of mixed Aboriginal and European descent. At the age of nineteen he went with his father to Wave Hill where they picked up 1525 bullocks and started them on the road to Walgett. Of course, they had to cross the Murranji and Reg remembered this all too well:

> *all I can say about the Murranji Track – it's a nightmare! Hardly any water, chalky ground, bulwaddy scrub and lancewood scrub. And many a drover lost a mob of cattle because the chalky ground, it rattles and makes noise louder than the cattle can stand being on ordinary ground, and of course, once they hit the bulwaddy scrub or the lancewood, no control. It's too thick*

> *to chase 'em. I believe John Darcy the year before we got there lost a whole mob… my father was cluey about how to handle chalky ground, and we had no incidents really*[730]

Reg said there were two turkeys nest bores on the Murranji then, and while they let the water run into the troughs from the turkeys nest, they had to release the windmill so that it would replenish the water they were using. Then when they finished watering the cattle they had to tie the windmill down so that it wouldn't keep pumping and overflow the turkeys nest. Because the amount of troughing wasn't great they had to hold the mob well out from the bore and only let about fifty bullocks in at a time, and it was while cutting off a mob of fifty bullocks that Reg was nearly killed:

> *Anyway, while I was cutting the cattle out I was on a large creamy horse. Oh, he was very heavily built, and…suddenly he put his foot in a hole and tossed me and landed on top of me. And when he got up my right foot was caught in the stirrup iron [and] it was twisted and I was laying on the ground, and he looked at me and he started to walk away, and he's draggin' me. And then he started to walk faster and I could see he was goin' to get into a little bit of a trot and…with my left leg I managed to plant it firmly in the ground and swing, and I got my hand on the pommel of the saddle. And once I got up there, I was able…to pull the stirrup leather out and let go and fall on the ground. And that stirrup was so twisted I had to take off my boot to get it out of the iron. Well that's the closest I've been over gettin' killed like that.*

Apart from this incident they had no more trouble or adventures, and delivered the bullocks at Walgett nine months later.

Bill Cussens grew up the son of a drover and worked as a drover almost all his life. He and his brother Mick first went across the Murranji with their father in 1933, taking horses out west for sale (see plates 37 & 53). Bill maintains that he and Mick were the only drovers to cross the entire continent from coast to coast, west to east. This was done in two legs, the first in 1938 when he and his father and brother lifted a mob from Yeeda station near Derby and took them to Alice Springs. Then in 1942 he and Mick each took a mob of Wave Hill bullocks right across to Rockhampton.[731]

Bill accepted that the Murranji was tough for the early drovers like the 'Farquharsons and all those fellas, Duracks, when they were goin' out, yeah. It was because there was no water, and…they had to travel with the wets', but in his own time he believed the Murranji, *was one of the best stock routes in Australia, no matter where they come from…there's always plenty of shade, there was plenty of grass, there was always plenty of water in the bores. Soft ground…Open camps. They talk about the Murranji scrub. All those scrubby patches, you could go around the end of 'em! Because they had clearin's through 'em, but if they'd taken particular notice and had a good look round they could'a gone 'round all those little scrub patches without goin' through 'em.*[732]

Bill said you could lose cattle or horses in the Murranji, or turn lame bullocks loose, and when you came back through a year later, 'you find them, and you'd have killers then to eat goin' back because they'd be fat when you went back'. He explained that there's a 'sort of a red grass grows under that bulwaddy…very sweet stuff', and the cattle grow fat on it. When asked why the Track got such a bad name Bill said it was probably because 'There's been some very big rushes in there', but he blamed these rushes on the drover's carelessness. Unlike Charlie Schultz, Bill thought moonlit nights were bad for droving on the Murranji:

See, moonlight nights [are] the worst thing in the world for bullocks on the road, if it's shady and a bloke stands underneath a tree… And then he'll move of course and the bullock asleep and he wake up and see something movin'. Nothing wrong with the Murranji road, track. I was on it for years and years and never had one bit of trouble on it. Careful, be careful. You can go a rush anytime. My old brother had two big rushes there – one at 11 and one at Number 10 – and old Eddie Jepp at Murranji, he lost the whole lot there. Johnny Darcy lost six hundred…and old Charlie Elliott, he done 360-odd – that was during the war, VRDs. There was a hell of a lot of luck into it, not all good management, don't get that into your head there. But anyone that come through that Murranji year after year, [there was] a bit of judgement [in it] but [also] a hell of a lot of luck. You do the right thing and…don't let them blokes stand under them shades and then they move, you know, on a bright moonlight night[733]

Edna Jessop has become famous as one of the few women boss drovers in Australia's history. The daughter of well-known drover Harry Zigenbine, Edna grew up with horses and cattle in western Queensland. Harry was a very large man (plate 57) and Edna remembers a particular horse that he used to ride:

He had an old chestnut horse, old Digger… And poor old Digger hated him! He used to hate carryin' old dad from camp to camp. God, he hated dad!

> *He'd see dad come with a bridle, and away he'd go. But yet the kids, any of us could catch him anywhere. You could ride him without a bridle or a saddle… But dad couldn't catch him. But I suppose, imagine that old horse carryin' twenty-two stone 'round all day.*[734]

Edna first went droving in 1942, aged fifteen, when she went with Harry to Wave Hill to take a mob of bullocks to Morestone in Queensland (plate 58). She learnt the trade well and continued droving with her father for nearly a decade, crossing the Murranji many times. On these long droving trips it was necessary to have a big plant of horses, as Edna explained:

> *yeah we…always had around bloody seventy or eighty horses. People used to wonder why you had so many. They were long old trips, and…we had… twelve or thirteen packs. You had to have a horse for either one of them. Then you had to have, oh we used to carry about twelve night horses I suppose, you know… Then every one had about three or four day horses, so if one got a sore back or something you had to keep changin', you know. Oh, you had to have 'em. We had 'em anyway.*[735]

Edna never experienced a rush in the Murranji, but said that,

> *of a morning when you took 'em off camp, you always had to be careful because you had to have somebody in the lead all the time, because bandicoots and I don't know what it was used to always stir 'em? And they'd go like buggery! You had someone in the lead all the time, but they would never give us any trouble in the night.*[736]

It was on a trip across the Murranji in 1950 that an incident occurred which set Edna on the road to fame. Some time previously a horse Harry was riding had fallen and rolled on him. He was left with damaged kidneys and these began to play up while they were on the Murranji. In Edna's words:

> *Well, we took delivery of the bullocks at Bedford and then we brought 'em in past Wave Hill, and we got into the Murranji.*[737] *The Murranji scrub they call it. And my dad had, oh he had bad kidneys, and anyway he was very sick all day and that hawker bloke [Sid Hawks] come along that night and camped with us, luckily, and I asked this hawker bloke would he bring him in to Newcastle? So he brought him in to Newcastle and he [Harry] just left me and the boys, and me brother Andy was cookin'. Me brother was cookin', and that's in the middle of the Murranji*[738]

When Edna arrived at Newcastle Waters the postmaster took a lot of photographs and sent them to the press, and the story of the 'girl drover' quickly spread around the world. Edna started to receive letters – hundreds of letters from around Australia and overseas – from men who wanted to marry her and women who wanted to go droving with her. The following year she acted as boss drover once again and her story has created interest ever since.

As a young man Kelly Dixon helped Drover John Darcy take cattle across the Murranji three times, the first time in 1948. According to Kelly, 'nothing exciting happened…other than a couple of rushes…[and]…the usual snake in your swag'. He remembers Darcy as 'a damned good drover' and though they had 'a couple of bad rushes, *really* bad rushes where we did lose seventy or eighty bullocks', he got all of them back. Kelly found the Murranji to be,

> *a grim sort of place to me – I was very young – and it was a bit of an uncomfortable sort of a place so I never enjoyed coming through it. Horses seemed to be on edge, cattle seemed to be on edge, men were on edge. Then when we did break out onto the open country just ah, north of Newcastle, it was quite a relief to see that open country. There's much been written about the Murranji and spoken about it. There's a certain amount of it's folklore, but it was not an easy piece of country to negotiate with a big mob of cattle, especially if you're short-handed and short of water, it was pretty tough going.*[739]

In the late 1940s the main problem they had was lack of water, even though there were windmills and tanks at reasonable distances all along the Track. Kelly said they once went eighty miles without water – 'three days…without bullock water, and two days and two nights without horse water for your horses, and as far as human water, you didn't know what a wash was'[740] – and he said that at the time this was a common experience for Murranji drovers. To do eighty miles without water on the Murranji track would require the tanks at two consecutive bores to be empty at the same time which could be caused by inadequate attention by the bore maintenance crews or by drovers letting the water run out of the tanks.

In Kelly's opinion the recurrent shortage of water had two causes. A lack of concern by Government, and poor planning by the big cattle companies to keep the herds far enough apart:

> *The thing is, the Vesteys' empire didn't seem to have very good planners in their head offices because they would schedule mob after mob after mob of cattle to come through there travelling a few days apart. Well then things change. After the actual first couple of mobs leave Wave Hill things would*

have changed. One drover'd be held up looking for some lost cattle after a rush or something, and the other mob would catch up to him. It would mean then that they would hit the [bores] pretty well the same day! If not the same day… one would water this morning and again this afternoon and go out on a dry camp, and another bloke would be in the bore first thing in the morning.[741]

In 1948 the bores relied on windmills to fill the tanks, but Kelly said it was common knowledge among bush people that in May, June and July there are windless days when the mills didn't turn (according to Administrator Abbott around the end of May there were windless periods of up to three weeks[742]). The Murranji bores were deep and needed large windmills to lift the rods, and these big mills needed a big wind to turn them. With mobs of 1000 to 1500 cattle coming every few days, it was easy for water problems to arise. Kelly believes 'the NT government were largely at fault for not having a…portable engine pump set up that could be put on a trailer and towed from bore to bore, and a couple of men manning it and keep the tanks at least half full.' Looking back to those times Kelly sees the situation then as 'just a debacle' and he said, 'I don't think it's an era that we should be really proud about, the way we…mistreated the animals just for the want of a bit of planning, and spend a few dollars and organise some portable pumps'.[743]

Scotty Watson is another drover who had a lot of experience of the Murranji country. His first trip over was with Sandy McIndoe's plant, taking a mob of Willeroo cows to Helen Springs in 1948, and he made other trips with mobs from Limbunya, VRD, Waterloo and Moola Boola. In later years he took many mobs from Beetaloo station, but these didn't go over the Murranji Track.

For Scotty, droving across the Murranji was never much fun, but one particular trip was especially trying. The trouble began on VRD where the cattle were being mustered:

George Lewis sent me up to give [the drover] a hand to put the mob together, hold them for him while he mustered. And of course, he was in charge, and he put together three thousand bullocks – that's a lot of bullocks – and we split 'em up into two mobs in the daytime. I took one mob, he took the other, and the silly bastard put 'em together of a night time. Have you ever ridden around three thousand bullocks? And they rushed, they rushed every night![744]

Once they were on the road the two mobs were kept separate, but there was still trouble. Near the Yellow Waterholes Scotty's mob rushed at about 1 am. He was on watch at the time and his experience highlights the dangers of trying to head a rushing mob in the Murranji country:

when they gallop in that Murranji, they stir up the bulldust and you can't see your hand in front of yer. How people never got killed in there I donno. And I wound up getting a piece of turpentine bush right up me nose, and it broke off inside. And of course, the tears – apart from the blood. I couldn't see! Couldn't see anything! ...my brother came round and he had to lead me back, back into camp. I had a cook called Bindy Burr with me and they laid me down and he had a pair of stake pliers and just pushed 'em up gently, 'cause that stuff'll break off easy, and he got it all out in one go. And I didn't move because he breathed garlic all over me and I just about passed out!

Apart from droving cattle across the Murranji, Scotty had another, quite different and unique experience of the region. When droving was suspended during the 1952 drought, Scotty had no work and nowhere to go where conditions were better. Instead, he spent six months camped at Murranji Waterhole looking after more than one hundred horses, a mob made up of his own plant horses, the horses from Hidden Valley station, and the plants of Alex Scobie, Doug Scobie, Alex Lewis and Norm Jansen. For something to do he would track-ride south-east as far as No. 10 Bore and west as far as No. 11[745], but the horses never went far and always came back to the water.

With no money and no means to get to a store, most of the time Scotty was very short of rations. He had a rough time:

you'd get very, very few vehicles through in those days, and you'd scrounge a bit of tucker off them when they'd come past, but you couldn't kill because everything was too poor. So what I used to do, I didn't have any money but I had a few bullets – ·22s – so I made two forky sticks and put the gun in it down near the trough [aimed along the edge of the trough], put a long string on it and hid behind one of the tanks, and when the pigeons and galahs'd come in, pull the trigger, and you'd get about six in one bullet. And they all went in for tucker. And I went off pigeons for life, I think.[746]

Rodney Watson (no relation to Scotty) worked as a ringer and drover all his life, including with Elmore Lewis who he regarded as the best all-round cattleman and horseman he ever worked with, and a polished horseman[747] (plate 59). Rodney travelled over the Murranji at least a dozen times, the first in 1946 when he was a boy and then in the 1950s when he had his own plant. He heard about some bad rushes in the Murranji and though he never had one himself he treated the Murranji with respect. He said some drovers were 'drivers' who made their cattle do big stages – fifteen or twenty miles from bore to bore – to get them through the scrub as quickly as possible. Normally the trip through the scrub took eight or nine days and Rodney explained the crossing step by step:

> *you come onto the Murranji at the head of the Armstrong Creek… You camp at the foot of the jump-up or back from the foot of the jump-up, you feed your cattle in the morning for a mile or so. The reason for that is, when you go up on top of the jump there's a lot of ironwood poison. That's especially when it's small – it grows into a big tree – [and] if you bring empty cattle onto it and they fill up on it, it'll poisoned 'em. Well you come up, you water there at 13 and you go out and camp at what they call Yellow Waterhole. That's, well it's semi-permanent, but perhaps it could've been permanent in the old days around the turn of the century. You camp there that night. Then you dry day to 12, go in and water at 11 next day and out, dry day again to Murranji, this side of Murranji. Then you go in to Murranji Bore. That's where the old Murranji Waterhole is and all the old graves. Beautiful water in the bore there too, it's the best. And you water and go out from there, and you dry day again next day and come out at 10. That's on the edge of the Murranji.*[748]

In 1954 Eugene Kostin crossed the Murranji with Drover Stan Fowler, known far and wide as 'Chook', and they had a couple of bad smashes on the Track. One was on Bandicoot Flat, near Pussycat Bore:

> *Yeah we had a bad smash there on that drummy ground. Come daylight we was fifty down the drain then. But it was all scrub cattle, you couldn't do bloody anything, it was a waste of time goin' lookin' for 'em. We got rid of them bastards, counted our losses and licked our wounds.*[749]

All went well through No. 13 Bore, the Yellow Waterholes and No. 12, but they had trouble again past No. 11 Bore when, 'about five o'clock in the mornin' some bloody curlews come and give an ungodly scream and awaaay they bloody went! I went after the bastards, we were down another fifty or sixty the next bloody morning.'[750] Eugene found one lame bullock, but he said, 'the lancewood and the bulwaddy put the fear of Christ up me.'

At the end of 1956 Aboriginal drover Charlie Yeeda helped take a mob of Moola Boola station cattle across the Murranji. They set out on December 5th and had trouble almost from the start: 'Oh well, when we started from Moola Boola, the first few weeks on the road, we had a bit a rush'. When they reached Pussycat Bore disease was detected in the mob and the cattle were quarantined for six weeks, but eventually were able to continue. Going through the Murranji Track the cattle rushed but Charlie and the other men didn't gallop after them to try and turn them back: 'That bullock he used to rush, we were always say, "well let it rush". We seen that bulwaddy tree, eh? Let it go an' the bulwaddy used to bring it back'.[751]

To get control of a mob that had rushed, Charlie said they used torches:

> *Every rush, we don't need to gallop, and just put the torch and every bullock and just bring it back. That's the secret what we found. Instead of you killin' yourself... we still livin', never get killed, never had a broken leg, never had a roll, you know? Not lots of people use a torch in the drovin'... When you gallopin' and just puttin' the torch in the front, you know.*[752]

Mick Coombes started up droving in the Northern Territory after leaving the army at the end of World War Two. He said he didn't mind the Murranji although there certainly were problems to be overcome. One was that, 'A lot of fellas went through there who never should've been in charge of cattle.' Another was that some of the night camps were too far from the bores and because of this,

> *you never had time to feed cattle. A lot of them bores was, I think from 12 goin' out to a night camp was the best part of six miles, and that's why they cut the mobs down from 1500 to 1350 to give 'em time to water 'em. By the time you watered them cattle and walked 'em out six mile to a night camp they was lookin' for...a feed* [753]

Combined with the heat, the distances being walked and the long time between drinks, the lack of adequate feeding meant that the cattle became weaker. This especially affected the cows with calves: 'Breeders...by the time you got to that Murranji tank with a mob of breeders they were finished. The little calves'd die, the mothers'd go dry and the calves'd die. It's too hot and [too far] in between water'.[754]

Over the years Mick heard about bad rushes on the Murranji. Drover Charlie Swan (plate 35) once told him about meeting another drover at the Yellow Waterholes who had about fifteen head of Bullshead (VRD) bullocks. Swan asked him, 'What are you doin' with them?' and the drover replied, 'That's all that's left from the mob, out of fifteen hundred!'[755]

Mick had a few rushes of his own. Once he had a mob of Willeroo cattle rush in the Murranji, but luckily for him,

> *They went about from here down to my gate, and they stopped themselves*

> *and I just trotted along behind 'em. Got around in front of 'em and lit another fire. Wouldn't try to shift 'em back onto camp [because] there might've been another start. Anyone that tells you they boxed a mob up in there [in the Murranji], well they were on the grog. Them and the bullocks!*[756]

In 1967 Mick took the second last mob of cattle over the Murranji Track, and between No. 12 Bore and No. 11 Bore he had a very bad smash. These were Wave Hill bullocks and Mick believes his smash is what led Vesteys to stop walking cattle to Queensland:

> *Yes, it was through me that Vesteys sent no more cattle. Now they'll all tell you how good they were and how they never made a mistake, but that's one thing I can claim, that I finished the drovin' up…we camped out from 12 now and a bullock…was draggin' an old hide. There was a lot of cattle died of ironwood poisoning through there, you know, anything up forty, fifty, a hundred head of cattle with ironwood poisoning, for the simple reason that they hadn't been fed and they'd eat anything, you see. Well these green ironwood bushes growin' along they'd eat 'em. And this bullock dragged this hide and the bones still in it… Anyhow, away they went, and they split into four mobs. Well we only had three night horses that time, and we held one mob…[and]…we couldn't let one mob go to go and chase another one. There was no point in that. Well they finished up some at Dunmarra, some at Beetaloo and some, the stock inspector yarded fifteen of them at Elliott. … they'd done over a hundred miles then. And they [Vesteys] said, 'Why didn't you look for them?' Well they decided that they'd road train everything from then on.*[757]

CHAPTER 18

THE 'GHOST ROAD' BEGINS

So what is left today of the Murranji Track and the men who moved the big herds along it during the eighty-one years of its functioning existence? Of the graves of the eight, eleven or perhaps twenty men who died there, no trace remains, the mounds washed and trampled away, and the names carved on the trees turned to ashes or covered by new bark. Illawarra and Paschendaele homesteads have long gone, marked only by fragments of glass, empty cartridge cases and worn out horseshoes, and the old Top Springs store has gone too, burnt down and rebuilt at a different location some kilometres away.

About the only visible reminder of the droving era is the bores and tanks, or what is left of them. Most are now in ruins or even completely destroyed, the tanks, windmills and troughs taken away, or smashed and twisted by storms (plates 60 and 62). A few are more or less intact although none of the windmills are now in operation. Several bores have been taken over by local landholders, with diesel pumps now drawing water for stock or domestic use, and Murranji Bore is being tapped to supply a nearby Aboriginal outstation.

In 1988, twenty years after the end of droving on the Murranji, a fine bronze statue of a drover and plaques with the names of many Murranji drovers were erected at the end of the Murranji Track, at Newcastle Waters (plate 62). This was followed in June 1998 with the declaration of a number of sites along the Track as historic places under the Northern Territory *Heritage Conservation Act 1991*. These included Murranji Bore and Waterhole, No. 11 Bore, No. 12 Bore, No. 13 Bore and Pussycat Bore (No. 14),[758] but the Murranji Track as a whole was given no legal status. It's now washed out in many places and movement along it is further barred by fence lines and scrub growth – as a physical entity, the Murranji Track is following the big herds and the drovers into oblivion.

Even the grassy spaces between the thickets of bulwaddy and lancewood are disappearing. Drover 'Pic' Willetts noticed scrub springing up soon after droving along the Track ended, a phenomenon he directly attributed to the absence of cattle.[759] Two Mudbura men who acted as guides during a survey of historic sites along the Murranji in 1991 constantly remarked that areas which formerly were open grassy flats were being taken over by saplings and scrub,[760] and when one of the Murranji drovers, Dave Allworth, visited the Track in 2000 he was shocked at how overgrown it had become. He made his complaint in traditional drover's fashion – he 'sent' a 'letter' to the Bagman's Gazette![761] (plate 63).

The drovers have all ridden away, to different lives in different places, far from the Murranji. Many have crossed the great divide. The ashes of their fires and the tracks of their cattle have long gone too, blown and washed away by the winds and rains of forty years and more. In the face of what these men and women achieved, a few ruined mills and a handful of old tanks, and even a bronze statue might seem a poor memorial, but the *legend* of the Murranji and its drovers will always remain a significant part of Australia's outback heritage.

On June 20th 1967 Noel 'Pic' Willetts dipped a mob of 1390 Auvergne and Newry cattle at Pussycat yard, and then started them over the Murranji.[762] This was the last mob to take the Track, and when the last tailers passed Newcastle Waters, the Murranji Track truly became 'The Ghost Road of the Drovers'.

BIBLIOGRAPHY

Abbreviations

CPP:	Commonweath Parliamentary Papers
NAA ACT:	National Archives of Australia, Australian Capital Territory.
NAA NT:	National Archives of Australia, Northern Territory.
NAA SA:	National Archives of Australia, South Australia.
NTRS:	Northern Territory Records Service (Northern Territory Archives).
SAPP:	South Australian Parliamentary Papers.
DPI&F	Department of Primary Industry & Fisheries

Abbott, C. Northern Territory Administrator, to Secretary, Department of the Interior, April 21 1938. NAA ACT, A284/1 B5244.

Abbott, C., Northern Territory Administrator, to Secretary, Department of the Interior, June 27 1938. NAA ACT, A284/1 B5244.

Abbott, C. Northern Territory Administrator, to Secretary, Department of the Interior, December 11 1940. NAA NT CRS F1 1940/508.

Abbott, C. Northern Territory Administrator, to A.S. Bingle, Australian Investment Agency, February 15 1941. NAA NT CRS F1 1940/508.

Abbott, C.L.A. telegram to Department of Interior, cited in Abbott to V.G. Carrington, June 7 1941, NAA, NT, series F1, item 1940/508.

Abbott, C. Northern Territory Administrator, to Secretary, Department of the Interior, May 5 1942. NAA NT CRS F1 1942/112.

Abbott. Administrator C.L.A., to the Secretary, Department of the Interior, May 12 1942, NAA NT CRS series F1, item 1942/112.

Abbott, C. Northern Territory Administrator, Report to Secretary, Department of the Interior, July 15 1942. NAA NT CRS F1 1942/112.

Abbott, C. Northern Territory Administrator, to A.S. Bingle, Australian Investment Agency, December 21 1942. NAA NT CRS F1 1942/112.

Abbott, C. Northern Territory Administrator, to Field Officer Clough, December 16 1943. NAA NT CRS F1 1943/10B.

Abbott, C. Northern Territory Administrator, list of essential and desirable requirements for east-west stock route, 1943, NAA NT CRS F1 1943/10B.

Abbott, C. Northern Territory Administrator, to Deputy Director-General of Allied Works,

Alice Springs, March 17 1944. NAA NT CRS F1 1943/10B.

Allen, J.W. to H. Connell, Director, Works Department, April 9 1932. NAA ACT, A284/1 B5244.

Allen, J.W. to Secretary, Department of the Interior, April 30 1936. NAA ACT, A284/1 B5244.

Allen, J.W. to Minister for the Interior, June 5 1936. NAA ACT, A284/1 B5244.

Allen, J.W. to Minister for the Interior, August 11 1936. NAA ACT, A284 B5244.

Althans, J., to A. Blain, MHR, Canberra, May 7 1947, Murranji Stock Route — Deviation of Route at Newcastle Waters, file 331/5/73. DPI&F, Alice Springs.

Artaud, Mounted Constable J.L., Temporary Inspector of Stock, January 1 1908, in 'Government Resident's Report on the Northern Territory, 1907', *SAPP*, vol. 3, no. 45, 1908.

Baldwin, S. 'When Mabel took the Reins', *The Bulletin*, January 26, 1988: 233-34.

Bancroft, T.D., internal memo, Department of External Affairs, October 23 1911. NAA ACT, series A3/1, item 14/3682.

Barclay, Captain H.V., to Secretary, Department of External Affairs, August 3 1911, NAA (ACT), series A3/1, NT 14/3682.

Bell, N.C. Director of Mines, to the Acting Administrator. January 9 1937. NAA NT, series F1/0, item 1936/456.

Biltris, L. 'The Passing of the Pioneers, *Walkabout*, May 1 1951: 44-45;

Bingle, A.S. *This Is Our Country*, privately published by author's widow, Sydney, 1978.

Bingle, A.S. Australian Investment Agency, to C. Abbott, Northern Territory Administrator, November 4 1940. NAA NT CRS F1 1940/508

Bingle, A.S., to Administrator, March 20 1942. NAA NT CRS F1 1942/112.

Bingle A.S., Australian Investment Agency, to The Government Secretary, Northern Territory Administration, March 25 1942, NAA NT, series F1, item 1942/112.

Bingle, A.S. Australian Investment Agency, to Government Secretary, Alice Springs, April 10 1942. NAA NT CRS F1 1942/112.

Bingle, A.S. Australian Investment Agency, to C. Abbott, Northern Territory Administrator, September 8 1942. NAA NT CRS F1 1940/508.

Bingle, A.S., Australian Investment Agency, to C. Abbott, Northern Territory Administrator, September 18 1942. NAA NT CRS F1 1942/112.

Bingle, A.S. Australian Investment Agency, to Secretary, Department of the Interior, December 7 1942. NAA NT CRS F1 1942/112.

Bingle, A.S. Australian Investment Agency, to C. Abbott, Northern Territory Administrator, December 8 1942. NAA NT CRS F1 1942/112.

Bingle, A.S. Australian Investment Agency, to C. Abbott, Northern Territory Administrator, January 2 1943. NAA NT CRS F1 1943/10B.

Bingle, W.D. Secretary Works and Railways, to Secretary, Commonwealth Treasury, May 14 1921, NAA (ACT), series A571/56, item 21/7152.

Birrell, C. to Chief Clerk, Lands and Survey Branch, Darwin, December 24 1951. NTRS F28 Box 44, GL1364.

Bishop, Captain F. to the Government Resident, October 6 1927, Wave Hill-Alice Springs Stock Route, NTRS F5, S258.

Bishop, Captain F. to the Northern Territory Administrator, April 29 1935, CRS, series F1, item 1940/508.

Bishop, Captain F. to the Administrator of the Northern Territory, October 14 1936, NAA ACT, series A284, item B5244.

Bishop, Captain F. report to Northern Territory Administrator, Darwin, May 14 1938. NAA ACT, A284/1 B5244.

Bishop, Captain F. to the Government Secretary, Darwin, May 21 1941. NAA (NT), CRS F1 1940/508.

Bishop, Captain F. extract from report by, November 27 1939. NAA ACT, A284/1 B5244.

Bolton, G. *A Thousand Miles Away: A History of North Queensland to 1920*, The Jacaranda Press, Brisbane, 1963.

Bowler, J. 'Water and Sand: Climate in Ancient Australia', in Mulvaney, D. J. and J. Peter White, (eds.) *Australians To 1788*, Fairfax, Syme & Weldon Associates, 1987: 25-45.

Braitling, W. to Secretary, Home and Territories, May 5 1921. NAA ACT, series A1 series 1930/2585.

Braitling, W. to the Secretary, Department of Home and Territories, May 4 1922. NAA, ACT, series A1, item 1930/2585.

Braitling, W. to E. Copely Playford, Director of Lands and Mines, July 21 1922, NTRS f28, GL 336.

Braitling, W. Application for Pastoral Licence, July 21 1922, NTRS F28 GL336.

Braitling, W. to Director of Lands, Darwin, June 18 1923, NTRS F28 GL336.

Braitling, W. to L.H. Giles, June 26 1926, NAA ACT, series A1/1, item 1930/2585.

Braitling, W. to L.H. Giles, August 20 1927. NAA ACT, series A1, item 1930/2585.

Braitling, W., Telegram to Director of Lands, Darwin, October 18 1928, NTRS F28 GL336.

Braitling, W. entry on W. Braitling in D. Carment, et al (eds.), *Northern Territory Dictionary of Biography, Volume One: To 1943*, Northern Territory University Press, Darwin, 1990: 33-34.

Brown, C. *1:250,000 Geological Series—Explanatory Notes. Daly Waters, Northern Territory, Sheet SE/53—1 International Index*. Bureau of Mineral Resources, Geology and Geophysics, Canberra, 1969: 4.

Brown, C. H., (Extract from) report for the Month of September 1950, Murranji Stock Route — General File, 331/4/15. DPI&F, Alice Springs.

Brown, C. H., (Extract from) report for the Month of April, 1951, Murranji Stock Route — General File, 331/4/15. DPI&F, Alice Springs.

Brown, C. Duplication of Bores — Barkly and Murranji Stock routes. Murranji Stock Route — General File. 331/4/15. DPI&F, Alice Springs.

Brown, C., Memorandum to Director of Animal Industry, October 10 1957. Murranji Water Hole. Murranji Stock Route, General File 331/5/72. DPI&F, Alice Springs.

Brown, F.G. *The Lost Mines and Treasures of Northern Australia*, Gemcraft Publications Pty. Ltd., East Malvern, 1983: 60-62.

Buchanan, B. *In the Tracks of Old Bluey: The Life Story of Nat Buchanan*, Central Queensland University Press, Rockhampton, 1997.

Buchanan, G. 'Pioneers of the Far North: Adventure and Achievement' *Sydney Stock & Station Journal*, April 28 1922.

Buchanan, G. General Inspection Report, October 29 1952. NTRS F28 Box 42 GL 1296

Buchanan. G. 'Recalling The Past: Some Notes on Nat Buchanan', *The Pastoral Review and Graziers' Record*, August 18 1961: 899-900.

Buchanan. G. *Packhorse and Waterhole: With the First Overlanders to the Kimberleys*. Hesperian Press, Perth, 1984 (Facsimile edition, first published by Angus & Robertson Limited, Sydney, 1933.

Buchanan, W.F. to Surveyor General, January 11 1901, Australian Archives, ACT, series A1640, item 1901/46; B. Buchanan, 1997.

Bucknall, R. entry on Thelma Hawks in D. Carment and H. Wilson (eds.), *Northern Territory Dictionary of Biography*, vol. 3, Northern Territory University Press, Darwin, 1996.

Burt, Mounted Constable F., Temporary Inspector of Stock, Victoria River District, December 30 1905, in 'Government Resident's Report on the Northern Territory, 1906', *SAPP*, vol. 2, no. 45, 1906: 23.

Byers, H.W. to A. Blain, MHR, Canberra, June 9 1947. Murranji Stock Route — Deviation of Route at Newcastle Waters, file 331/5/73. DPI&F, Alice Springs.

Cahill, T. cited in the 'Government Resident's Report on the Northern Territory, 1905', *SAPP*, vol. 2, no. 45, 1906.

Carment, D. et al (eds.), *Northern Territory Dictionary of Biography, Volume One: To 1945*. Northern Territory University Press, Darwin, 1990.

Carrodus, J. Secretary, Department of the Interior, memorandum to Assistant Secretary, Works and Services Branch. March 19 1937. NAA ACT, A284/1 B5244.

Carrodus, J., Secretary, Department of the Interior, to the Administrator, April 16 1946. Murranji Stock Route General File, 331/4/15. DPI&F, Alice Springs.

Carrington, V. District Officer, to the Northern Territory Administrator, June 13 1941. NAA NT CRS F1 1940/508.

Chewings, C. 'A Journey from Barrow Creek to Victoria River', *The Geographical Journal*, vol. 76, no. 4, October 1930: 316-338.

Clough, F. to Government Secretary, April 7 1942. NAA NT, F1 1942/112.

Clough, Field Officer W., to the Chief Clerk, Lands Department, November 19 1940 NAA NT, F1 item 1940/508.

Clough, Field Officer W., to Government Secretary, Alice Springs, May 20 1942. NAA NT CRS F1 1942/112.

Clough, Field Officer W. Report on Murranji, to Administrator, October 5 1943. NAA NT CRS F1 1943/10B.

Cole, T. *Hell West and Crooked*, Collins Publishers Australia, Sydney, 1988.

Cole, T. *Riding the Wildman Plains; The Letters and Diaries of TOM COLE 1923-1943*, Sun Books, Sydney, 1992.

Collier, J. *The Pastoral Age in Australia*, Whitcombe & Tombs, Limited, Melbourne, 1911.

Colson. F. to the Resident Engineer, Alice Springs, October 12 1943. NAA NT CRS F1 1943/10B.

Commonwealth Gazette, August 2 1956.

Conacher, C.W.D. to the Chairman, North Australia Commission, June 18 1928, NTRS F5 S258.

Conacher, C. Australian Investment Agency, to J. Carrodus, Department of the Interior, July 2 1936. NAA ACT, A284/1 B5244.

Connellan, E.J. *Failure of Triumph: the story of Connellan Airways*, Paradigm Investments, Alice Springs, 1992.

Corfield, J. *The Ned Kelly Encyclopaedia*, Lothian Books, Melbourne, 2003.

Dashwood, C., Government Resident, to the 'Minister Controlling the Northern Territory', January 8 1900, NAA ACT, series A1640/1, item 99/502.

Dashwood, C., Government Resident, to C.C. Kingston, the Premier of South Australia, January 20 1896, NAA ACT, series A/1640 item 96/35.

Davidson, W.J., Chief Clerk, to Newcastle Waters Ltd., February 9, 1951, NAA NT series F1/0, item 1951/763.

Davis, P. *Kookaburra. The most compelling story in Australia's aviation history*, Sydney, 1980.

Day, E. Crown Lands and Survey Department, to Surveyor A.B. Scandrett, May 16 1913, NTRS F9, 364/39.

Delbridge, A. et al (eds), *The Macquarie Dictionary*, Second Edition, the Macquarie Library, Sydney, 1991.

Derby Police Occurrence book, September 4 1889, Western Australian State Records Office, Ms 241.

Ditchfield, J. *Angels Don't Go Droving*, Central Queensland University Press, Rockhampton, 2003.

Donovan, P. *At the Other End of Australia: The Commonwealth and the Northern Territory 1911-1978*, Queensland University Press, Brisbane, 1984.

Duncan, R. *The Northern Territory Pastoral Industry*, Melbourne University Press, Melbourne, 1967.

Durack, M. *Sons In The Saddle*, Corgi Books, Condell Park (NSW), 1985.

Durack, M.P. to W. Griffiths, November 29 1899, NAA ACT A1640/1 99/502.

Edwards, G. Manager of the Australian Investment Agency (Vesteys), to the Secretary, Department of Home and Territories, June 18 1924. NAA ACT, series A1/1, item 1926/12258.

Egan, Pastoral Inspector, December 2 1958. NTRS F28 Box 42 GL 1296.

Elder, P. et al, *Northern Territory Dictionary of Biography*, vol. 2.

Esson, L. 'The Drovers' in A. Sykes (ed.), *Five Plays for stage, radio, and television*, University of Queensland Press, Brisbane, 1977.

Farwell, G. *Cape York to the Kimberleys*, Rigby, Adelaide, 1962.

Farwell, G. 'Down the Murranji Track', *The Pastoral Review and Graziers' Record*, April 16 1952.

Fleetwood, A. Engineer, Water Supply and Sewerage, report to Assistant Secretary, Department of the Interior, August 7 1936. NAA ACT, A284 B5483.

Fleming, A. 'Tales of the Murrunji' [sic], *Brisbane Courier Mail*, August 11 1938

Flemming, J. Chief Mechanical Engineer, to Assistant Secretary, Works and Services Branch, Department of the Interior, December 13 1935. NAA NT CRS F1 1940/508.

Footell, D. (Vesteys) to the Secretary, Northern Territory Pastoral Lessees' Association, July 15 1936. NTRS, Northern Territory Cattlemen's Association Inc. PAC 106. vol. 39, 'Stock Routes and Reserves'.

Forrest, A. *North-West Exploration: Journal Of Exploration From DeGrey To Port Darwin*. Government Printer, Perth, 1880.

Foster, J.S. to the Resident Magistrate in Wyndham, July 29 1890, cited as Appendix 2 in G. Bolton, *A Survey of the Kimberley Pastoral Industry from 1885 to the Present*, unpublished Masters thesis, University of Western Australia, 1953.

Gaunt, C.E., 'Old Time Memories: The Birth of Borroloola', *Northern Standard*, October 16 1931.

Gaunt, C.E., 'Old Time Memories: The Lepers of Arnhem Land and Sketches', *Northern Standard*, July 10 1934.

Giles, A. *Exploring in the 'Seventies and the Construction of the Overland Telegraph Line*, Facsimile edition, Friends of the State Library of South Australia, 1995 (First published by W.K. Thomas & Co. [The Register] Adelaide, 1926).

Giles, A. *The First pastoral Settlement in the Northern Territory*, copy held at the National Trust of Australia (NT), Darwin, nd.

Gilruth, Dr. J.A. 'Report of the Administrator for the Year Ended 30th June 1918', *CPP*, sessions 1917-19, vol., 6.

Geo. A. H., Secretary, to Assistant Secretary, Department of Home Affairs, September 23 1930, NTRS series F5, item S258

Goodliffe, C. 'The Condamine Bell'. *Walkabout*, October 1 1945.

Gordon Creek Police Journal, NTRS F302.

Goss, F. *Life in the Never-Never Country of South Australia in the 70s. to 90s*, Mortlock Library, D4436(L), 1956.

Gregory, A.C. and F. Gregory. *Journals of Australian Explorations*, James C. Beal, Government Printer, Brisbane, 1884.

Griffiths, W. (M.P.), to 'the Minister for the Northern Territory', December 15 1899, NAA ACT series A1640/1, item 99/502.

Groom, A. *Wealth in the Wilderness*, Angus and Robertson, Sydney 1955.

Gunn, J. *We of the Never Never*, Hutchinson, London, 1908.

Hare, W. *The Early History of Animal Industry In The Northern Territory*, Conservation Commission Of The Northern Territory, Government Printer, Darwin, 1985.

Harney, W. 'Water in the Dry Lands', *Walkabout*, February 1 1952.

Harney, W. *Life Among the Aborigines*, Robert Hale Limited, London, 1957.

Harney, W. *Content to Lie in the Sun*, Rigby Limited, Sydney, 1974 [1958].

Harney, W. 'The Maluka's Grave', *Walkabout*, November 1948.

Hartt, H. 'Out On The Murranji', *Walkabout*, October 1 1944.

Haslam, W., Deputy Director-General of Allied Works for Northern Territory, memorandum to Government Secretary, Alice Springs, June 16 1943. NAA NT CRS F1 1943/94.

Hawks, C.J. to the Minister for Lands, April 1955, NTRS Box 52, GL 1555.

Hemphill, C. Letter to the editor headed, 'Mr. N. Buchanan's Exploration', *South Australian Register*, October 15 1896.

Herbert, C., Government Resident, to the Minister Controlling the Northern Territory, August 22 1906, NAA, ACT, series A1640, item 1906/492.

Herbert, C. Government Resident's Report on the Northern Territory, 1906', *SAPP*, vol. 3, no. 45, 1907.

Herbert, C. 'Government Resident's Report on the Northern Territory, 1907', *SAPP* vol. 3, no. 45, 1908.

Herbert, C. 'Government Resident's Report on the Northern Territory, 1908', *SAPP* vol. 3, no. 45, 1909.

Herbert, C. 'Northern Territory. Report of the Government Resident for the year 1910', *SAPP*, vol. 3, no. 66, 1911.

Hilgendorf, M. *Northern Territory Days*, Historical Society of the Northern Territory, 1994.

Hill, E. 'Along the Murran-ji', *Walkabout*, November 1 1949.

Hill, E. *The Territory*, Angus and Robertson, Sydney, 1951.

Hill, E. to Billy Linklater, June 21 1946, Mitchell Library, CY 3480 Al 10/18.

H. Ernestine, *Suicide Track of Continent*, unprovenanced newspaper cutting, 1936.

'H7H' (Hely Hutchinson), 'Record Droving Trips', *The Pastoralists' Review*, May 15 1905.

'H7H' (Hely Hutchinson), 'Odd Stock and Other Notes', *The Morning Bulletin*, June 20 1905.

'H7H' (Hely Hutchinson), 'Odd Stock and Other Notes' *Morning Bulletin*, Rockhampton, July 15 1905.

'H7H' (Hely Hutchinson), 'Odd Stock and Other Notes', *The Morning Bulletin* (Rockhampton), December 2 1905.

'H7H' (Hely Hutchinson), 'Odd Stock and Other Notes', *The Morning Bulletin* (Rockhampton), January 20 1906.

'H7H' (Hely Hutchinson), *North Queensland Herald*, January 22 1906.
'H7H' (Hely Hutchinson), 'A Big Overland Trip. Notes By The Way', *Morning Bulletin* (Rockhampton), April 28 1906.
'H7H' (Hely Hutchinson), 'Early Drovers in the Northern Territory – Leaves from the Diary of Alfred Giles', *The Pastoralists' Review*, March 15 1906.
'H7H' (Hely Hutchinson), 'The Men Who Blazed The Track', *The Pastoralists' Review*, August 15 1912.
Holland, U.W. (Mounted Constable) to Inspector N. Waters, January 3 1910, cited in the 'Government Resident's Report on the Northern Territory, 1909', *SAPP*, vol. 3, no. 45, 1910.
Ingham, A.M., *The Boss Drover and his Mates*, Halstead Press, Sydney, 1996.
'John Stockman' (Constable Bert Mettam), 'Territory Letter', *Hoofs and Horns*, May 1951.
'John Stockman' (Constable Bert Mettam), 'Territory Letter', *Hoofs and Horns*, September 1955.
'John Stockman' (Constable Bert Mettam), 'Territory Letter', *Hoofs and Horns*, August 1959.
'John Stockman' (Constable Bert Mettam), 'Territory Letter', *Hoofs and Horns*, April 1961.
Johnston, C. (Mounted Constable), Temporary Inspector of stock, December 31 1905, cited in the 'Government Resident's Report on the Northern Territory, 1905', *SAPP*, vol. 2, no. 45, SAPP, 1906.
Jones, R.C. Director of Works, to The Government Secretary, Northern Territory Administration, September 7 1950. NAA NT CRS F1/0, item 1947/198.
Jones, R. and J. Bowler, 'Struggle for the Savanna: Northern Australia in Ecological and Prehistoric Perspective', *In* R. Jones (ed.) *Northern Australia: Options and Implications*, Research School of Pacific Studies, Australian National University, Canberra, 1980.
Jones, R. 'The Alligator Rivers: A Mirror to Continental Prehistory', in D. Wade-Marshall and P. Loveday (eds.), *North Australia: Progress and Prospects, Volume 2. Floodplains Research*, North Australia Research Unit, Darwin, 1988.
Katherine Mortuary Book, NTRS, F1060.
Kimber, R. *Arltunga Man: Walter Smith Australian Bushman*, Hesperian Press, Perth 1986.
Kimber, R. entry on Joe Brown in D. Carment, et al (eds.), 1990.
Lamond, G. *Tales Of The Overland: Queensland To Kimberley In 1885*, Hesperian Press, Victoria Park [W.A.], 1986.
Lewis, D. *The Final Muster: A Survey of Previously Undocumented Sites throughout the Victoria River District*, 2000. Report prepared for the Australian National Trust (N.T.).
Lewis, D. entry on Charlie Schultz in D. Carment and H. Wilson (eds.), *Northern Territory Dictionary of Biography*, vol., 3, 1996.
Lewis, D. letter to the editor of the *Stockman's Hall of Fame paper*, December, 2000.
Lewis, D. *Slower than the Eye Can See: Environmental change in northern Australia's cattle lands*, Tropical Savannas CRC, Darwin, 2002.
Lewis, D. *A Wild History*, unpublished PhD thesis, Australian National University, 2004.
Linklater, W. and L. Tapp, *Gather No Moss*, Hesperian Press facsimile edition, 1997 (originally published in 1968 by the Macmillan Company).
Linklater, W. 'Pioneer Women of N.T.', Miscellaneous letters and other documents, 1895-1949, Mitchell Library, Al 10/3-37, CY3480.
Linklater, W. 'Billy Miller of O.T. Station N.T.', December 26 1941, unpublished unprovenanced ms (possibly from Mitchell Library).
Little, J.A.G. 'Notice of Annual, Inspecting Journey of Overland Telegraph Line, from Port Darwin to Attack Creek', *Northern Territory Times*, August 30 1901.

Little, J.K. 'Droving of Yore', *The Pastoral Review and Graziers' Record*, November 16, 1950.

Little, J.K. 'The Murranji Waterhole', *The Pastoral Review and Graziers' Record*, February 16 1952.

Littlejohn, W. to Government Secretary, Alice Springs, June 6 1942. NAA NT CRS F1 1942/112.

Lunney, Bob. *Fifteen Hundred Down The Murranji*, Crawford House Publishing Pty. Ltd., Bathurst, 1997.

Maddock, J. *A History of Road Trains in the Northern Territory, 1934-1988*. Kangaroo Press, Sydney, 1988.

Makin, J. *The Big Run: The Story of Victoria River Downs*, Rigby, Sydney, 1983.

Mallison, M. 'Adventures on the Murranji Track: Droving and Spear-throwing', *Sydney Morning Herald*, June 27 1942.

Mallison. M. 'Across the Territory by Covered Waggon: How the Bridges made History', *Quirindi Advocate*, October 3 1958.

Marsh, R. to Director of Animal Industry Division, Alice Springs, May 13 1958. Top Springs Dip (Pussycat) File 331/7/8. DPI&F, Alice Springs.

Martin, A. to J.W. Allen, Secretary, Northern Territory Pastoral Lessees Association, November 2 1931. NTRS, Northern Territory Cattlemen's Association Inc., PAC 106. vol. 39, 'Stock Routes and Reserves'.

Martin, A. to Lord Luke, July 21 1941. Bovril Australian Estates Ltd.: Records, Correspondence between Australian Mercantile Land and Finance Co. Ltd., Sydney, and B.A.E. Ltd., London, and station manager. Noel Butlin Archives, 119/6.

Martin, A. manager of VRD, to Lord Luke, Chairman of Bovril, April 27 1942. Bovril Australian Estates Ltd. Records, Correspondence between Australian Mercantile Land and Finance Co. Ltd., Sydney, and B.A.E. Ltd., London, and station manager, Noel Butlin Archives,119/6.

Martin, A. manager of VRD, telegram to Administrator (?), April 1942. NAA NT CRS F1 1942/112.

Martin, A. manager of VRD, to Lord Luke, Chairman of Bovril, September 23 1943. Bovril Australian Estates Ltd. Records, Correspondence between Australian Mercantile Land and Finance Co. Ltd., Sydney, and B.A.E. Ltd., London, and station manager. Noel Butlin Archives, 119/6.

Martin, B. 'Droving in Northern Territory' (letter to the editor), *The Pastoralists' Review*, June 15 1906.

Meldrum, T. to drover J.A. Davis, July 6 1897. Goldsbrough Mort and Co. Ltd: Head Office, Melbourne: letters received from H. W. H. Stevens, Port Darwin, re NT property and butchering business, 1889-1892. Noel Butlin Archives, 872.

McConvell, P. and A. Palmer *A Claim To An Area Of Traditional Land By The Mudbura Traditional Owners*, Northern Land Council, Darwin, 1979.

McIndoe, D. to A.S. Bingle, Australian Investment Agency, June 22 1942. NAA NT CRS F1 1942/112.

McInnes, D., Field Officer, to the Chief Clerk, Lands Department, Darwin, December 4 1940. NAA NT CRS F1, item 1940/508.

McKellar, C.R. to The Secretary, Commonwealth Railways, May 11 1929, NAA SA, Series B300/2, item 7257.

Middleton, W. Secretary of the Australian Investment Agency Ltd. (Vesteys), to The Secretary, Department of the Interior, April 18 1933. NAA ACT, series A284/1, series B5244.

Middleton, W. Secretary, Australian, Investment Agency, to Secretary, Department of the Interior, September 28 1937. NAA ACT, A284/1 B5244.

Moray, A. to Managing director of the Northern Agency, September 8 1918, NTRS series F5, item N64.

Moray, A. letter cited by W. Middleton, Secretary, Australian Investment Agency, to Secretary, Department of the Interior, April 18 1933. NAA ACT, series A284/1, item B5244.

Morey, E. Constable, Newcastle Waters police station, report to Administrator, September 29 1941. NAA NT CRS F1 1940/508.

Mulhearn, C. Veterinary Officer: Proposed Quarantine Reserve — Lease No. 208, Murringi [sic]. August 4 1948. Murranji Stock Route — No. 10 Bore. File No. 331/6/4. DPI&F, Alice Springs.

Mulvaney, J. and J. Kamminga, *Prehistory of Australia*, Allen & Unwin, Sydney, 1999.

Mulvaney, D. *Paddy Cahill of Oenpelli*, Aboriginal Studies Press, Canberra, 2005.

Murranji Survey Plan made by Surveyor Scandrett in 1914. CP 607, Northern Territory Lands Department, Darwin.

Nash, D. 'Aboriginal Knowledge of the aeroplane "Kookaburra"', *Aboriginal History*, vol. 6, no. 1, 1981.

Newcastle Waters Mortuary Book, 1893-1951. NTRS, CRS F608.

Nixon, M. *The Rivers of Home: Frank Lacy – Kimberley Pioneer*, Vanguard Service Print, Perth, 1978.

Noblett, C. 'Report of Sub-Inspector of Stock, Powell's Creek District', cited in 'Northern Territory, Report of the Government Resident for the year 1910', *CPP*, vol. 3, no. 66, 1911.

Northern Territory Cattleman's Association, Miscellaneous – correspondence & cuttings 1929-71. NTRS, D3/3A.

Northern Territory Government Gazette, No. G23.

O'Keefe, Mounted Constable E., cited in 'Government Resident's Report on the Northern Territory, 1905, *SAPP*, vol. 2, no. 45, 1906.

Peacock. S. to Commissioner of Lands, Darwin, April 30 1919. NTRS, F5, P137;

Peacock, S. to the Secretary, Home and Territories, October 29 1921. NAA ACT, series A1, item 1926/12258.

Peacock, S. Notes of interview conducted by the Hon. R.W. Foster, M.P., January 10 1922, NAA ACT, series A1, item 1926/12258.

Peacock, S. to Senator Pearce, July 24 1923, NAA ACT, series A1, item 1926/12258.

Peacock, S. to Northern Territory Administrator F.C. Urquhart, July 15 1924. NAA ACT, series A1/1, item 1926/12258.

Peacock, S. to the Secretary, Home and Territories, October 24 1925, NAA ACT, series A1/1, item 1926/12258.

Pearson, S.E. 'Pioneer Drovers', *The Pastoral Review*, July 16 1929: 653.

Percival, A. Assistant Secretary, Property and Survey Branch, Department of Interior, memorandum to Assistant Secretary, Works and Services Branch, December 2 1932. NAA ACT, A284/1 B5244.

Playford, C. Director of Lands and Mines, to the Government Secretary, February 23 1922, NAA ACT, series A1, item 1926/12258.

Pownall, E. and W. Stackpool, *The Singing Wire*, Collins, Sydney, 1973.

Radford, M.A. [manager of Newcastle Waters] to John Lewis, August 1902 [undated but contextual clues suggest this date]. South Australian State Library, PGR 247/10/1.

Radford, M.A. to John Lewis, September 3 1902, South Australian State Library, PGR 247/10/1.

Radford, M.A. to John Lewis, February 17 1903. South Australian State Library, PGR 247/10/1.

Radford, M.A. to J. Lewis, May 25 1904. South Australian State Library, PGR 247/10/1.

Ramson, W.A. (ed.), *The Australian National Dictionary*, Oxford University Press, Melbourne, 1988.

Ravenscroft, A.G.B., 'Some Habits and Customs of the Chingalee Tribe, Northern Territory, S.A.', *Transactions of the Royal Society of South Australia*, vol. 15, part 1, 1892.

Rees. W. 'Murranji Track'. *Walkabout*. June 1 1950.

Rees, W. 1945. *A Few Notes on the Early Settlement of Victoria River Downs, Northern Territory*. July 12 1945 (copy in possession of author).

Rideout, B.L. Chief Inspector of Stock, to Assistant Secretary, Mines Branch, December 4 1974. Top Springs and Bore Quarantine and Holding Reserve. File 331/6/202. DPI&F, Alice Springs.

Rideout, F.C. Project Officer, to Director of Animal Industry Branch, Darwin, November 16 1978. Murranji Stock Route — General File. 331/4/15. DPI&F, Alice Springs.

Roberts, R. Jones, R. and M. Smith. 'Thermoluminescence dating of a 50,000-year-old human occupation site in northern Australia', *Nature*. 1990: 345: 153-56.

Roberts, T. *Frontier Justice: A History of the Gulf Country to 1900*, University of Queensland Press, St Lucia, 2005.

Rolland, H. Works Director, to Assistant Secretary, Works and Services Branch, Department of the Interior, June 16 1933. NAA ACT, A284/1 B5244.

Ronan, T. *The Deep of the Sky: An Essay in Ancestor Worship*, Cassell Australia, Melbourne, 1963.

Rose, A., Chief Veterinary Officer, to Field Officer Clough, June 4 1946. NAA NT CRS F1 1946/100, Pt 1.

Rose, A. Chief Veterinary Officer, to Northern Territory Administrator, July 7 1947. Murranji Stock Route — Deviation of Route at Newcastle Waters, file 331/5/73. DPI&F, Alice Springs.

Rose, A., Chief Veterinary Officer, to Northern Territory Administrator, August 6 1947. Murranji Stock Route — Deviation of Route at Newcastle Waters, File 331/5/73. DPI&F, Alice Springs.

Rose, A. No. 10 bore, Murranji — Stock and Quarantine Reserve, June 18 1948. Murranji Stock Route — No. 10 Bore. File No. 331/6/4. DPI&F, Alice Springs.

Rose, A., Chief Veterinary Officer, to The Government Secretary, N.T. Administration, September 3 1948, Murranji Stock Route — General File. 331/4/15. DPI&F, Alice Springs.

Rose, A. to the Government Secretary, N.T. Administration, September 15 1948, NAA ACT, series F1/0, item 1947/198.

Rose, A. Chief Veterinary Officer, internal memo by, November 8 1948, Murrangi [sic] Stock Route General File, 331/4/15, DPI&F, Alice Springs.

Rose, A. Chief Veterinarian, to Charlie Schultz, March 29 1949. Murrangi [sic] Stock Route General File, 331/4/15, DPI&F, Alice Springs.

Rose, A. minute to various Government Departments, June 24 1949. Murranji Stock Route — General File. 331/4/15. DPI&F, Alice Springs; NTRS F1 1946/100 Pt 2

Rose, A. Chief Veterinary Officer, Animal Industry Division, File No. 331/6/4. Murranji Stock Route — No. 10 Bore Stock Reserve. DPI&F, Alice Springs

Rose, A. to Director of Lands, April 8 1954. Top Springs and Bore Quarantine and Holding Reserve. File 331/6/202. DPI&F, Alice Springs.

Rose, A (?), to Works Director, Department of Works, Elliott, May 14 1954, Top Springs and Bore Quarantine and Holding Reserve. File 331/6/202. DPI&F, Alice Springs.

Rose, A. to A.S. Bingle, Australian Investment Agency, May 20 1954. Murranji Stock Route — General File. 331/4/15. DPI&F, Alice Springs.

Rose, A. to Director of Lands, October 7 1955. Top Springs and Bore Quarantine and Holding Reserve. File 331/6/202. DPI&F, Alice Springs.

Rose, A., Note re stock route improvements, nd., Murranji Stock Route — General File, 331/4/15. DPI&F, Alice Springs.

Rose, D. 'Ned Lives!', *Australian Aboriginal Studies*, 2, 1989.

Rose, D. *Dreaming Ecology: Nomadics and Indigenous Knowledge, Victoria River, North Australia.* Mss in preparation for publication.

Ruhen, O, et al, *This Is Australia*, Paul Hamlyn Pty Ltd, Sydney, 1975.

Russell-Smith, J. 'Classification, species richness, and environmental relations of monsoon rain forest in northern Australia', *Journal of Vegetation Science*, 2, 1991.

Saltmer, Drover, to W. Carroll, July 8 1936. NAA ACT, A284/1 B5483.

Scandrett, A.B. to the Chief Surveyor, Darwin, March 6, September 6, October 14 and October 20, 1913, NTRS, F9, 364/39.

Seal, H. cited in the 'Government Resident's Report on the Northern Territory, 1906', *SAPP*, vol. 3, no. 45, 1907.

Schultz, C.N. to the Northern Territory Administrator, July 11 1948. NAA NT, F1/0, item 1947/198.

Charles Schultz to Chief Veterinary Officer, Colonel A.L. Rose, August 25 1948. Murranji Stock Route — General File, 331/4/15, DPI&F, Alice Springs.

Schultz, C. and D. Lewis, *Beyond the Big Run: Station Life in Australia's Last Frontier*, University of Queensland Press, Brisbane, 1995.

Scully, W. Minister for Agriculture and Commerce, 1944. NAA NT, series F1, item 1943/10B.

Skuthorpe, J. 'Correspondence: Long Droving Trips', *The Morning Bulletin* (Rockhampton), June 23 1905.

Smart, manager of Newcastle Waters, to the Northern Territory Administrator, J.A. Gilruth, February 1918, NTRS F5 S140.

Smith, D.D. Resident Engineer, to Assistant Secretary, Works and Services Branch, Department of the Interior, April 16 1934. NAA ACT A284/1 B5244.

Smith, D.D. Resident Engineer, to the Deputy Administrator of the Northern Territory, June 15 1936. NAA ACT, A284/1 B5244

Smith, D.D. Resident Engineer, (telegram) July 28 1936. NAA ACT, A284/1 B5483.

Smith, D.D. telegram from, November 23 1936, NAA ACT, Series A284/1, item B5483.

Smith, D.D. Resident Engineer, memorandum to Assistant Secretary, Works and Services Branch, Department of the Interior, October 21 1937. NAA ACT, A284/1 B5244.

Smith, D.D. Resident Engineer, to the Northern Territory Administrator, October 25 1940. NAA NT, F1 1940/508.

Smith, D.D. Resident Engineer, to His Honour the Administrator, May 30 1941. NAA NT, F1, item 1940/508.

Smith, D.D. Resident Engineer, Alice Springs, to Secretary, Lands Department, Darwin, March 29 1941. NAA NT, F1 1940/508.

Smith, D.D. Resident Engineer, Alice Springs, to the Northern Territory Administrator, June

13 1941. NAA NT, F1 1940/508.
Smith, D.D. Resident Engineer, to Deputy Director-General of Allied Works, Alice Springs, January 7 1944. NAA NT, F1 1943/10B.
Smith, D.D. Resident Engineer, to Deputy Director-General of Allied Works, Alice Springs, May 19 1944. NAA NT, F1 1943/10B.
Smith, D.D. Divisional Works Officer, to the Chief Veterinary Officer, Animal Industry Division, July 13 1950, DPI&F, Alice Springs, file 331/4/15.
Smith, M. 'The case for a resident human population in the Central Australian Ranges during full glacial aridity'. *Archaeology in Oceania,* 24: 1989.
Smith, S. Acting Administrator, 'Annual Report of the Acting Administrator for the Year Ending 30th June 1920', *CPP*, session 1920-21, vol. 3, no. 28.
Steele, W. 'Pioneer Drovers – A Disappearing Band', *Queensland Agricultural Journal*, August 1 1929.
Steele, W. and C. Steele, *To the Great Gulf: The Surveys and Explorations of L.A. Wells*, Lynton Publications, Adelaide, 1978.
Stevens, H.W.H., report to Goldsbrough Mort, July 22 1890. Goldsbrough Mort and Co. Ltd.: Head Office, Melbourne: letters received from HWH Stevens, Port Darwin, re NT property and butchering business, 1889-1892. Noel Butlin Archives, 2/872.
Stevens, H.W.H., cited in 'Government Resident's Report on the Northern Territory for the Year 1888', *SAPP*, vol. 2, no. 28, Jan 1889.
Stevens, H.W.H. cited in 'Government Resident's Report on the Northern Territory for 1895', *SAPP*, vol. 2, no. 45, 1896.
Stevens, H.W.H., report to Goldsbrough Mort and Co. Ltd., November 7 1887. Goldsbrough Mort and Co. Ltd.: Head Office, Melbourne: letters received from HWH Stevens, Port Darwin, re NT property and butchering business, 1889-1892. Noel Butlin Archives, 2/872.
Stevens, H.W.H., Report on NT Stations to Goldsbrough Mort & Co. Ltd., January 8 1891. Goldsbrough Mort and Co. Ltd: Head Office, Melbourne: letters received from HWH Stevens, Port Darwin, re NT property and butchering business, 1889-1892. Head Office, Melbourne: letters received from H. W. H. Stevens, Port Darwin, re NT property and butchering business, 1889-1892. Noel Butlin Archives, 2/872.
Stocker, G. and J. Mott, 'Fire in the tropical forests and woodlands on northern Australia', in A. Gill, R. Groves and I. Noble [eds.], *Fire and the Australian Biota*, Academy of Science, Canberra, 1981.
Stoddard, E. to the Director General of Works, October 23 1926, NAA ACT, series A281/1, item DGW 27/1677.
Stoddardt, E. April 6 1927, NAA ACT, series A1640, item 1906/492.
Stoddart, E., Works Director, report to Director-General of Works, Department of the Interior, April 7 1938. NAA ACT, A284/1 B5244.
Strong, B. entry on H.V. Barclay in D. Carment, et al (eds.), *Northern Territory Dictionary of Biography: Volume One to 1945*, Northern Territory University Press, Darwin, 1990.
Stuart, John McDouall. *Explorations in Australia. The Journals of John McDouall Stuart during the years 1858, 1859, 1860, 1861, and 1862*. Hesperian Press facsimile edition, 1984. (originally published by Saunders, Otley and Co., London, 1865.
Sutton, P., et al. The *Murranji Land Claim*. Northern Land Council, Darwin, 1983.
Tabrett, D. to Assistant Director of the Land Development Branch, Department of Lands, Darwin, 1981. Murranji Stock Route — General File. 331/4/15. DPI&F, Alice Springs.
Terry, M. *Across Unknown Australia,* Herbert Jenkins, London, 1925.

Terry, M. *Across Unknown Australia, The Sun* (Sydney), January 18 1924.
Terry, M. *Through a Land of Promise*, Herbert Jenkins, London, 1927.
Timber Creek Police Letter Book, photocopy held at Berrimah police station, Darwin.
Timber Creek Police Journal, May 4 1896, NTRS F302.
Traine, T. *Across the Barkly Tableland to the Kimberleys: Memories and Experiences of a Pioneer*, Unpublished manuscript, Northern Territory State Library, 1920.
Travers, M. *Newcastle Waters*, Report prepared for the National Trust of Australia (N.T.), 1986.
Urquhart, F.C. Report of the Administrator for the Year ended 30th June 1921. *CPP*, session 1922, vol. 2, no. 44: 14.
'Vanguard', 'North Australia: The Real Backblocks', *Cummins & Campbell's Monthly Magazine*, January 1934.
Walker, D., Chief Stock Inspector, extract from report to Director General of Health, November 6 1942. NAA NT, CRS F1 1942/112.
Wave Hill Police Journal, NTRS F292.
Weddell, Lt-Col. R.H., cited in 'Report on the Administration of the Northern Territory for the year ended 30th June 1932'. *CPP*, session 1932-34, vol. 3, no. 124.
Weir, J. to Mines Branch, Darwin, 1974. Top Springs and Bore Quarantine and Holding Reserve. File 331/6/202. DPI&F, Alice Springs.
Wells, Surveyor L.A. 'Report on Northern Territory Trigonometrical Survey Expedition', *SAPP*, vol. 3, no. 64, 1910.
Whatley, N. letter to the Stockman's Hall of Fame paper, June 1996.
White, Mounted Constable T., to N. Bell, Chief Warden of Mines, June 5 1931, NTRS, F5, item S258
White, J.P. and J.F. O'Connell. *A Prehistory of Australia, New Guinea and Sahul*, Academic Press, New York, 1982.
White, K. *True Stories of the Top End*, Indra Publishing, Briar Hill, Victoria, 2005.
Whittem, J., to Assistant Administrator, Darwin, December 10 1958. Murranji Stock Route — Deviation of Route at Newcastle Waters, file 331/5/73. DPI&F, Alice Springs.
Whittem, J.H. Director of Animal Industry Branch, to the District Veterinary Officer (North), March 11 1959. NAA NT, series F1/0, item 1951/763.
Willmington, Frank, interview by Reg Wilson, Northern Territory Archives Oral History Unit, TS 359.
Willey, K. *The Drovers*, The Macmillan Company of Australia Pty. Ltd., Melbourne, 1982.
Wilson, A.H. manager of Newcastle Waters station, to J. Lewis & Co., Adelaide, February 10 1943, Northern Territory Cattleman's Association, Circulars 1930-40. NTRS, A1/2A.
Wilson A.H. to J. Lewis & Co., February 21 1943 and March 1 1943, Northern Territory Cattleman's Association, Circulars 1930-40. NTRS, A1/2A.
Wilson, A.H. to J. Lewis & Co., May 6 1943, Northern Territory Cattleman's Association, Circulars 1930-40. NTRS, A1/2A.
Woodley, P. *"Young Bill's Happy Days": Reminiscences of Rural Australia 1910-1915*, pp 348-387. (Reminiscences of T W Lavender, nd), Unpublished Masters thesis, Australian National University, Canberra, 1982.
Woolnough, W.G. 'Supposed Oil Indications at Murranji Waterhole, Northern Territory', NAA NT series F1/0, item 1936/456.
Wright, R. Lands Allocation Branch, Department of Lands, to Secretary, Department of Primary Production, Darwin, July 9 1981. Murranji Stock Route — General File.

331/4/15. DPI&F, Alice Springs.

Newspapers

Northern Territory Times, 1878.
Northern Territory Times, 1883.
Northern Territory Times, 1885.
Northern Territory Times, 1888.
Northern Territory Times, 1892.
Northern Territory Times, 1894.
Northern Territory Times, 1899.
Northern Territory Times, 1900.
Northern Territory Times, 1901.
Northern Territory Times, 1902.
Northern Territory Times, 1903.
Northern Territory Times, 1904.
Northern Territory Times, 1905.
Northern Territory Times, 1906.
Northern Territory Times, 1907.
Northern Territory Times, 1908.
Northern Territory Times, 1910.
Northern Territory Times, 1917.
Northern Territory Times, 1918.
Northern Territory Times, 1927.
Northern Territory News, 1952.
Northern Territory News, 1953.
Northern Territory News, 1981.
The Townsville Register, 1953.
North Queensland Herald, 1906.
The Register (Adelaide), 1904.
The Register (Adelaide), 1905.
The Register (Adelaide), 1906.
The Register (Adelaide), 1908.
South Australian Register, 1881.
South Australian Register, 1896.
The Observer (Adelaide), 1905.
The Observer (Adelaide), 1906.
The Observer (Adelaide), 1926.
The Adelaide Advertiser, 1936.
The Morning Bulletin (Rockhampton), 1905.
Sydney Morning Herald, 1881.
Sydney Morning Herald, 1942.
Sydney Morning Herald, 1954.
The Age, (Melbourne) 1883.
The Age, 1921.
The Age, 1916.
The Argus, 1884.

South Australian Records Office

Unprovenanced newspaper cutting, October 29 1892, GRS 9/3.

Journals

The Australasian Pastoralists' Review, 1893.
The Pastoralists' Review, 1905.
The Pastoralists' Review, 1906.
The Pastoralists' Review, 1907.
The Pastoralists' Review, 1909.
The Pastoralists' Review, 1910.
The Pastoral Review, 1929.
The Graziers' Review, 1921.
The Bulletin, 1881.
North Australian Monthly, 1955.
The Town and Country Journal, 1905.
Hoofs and Horns, 1951.
Horns and Horns, 1953.
Hoofs and Horns, 1954.
Hoofs and Horns, 1955.
Hoofs and Horns, 1957.
Hoofs and Horns, 1958.
Hoofs and Horns, 1961.

Department of Primary Industries, Alice Springs.

Top Springs Dip (Pussycat), File 331/7/8.
Murranji Stock Route General File, 331/4/15.
Murranji stock Route — Deviation of Route at Newcastle Waters, File 331/5/73.
Murranji Stock Route — No. 10 Bore. File No. 331/6/4.

South Australian Parliamentary Papers

'Report of the Northern Territory Commission together with Minutes of Proceedings, Evidence, and Appendices', vol. 2, no. 19, 1895.

Commonwealth Parliamentary Papers

Vol. 2, 1914-15-16-17.

National Archives of Australian (Northern Territory)

A3, 18/2017.
F1 1943/10B.
F1 1943/10B.
F1 1943/10B.
F1 1946/100 Pt 2.
F1, 52/758.
F1 1943/10B.

National Archives of Australian (Australian Capital Territory)

A3, item 18/2017.
A571/56, item 21/17152.
A281/1, item DGW 27/1677.
A3/1 item NT 14/3682.
A1, item 1936/1701.
A659 item 40/1/899.
A284/1 item B5244.
A284/1 item B5483.
A284/1 item B5244.
A1/1 item 1930/2585.
A3, item 18/2017.

Northern Territory Archives

NTRS F5 S258.
NTRS, series F5 item S258.
NTRS F28 GL336.
NTRS, F28 GL1200.
NTRS, F28 GL 1296.
NTRS, F28 GL1724.
NTRS, F28 GL 336.
NTRS, F8 GL 1555.
NTRS, F28 GL 1703.
NTRS 1718.
NTRS, F670 vol. 1, pastoral lease 2198.

Cattleman's Association Records

PAC 106, NTRS A1/2A.
PAC 106. vol. 39, 'Stock Routes and Reserves'.

ENDNOTES

1. This poem was first published in Ernestine Hill's article, 'Along the Murran-ji', *Walkabout*, November 1 1949: 16-19. It may have been composed by Hill herself, but there's no evidence that she wrote poetry and I suspect she recorded it from one of her innumerable unnamed sources.
2. Haliden Hartt, 'Out On The Murranji', *Walkabout*, October 1 1944: 25-28. According to the *Northern Territory Dictionary of Biography*, vol. 2: 1, Haliden Hartt was a pen name used by Hilda Abbott, the wife of Northern Territory Administrator, Charles Abbott.
3. Ernestine Hill, *The Territory*, Angus and Robertson, Sydney, 1951: 300.
4. G. Farwell, *Cape York to the Kimberleys*, Rigby, Adelaide, 1962: 198.
5. Ernestine Hill, *Suicide Track of a Continent*, unprovenanced newspaper cutting, 1936.
6. Captain F. Bishop, Chief Inspector of Stock, refers to the 'Murranji Jungle' in a letter to the Government Secretary, Darwin, May 21 1941. NAA NT, CRS F1 1940/508; A. Groom mentions 'lancewood jungles' in *Wealth in the Wilderness*, Angus and Robertson, Sydney 1955: 68, and in *Walkabout*, October 1 1944: 26, Haliden Hartt talks about 'jungle-like' bush. Botanically speaking, the term 'jungle' has some validity. According to some botanists the bulwaddy-lancewood plant community may be considered an inland (low rainfall) category of monsoon rainforest! (see G. Stocker and J. Mott, 'Fire in the tropical forests and woodlands on northern Australia', in A. Gill, R. Groves and I. Noble [eds.], *Fire and the Australian Biota*, Academy of Science, Canberra, 1981: 425-39; J. Russell-Smith, 'Classification, species richness, and environmental relations of monsoon rain forest in northern Australia', *Journal of Vegetation Science*, 2, 1991: 259-78).
7. E. Hill, 1951: 298.
8. J.K. Little, 'Droving of Yore', *The Pastoral Review and Graziers' Record*, November 16, 1950: 1213 & 1215; J.K. Little, 'The Murranji Waterhole', *The Pastoral Review and Graziers' Record*, February 16 1952: 147.
9. E. Hill, 1951: 300.
10. G. Farwell, 1962: 198.
11. G. Farwell, 'Down the Murranji Track', *The Pastoral Review and Graziers' Record*, April 16 1952: 365.
12. *Acacia shirleyii*.
13. *Macropteranthes kekwickii*

14. John McDouall Stuart, *Explorations in Australia. The Journals of John McDouall Stuart during the years 1858, 1859, 1860, 1861, and 1862*. Hesperian Press fasimile edition, 1984: 306 (originally published by Saunders, Otley and Co.).
15. G. Farwell, 'Down the Murranji Track, N.T.' *The Pastoral Review and Graziers' Record*, March 15 1952: 241.
16. R. Jones, and J. Bowler, 'Struggle for the Savanna: Northern Australia in Ecological and Prehistoric Perspective', *In* R. Jones (ed.) *Northern Australia: Options and Implications*, Research School of Pacific Studies, Australian National University, Canberra, 1980: 3-31; Jim Bowler, 'Water and Sand: Climate in Ancient Australia', in Mulvaney, D. J. and J. Peter White, (eds.) *Australians To 1788*, Fairfax, Syme & Weldon Associates, 1987: 25-45.
17. R. Jones and J. Bowler, 1980: 10.
18. R. Jones, 'The Alligator Rivers: A Mirror to Continental Prehistory', in D. Wade-Marshall and P. Loveday (eds.), *North Australia: Progress and prospects, Volume 2. Floodplains Research*, North Australia Research Unit, Darwin, 1988: 9.
19. C. Brown, *1:250,000 Geological Series—Explanatory Notes. Daly Waters, Northern Territory, Sheet SE/53—1 International Index*. Bureau of Mineral Resources, Geology and Geophysics, Canberra, 1969: 4.
20. A 'jump-up' is a sudden change in the level of flat country, marked by an escarpment.
21. J.P. White and J.F. O'Connell. *A Prehistory of Australia, New Guinea and Sahul*, Academic Press, New York, 1982: 119.
22. R. Roberts, R. Jones and M. Smith. 'Thermoluminescence dating of a 50,000-year-old human occupation site in northern Australia', *Nature*, 1990: 345: 153-56.
23. M. Smith, 'The case for a resident human population in the Central Australian Ranges during full glacial aridity'. *Archaeology in Oceania,* 1989: 24: 93-105.
24. E. Hill, 1951: 301; K. Willey, *The Drovers*, The Macmillan Company of Australia Pty. Ltd., Melbourne, 1982: 77.
25. P. Sutton, et al. The *Murranji Land Claim*. Northern Land Council, Darwin, 1983: 118.
26. Personal communication, Nugget Kiriyalangungu, during fieldwork along the Murranji Track in 1991.
27. P. Sutton et al, 1983: 126.
28. Ibid.
29. D. Rose, *Dreaming Ecology: Nomadics and Indigenous Knowledge, Victoria River, North Australia*. Mss in preparation for publication.
30. P. Sutton, et al, 1983: 151.
31. P. McConvell and A. Palmer *A Claim To An Area Of Traditional Land By The Mudbura Traditional Owners*, Northern Land Council, Darwin, 1979; P. Sutton, 1983.
32. P. McConvell and A. Palmer, 1979: 11.
33. For example, J.M. Stuart, 1984 (1865): 298, 299, 343, 344; Charles Goodliffe, 'The Condamine Bell'. *Walkabout*, October 1 1945: 26-27.
34. P. Sutton, et al., 1983: 149.
35. W. Linklater and L. Tapp, *Gather No Moss*, Hesperian Press facsimile edition, 1997: 118 (originally published in 1968 by The Macmillan Company).
36. A.G.B. Ravenscroft describes wells from Jingili country and mentions that they were often at least partly angled, and usually contained water undrinkable to Europeans ('Some Habits and Customs of the Chingalee Tribe, Northern Territory, S.A.', *Transactions of the Royal Society of South Australia*, vol. 15, part 1, 1892: 121).

37. Personal communication, Long Captain Marajala.
38. W. Harney, 'Water in the Dry Lands', *Walkabout*, February 1 1952: 18-19.
39. A.B. Scandrett to the Chief Surveyor, Darwin, October 14 1913. NTRS, F9 364/39.
40. P. Sutton, et al, 1983.
41. Personal observation.
42. P. Sutton, et al, 1983: 118.
43. P. Sutton, et al, 1983: 93-96.
44. J.M. Stuart, 1984 (1865): 296, 333, 334, 335, 342, 348.
45. J. Mulvaney and J. Kamminga, *Prehistory of Australia*, Allen & Unwin, Sydney, 1999: 58-62.
46. J.M. Stuart, 1984 (1865): 297.
47. A. Giles, *Exploring in the 'Seventies and the Construction of the Overland Telegraph Line*, Facsimile edition, Friends of the State Library of South Australia, 1995: 144-45, 150-51 (First published by W.K. Thomas & Co. [The Register] Adelaide, 1926).
48. F. Goss, *Life in the Never-Never Country of South Australia in the 70s. to 90s*, Mortlock Library, D4436(L), 1956: 15.
49. A. Giles, *The First Pastoral Settlement in the Northern Territory*, copy held at the National Trust of Australia (NT), Darwin, nd: 39-42.
50. 'Murder by the blacks at Lawson Springs', *Northern Territory Times*, September 8 1883.
51. 'The Death of an Exploring Party', *The Age*, November 15 1883.
52. J.K. Little, 1952: 147.
53. M. Mallison 'Adventures on the Murranji Track: Droving and Spear-throwing', based on an interview with Billy Miller (alias William Linklater), *Sydney Morning Herald*, June 27 1942. The spearing of Hardcastle was mentioned in the *Northern Territory Times*, September 28 1900.
54. W. Linklater and L. Tapp, 1997: 118.
55. Ibid.
56. M.A. Radford [manager of N'Waters] to John Lewis, August 1902 [undated but apparently this date]. South Australian State Library, PGR 247/10/1.
57. M.A. Radford to John Lewis, September 3 1902, South Australian State Library, PGR 247/10/1.
58. M.A. Radford [manager of Newcastle Waters] to John Lewis, August 1902 [undated but apparently this date]. South Australian State Library, PGR 247/10/1.
59. M.A. Radford to John Lewis, September 3 1902.
60. M.A. Radford to John Lewis, February 17 1903. South Australian State Library, PGR 247/10/1.
61. D. Lewis, *A Wild History*, unpublished PhD thesis, Australian National University, 2004.
62. W. Harney, *Life Among the Aborigines*, Robert Hale Limited, London, 1957: 185.
63. Personal observation at Nongra Lake, Inverway station, on VRD and at Finnis River.
64. Personal communication, Agnes Draper, whose mother, Lizzie, was one of the last Mudbura people to 'come in'.
65. Personal communication, Dr. Deborah Rose.
66. Personal observation at Yarralin community (VRD), at Elliott and on the Murranji.
67. A.C. Gregory and F. Gregory. *Journals of Australian Explorations*, James C. Beal, Government Printer, Brisbane, 1884: 99-194.
68. J.M. Stuart, 1984 (1865).

69. Ibid: 288.
70. Ibid: 289.
71. W.S. Ramson (ed.), *The Australian National Dictionary*, Oxford University Press, Melbourne, 1988: 107, 307. The name 'bulwaddy' first appears in historical records in 1918 (A. Moray to Managing director of the Northern Agency, September 8 1918, NTRS series F5, item N64).
72. J.M. Stuart, 1984 (1865).
73. Ibid: 299-300.
74. Ibid: 304.
75. Ibid: 305.
76. Ibid: 306-7.
77. Ibid: 308.
78. Ibid: 308-09.
79. Ibid: 309.
80. Ibid: 332-346. This spring later became known as Nash's Spring, Nash's Soak or Nash's Well.
81. Ibid: 343-345.
82. Ibid: 347-408.
83. Ibid: 333-35, 348.
84. Ibid: 303, 310-11,
85. Ibid: 288, 293, 294,
86. Ibid: 344
87. Ibid: 286.
88. Ibid: 299, 303, 343-44,
89. Ibid: 343, 331-32, 342-43
90. Ibid: 295-97, 301-02, 343
91. Ibid: 295-297.
92. Ibid: 346
93. A. Forrest, *North-West Exploration: Journal Of Exploration From DeGrey To Port Darwin*. Government Printer, Perth, 1880.
94. Ibid: 33-34.
95. E. Pownall and W. Stackpool, *The Singing Wire*, Collins, Sydney, 1973.
96. A. Giles nd: 184, 189.
97. Jock Makin, *The Big Run: The Story of Victoria River Downs*, Rigby, Sydney, 1983: 62.
98. 'Trip to the Victoria River', *Northern Territory Times*, September 29 1878.
99. 'Exploration and Prospecting', *Northern Territory Times*, March 24 1883.
100. 'An Exploring Expedition', *The Argus*, January 5 1884 and January 17 1884.
101. Charles Goodliffe, 1945.
102. G. Buchanan. *Packhorse and Waterhole: With the First Overlanders to the Kimberleys*. Hesperian Press, Perth, 1984: 189-90 (Facsimile edition, first published by Angus & Robertson Limited, Sydney, 1933); 'Notes from the Victoria River', *Northern Territory Times*, August 29 1885. Both Buchanan and the *Northern Territory Times* report give the name of Hedley's mate as Morgan, but a *Times* report two months later refers to Hedley's mate as 'Moore' (*Northern Territory Times*, October 24 1885).
103. 'Notes from the Victoria River', *Northern Territory Times*, August 29 1885.
104. T. Roberts, *Frontier Justice: A History of the Gulf Country to 1900*, University of Queensland Press, St Lucia, 2005: 8.
105. Ibid: 46, 244.

106. G. Buchanan, 'Pioneers of the Far North: Adventure and Achievement' *Sydney Stock & Station Journal*, April 28 1922. This is number twenty-one in a series of articles about northern Australia published by this journal. The authorship of the articles isn't stated, but many of them are almost word for word for chapters in G. Buchanan's *Packhorse and Waterhole*, and there can be no doubt that they were written by Buchanan.
107. 'Notes from the Victoria River', *Northern Territory Times*, August 29 1885.
108. G. Lamond, *Tales Of The Overland: Queensland To Kimberley In 1885*, 1986: 32-34. Hesperian Press, Victoria Park [W.A.].
109. G. Buchanan, April 28 1922.
110. Guchanan, 1984: 121.
111. Ibid: 142.
112. Ibid: 36, 54.
113. Ibid: 70, 72.
114. Unprovenanced newspaper cutting, October 29 1892, South Australian Records Office, GRS 9/3.
115. 'Murder of Samuel Croker by a Half-caste', *Northern Territory Times*, October 7 1892.
116. G. Buchanan, 1984: 121; G. Buchanan, 'Recalling The Past: Some Notes on Nat Buchanan', *The Pastoral Review and Graziers' Record*, August 18 1961: 899-900.
117. G. Buchanan, 1984: 120-21.
118. C. Hemphill, 'Mr. N. Buchanan's Exploration', letter to the editor, *South Australian Register*, October 15 1896.
119. C. Hemphill, 'Central Australian Exploration' (letter to the editor), *The Adelaide Observer*, April 4 1901: 27, column 1.
120. D. Nash, 'Aboriginal Knowledge of the aeroplane "Kookaburra"', *Aboriginal History*, vol. 6, no. 1, 1981: 62-73.
121. G. Buchanan, 1961: 899-900.
122. B. Buchanan, *In the Tracks of Old Bluey: The Life Story of Nat Buchanan*, Central Queensland University Press, Rockhampton, 1997.
123. G. Buchanan, 1984: 127-28.
124. G. Buchanan, April 28 1922. I've drawn upon this article instead of *Packhorse and Waterhole* because of a minor difference in detail. Here Buchanan states that the party made a camp 'between Frew's Pond and Newcastle', rather than *at* Frew's Pond, which suggests that they followed up Newcastle Creek rather than the Overland Telegraph line.
125. C. Goodliffe, 1945.
126. 'H7H' (Hely Hutchinson), 'Long Droving Trips', *The Morning Bulletin* (Rockhampton), June 23 1905.
127. 'H7H' (Hely Hutchinson), 'Odd Stock and Other Notes', *The Morning Bulletin* (Rockhampton), January 20 1906.
128. 'H7H' (Hely Hutchinson), 'A "Gum-Tree Journalist"', *Northern Territory Times*, June 22 1906.
129. 'A Big Overland Trip', citing a letter from 'H7H' (Hely Hutchinson), *Northern Territory Times*, June 1 1906.
130. D. Mulvaney, *Paddy Cahill of Oenpelli*, Aboriginal Studies Press, Canberra, 2005: 31.
131. 'H7H' (Hely Hutchinson), January 20 1906.
132. 'Some Bush Yarns', *The Australasian Pastoralists' Review*, February 15 1893: 1073.
133. 'The Fate of Leichhardt', *Sydney Morning Herald*, 27 January 1881.

134. 'Relics of Leichhardt', *South Australian Register*, September 29 1881.
135. 'The Skuthorpe Libel Case', *Sydney Morning Herald*, 8 February 1881.
136. *The Bulletin*, 19 March 1881.
137. 'A Narrow Escape', *Northern Territory Times*, April 20 1906.
138. T. Roberts, 2005: 23, 40, and personal communication.
139. G. Buchanan, 1984: 122.
140. W. Rees. 'Murranji Track'. *Walkabout*. June 1 1950: 8.
141. 'Record Droving Trips', *The Pastoralists' Review*, May 15 1905: 208.
142. 'The Recent Record Droving Trips', *The Pastoralists' Review'*, June 15 1905: 294.
143. W. Rees, 1945. *A Few Notes on the Early Settlement of Victoria River Downs, Northern Territory*. July 12 1945.
144. W. Rees, 1950.
145. 'Murder of Samuel Croker by a Half-caste', *Northern Territory Times*, October 7 1892; H.W.H. Stevens to Goldsbrough Mort, July 22 1890. Goldsbrough Mort and Co. Ltd.: Head Office, Melbourne: letters received from HWH Stevens, Port Darwin, re NT property and butchering business, 1889-1892. Noel Butlin Archives, 2/872.
146. Gordon Creek Police Journal, entries for May 23 1895 to May 27 1895, Northern Territory Archives, NTRS F302.
147. E. Hill, 1951: 299.
148. W. Linklater, 'Pioneer Women of N.T.', Miscellaneous letters and other documents, 1895-1949, Mitchell Library, Al 10/3-37, CY3480.
149. Ibid; S. Baldwin, 'When Mabel took the Reins', *The Bulletin*, January 26, 1988: 233-34.
150. M. Mallison. 'Across the Territory by Covered Waggon: How the Bridges made History', *Quirindi Advocate*, October 3 1958. Mallison's story is based on an interview with Charles Bridge, a cousin of Joe Bridge who actually made the trip.
151. 'The Northern Territory. Its' Pastoral Possibilities', *The Age* (Melbourne), October 4 1921.
152. M. Terry, *Through a Land of Promise*. Herbert Jenkins, London, 1927: 89.
153. M. Terry, *Across Unknown Australia*, Herbert Jenkins, London, 1925: 192.
154. Report by H.W.H. Stevens to Goldsbrough Mort and Co. Ltd., November 7 1887. Goldsbrough Mort and Co. Ltd.: Head Office, Melbourne: letters received from HWH Stevens, Port Darwin, re NT property and butchering business, 1889-1892. Noel Butlin Archives, 2/872.
155. G. Buchanan, 1933: 126 (Hesperian Press Facsimile edition, 1984); M. Durack, *Sons In The Saddle*, Corgi Books, Condell Park (NSW), 1985: 520.
156. 'H7H' (Hely Hutchinson), 'Odd Stock and Other Notes', *The Morning Bulletin* (Rockhampton), December 2 1905.
157. J.S. Foster to the Resident Magistrate in Wyndham, July 29 1890, cited as Appendix 2 in G. Bolton, *A Survey of the Kimberley Pastoral Industry from 1885 to the Present*, unpublished Masters thesis, University of Western Australia, 1953; T. Traine, *Across the Barkly Tableland to the Kimberleys: Memories and Experiences of a Pioneer*, Unpublished manuscript, Northern Territory State Library, 1920: 30.
158. Derby Police Occurrence Book, September 4 1889, Western Australian State Records Office, Ms 241.
159. 'Katherine Items', *Northern Territory Times*, December 1 1892.
160. M. Durack, 1985: 25, 57.
161. Ibid: 1985: 76, 91.

162. Ibid: 1985: 76.
163. B. Buchanan, 1997: 111.
164. 'Wyndham (W.A.) Notes', *Northern Territory Times*, December 22 1899.
165. M. Durack, 1985: 108.
166. 'Wyndham (W.A.) Notes', *Northern Territory Times*, December 22 1899.
167. M. Durack, 1985: 108.
168. 'News and Notes', *Northern Territory Times*, June 29, 1900.
169. 'The Katherine', *Northern Territory Times*, January 30 1903.
170. L. Biltris, 'The Passing of the Pioneers, *Walkabout*, May 1 1951: 44-45; M. Hilgendorf, *Northern Territory Days*, Historical Society of the Northern Territory, 1994: 35; J.A.G. Little, 'Notice of Annual, Inspecting Journey of Overland Telegraph Line, from Port Darwin to Attack Creek', *Northern Territory Times*, August 30 1901; 'News and Notes', *Northern Territory Times*, November 22 1901; 'News and Notes', *Northern Territory Times*, November 22 1901.
171. L. Biltris,1951: 34.
172. E. Hill, 1951: 300; G. Pike, *Frontier Territory*, Cosmos Printing Press, Hong Kong, 1972: 173; G. Farwell, 1962: 200.
173. M.P. Durack to W. Griffiths, November 29 1899, NAA ACT A1640/1 99/502.
174. 'H7H' (Hely Hutchinson), 'The Men Who Blazed The Track', *The Pastoralists' Review*, August 15 1912: 594.
175. Dick Scobie, interviewed at Charters Towers in December 1994.
176. Personal communication, Rodney Watson, 2005.
177. C.N. Schultz to A.L. Rose, August 25 1948, Murrangi Stock Route General File. File no. 331/4/15, Department of Primary Industries and Fisheries, Alice Springs.
178. Sid Hawks, interviewed in Darwin in October 1998.
179. A. Fleming, 'Tales of the Murrunji', *Brisbane Courier Mail*, August 11 1938; G. Farwell, 1962: 204.
180. G. Farwell, 1962: 210; L. Esson, 'The Drovers' in A. Sykes (ed.), *Five Plays for stage, radio, and television*, University of Queensland Press, Brisbane, 1977: 5-19.
181. E. Hill, 1951: 302-03.
182. Frank Willmington interview by Reg Wilson, Northern Territory Archives Oral History Unit, TS 359.
183. Sid Hawks, interviewed in Darwin in October 1998.
184. Ibid.
185. Norm Whatley, letter to the Stockman's Hall of Fame paper, June 1996.
186. A. Ingham, *The Boss Drover and his Mates*, Halstead Press, Sydney, 1996: 159.
187. Transcript of the taped memoir of William Leslie McDonald, in possession of his daughter, Jill Campbell of Kybo station, Western Australia.
188. Timber Creek Police Journal, May 4 1896, NTRS F302; 'Ben Bridge the "Outlaw"', *Northern Territory Times*, January 1 1900, and January 12 1900.
189. 'Ben Bridge the "Outlaw"', *Northern Territory Times*, January 1 1900, and *Northern Territory Times*, January 12 1900.
190. 'Ben Bridge, the "Outlaw"', *Northern Territory Times*, January 12 1900.
191. Ibid.
192. Ibid.
193. Timber Creek Police Journal, May 4 1896, NTRS F302.
194. 'Notes of the Week', *Northern Territory Times*, January 12 1900.
195. Ibid.

196. E. Hill, 1951: 303.
197. Timber Creek Police Journal, June 23 1899. NTRS F302.
198. E. Hill, 1951: 302
199. 'A Bush Tragedy', *Northern Territory Times*, July 15 1904.
200. Timber Creek Police Journal, December 15 1905, NTRS F302.
201. 'Bush Horrors' *Northern Territory Times*, April 3 1908.
202. Timber Creek Police Journal, entry for April 15 1914, NTRS F302.
203. Memo from Mounted Constable Uriah W. Holland to Mounted Constable Dempsey, July 13 1908. Timber Creek Police Letter Book, photocopy held at Berrimah police station, Darwin.
204. Timber Creek Police Journal, December 16 1908. NTRS, F302.
205. 'Perished From Thirst', *Northern Territory Times*, February 9 1906.
206. Timber Creek Police Letter Book, March 5 1906, photocopy held at Berrimah police station, Darwin.
207. The White Range goldfield is actually in the Northern Territory, in the McDonnell Ranges.
208. 'Perished From Thirst', *Northern Territory Times*, February 9 1906.
209. 'H7H' (Hely Hutchinson), 'Odd Stock and Other Notes', *The Morning Bulletin* (Rockhampton), January 20 1906.
210. E. Hill, 1951: 301.
211. Ibid.
212. Timber Creek Police Letter Book, March 5 1906, photocopy held at Berrimah police station, Darwin; Hely Hutchinson, 'A Big Overland Trip', *The Morning Bulletin* (Rockhampton), April 28 1906.
213. E. Hill, 1949; M. Terry, *Across Unknown Australia, The Sun* (Sydney), January 18 1924.
214. Memo from Mounted Constable Uriah W. Holland to Mounted Constable Dempsey, July 13 1908. Timber Creek Police Letter Book, photocopy held at the Berrimah police station, Darwin.
215. Katherine Mortuary Book, NTRS F1060.
216. E. Hill, 1951: 302.
217. G. Farwell, 1962: 209-10.
218. M. Terry', 1924.
219. M. Nixon, *The Rivers of Home: Frank Lacy – Kimberley Pioneer*, Vanguard Service Print, Perth, 1978: 4-7.
220. J. Corfield, *The Ned Kelly Encyclopaedia*, Lothian Books, Melbourne, 2003: 507-08.
221. Ibid: 508; W. Harney, 'The Maluka's Grave', *Walkabout*, November 1 1948.
222. Mortuary Book, Newcastle Waters Police, 1893-1951. Northern Territory Archives, CRS F608; for additional details see D. Rose, 'Ned Lives!', *Australian Aboriginal Studies*, 2, 1989: 51-59.
223. P. Davis, *Kookaburra. The most compelling story in Australia's aviation history* (Research by Dick Smith, story by Pedr Davis), Sydney, 1980.
224. 'Fliers Fit But Weary', *The Adelaide Advertiser*, April 27 1936.
225. T. Cole, *Hell West and Crooked*, Collins Publishers Australia, Sydney, 1988: 111.
226. T. Cole, *Riding the Wildman Plains; The Letters and Diaries of TOM COLE 1923-1943*, Sun Books, Sydney, 1992: 39-41.
227. T. Cole, 1988: 120.
228. T. Cole, 1992: 230.

229. Northern Territory Cattleman's Association, Miscellaneous – correspondence & cuttings 1929-71. NTRS D3/3A; T. Cole, 1992: 231.
230. A.H. Wilson, manager of Newcastle Waters station, to J. Lewis & Co., Adelaide, February 10 1943, Northern Territory Cattleman's Association, Circulars 1930-40, NTRS, A1/2A.
231. A.H. Wilson to J. Lewis & Co., February 21 1943 and March 1 1943, Northern Territory Cattleman's Association, Circulars 1930-40, NTRS, A1/2A; Personal communication, Dick Scobie.
232. A.H. Wilson to J. Lewis & Co., May 6 1943, Northern Territory Cattleman's Association, Circulars 1930-40, NTRS, A1/2A.
233. Wave Hill Police Journal, November 11 1955. NTRS, F292.
234. Sid Hawks, Interviewed in Darwin in October 1998.
235. E. Hill, 1951: 301; 'H7H' (Hely Hutchinson), 'Early Drovers in the Northern Territory—Leaves from the Diary of Alfred Giles', *The Pastoralists' Review*, March 15 1906: 39-41; B. Martin, 'Droving in Northern Territory' (letter to the editor), *The Pastoralists' Review*, June 15 1906: 314; W. Steele, 'Pioneer Drovers – A Disappearing Band', *Queensland Agricultural Journal*, August 1 1929. Steel was with one of the original parties in 1904; M. Mallison, *Sydney Morning Herald*, June 27 1942. Mallison's story is based on an interview with Billy Miller (alias William Linklater).
236. H.W.H. Stevens, cited in 'Government Resident's Report on the Northern Territory for the Year 1888', *SAPP*, vol. 2, no. 28, Jan 1889: 2.
237. R. Duncan, *The Northern Territory Pastoral Industry*, Melbourne University Press, Melbourne, 1967: 58, 86.
238. M. Durack, 1985: 380; G. Bolton, *A Thousand Miles Away: A History of North Queensland to 1920*, The Jacaranda Press, Brisbane, 1963: 220.
239. R. Duncan, 1967: 60-65.
240. G. Bolton, 1963: 221; R. Duncan, 1967: 131.
241. G. Bolton, 1963: 220.
242. J. Collier, *The Pastoral Age in Australia*, Whitcombe & Tombs, Limited, Melbourne, 1911: 222.
243. R. Duncan, 1967: 163-65.
244. H.W.H. Stevens, cited in 'Government Resident's Report on the Northern Territory for 1895', *SAPP*, vol. 2, no. 45, 1896: 3.
245. Mounted Constable F.G. Burt, Temporary Inspector of Stock, in the 'Government Resident's Report on the Northern Territory, 1905, SAPP, vol 2, no. 45, 1906: 23-24.
246. "Our Eastern Pastoral Letters', *Northern Territory Times*, January 18 1907.
247. 'Mr. Sidney Kidman and Sale of Pastoral Properties', *The Pastoralists' Review*, April 16 1909: 108.
248. WF Buchanan to Surveyor General, January 11 1901, Australian Archives, ACT, series A1640, item 1901/46; B. Buchanan, 1997: 106.
249. 'Mr. Sidney Kidman and Sale of Pastoral Properties', *The Pastoralists' Review*, April 16 1909: 108.
250. 'Rural Industries', *The Register* (Adelaide), December 4 1906.
251. 'Droving in Northern Australia, *The Adelaide Observer*, December 1 1906: 28-29; 'News Jottings', *The Pastoralists' Review*, October 16 1905: 639; 'A Record Droving Trip across Australia from West to East, through Drought, Disease, and Death', *The Pastoralists' Review*, January 15 1907: 948.
252. T. Cahill, cited in 'Government Resident's Report on the Northern Territory, 1905',

vol. 2, no. 45: 7, *SAPP*, 1906.

253. 'The Northern Territory', *Adelaide Register*, March 31 1904; 'A Wet Trip – Splendid Rains – A Sudden Death', *Northern Territory Times*, February 5 1904.
254. 'Victoria River Notes' (From various Correspondents), *Northern Territory Times*, July 15 1904.
255. Ibid; 'Pioneer Drovers', *The Pastoral Review*, July 16 1929: 653.
256. 'Victoria River Notes (From various Correspondents)', *Northern Territory Times*, July 15 1904; *The Pastoralists' Review*, June 15 1905: 294.
257. Jeannie Gunn, *We of the Never Never*, Hutchinson, London, 1908.
258. 'The Elsey', *Northern Territory Times,* January 9 1903.
259. 'Rural Industries', *Adelaide Register*, January 21, 1904.
260. M. Mallison, *Quirindi Advocate,* 1958; W. Linklater, 'Bill Miller of O.T. Station N.T.', December 26 1941, unpublished unprovenanced ms (possibly from Mitchell Library); M. Durack, 1985: 107.
261. Newcastle Waters was generally regarded as belonging to Steve and Harry's brother, the Honourable John Lewis, who was a member of the South Australian Parliament and a founder of Broken Hill Propriety Limited. It would appear that Steve and Harry held shares in the station.
262. M. Durack, 1985: 107.
263. 'Notice of Annual Inspecting Journey of Overland Telegraph Line, from Port Darwin to Attack Creek', *Northern Territory Times*, August 30 1901.
264. According to Mrs Betty Burrowes (nee Phillott; personal communication) this information is written in her father's hand on the back of a photograph of the team of men that Phillott took to Wave Hill.
265. 'The Queensland Border', *The Adelaide Register*, March 9 1904.
266. 'Victoria River Notes', *Northern Territory Times*, July 15 1904.
267. 'News Jottings', *The Pastoralists' Review*, February 15 1905: 949; 'A Record Droving Trip across Australia from West to East, through Drought, Disease, and Death', *The Pastoralists' Review*, January 15 1907: 948.
268. 'H7H' (Hely Hutchinson), 'A Big Overland Trip. Notes By The Way', *Morning Bulletin* (Rockhampton), April 28 1906.
269. 'H7H' (Hely Hutchinson), 'Odd Stock and Other Notes' *Morning Bulletin* (Rockhampton), July 15 1905. In a later edition of the *Morning Bulletin* (April 28 1906), Hutchinson reported that Skuthorpe had intended to obtain supplies from the Wave Hill station store, but before he arrived the store burnt down so he had to get supplies from Newcastle Waters to tide him over until seven tons of rations he'd ordered arrived from Katherine.
270. 'A Big Droving Contract', *The Register* (Adelaide), February 28 1905.
271. 'News Jottings', *The Pastoralists' Review*, November 16 1909: 948.
272. 'Station Life', *Northern Territory Times*, June 10 1910.
273. 'Record Droving Feat', *The Town and Country Journal*, February 15 1905: 13.
274. 'H7H' (Hely Hutchinson), May 15 1905: 208 and March 15 1906: 39-41.
275. Ben Martin, who piloted the various mobs across Illawarra station, claimed that Miller had 1000 head (*The Pastoralists' Review*, June 15 1906: 314). The *Northern Territory Times* reported that Miller had 1500 ('Victoria River Notes', *Northern Territory Times*, July 15 1904).
276. M.A. Radford to J. Lewis, May 25 1904. South Australian State Library, PGR 247/10/1.

277. Ben Martin, 'Droving in Northern Territory', *The Pastoralists' Review*, March 15 1906: 314.
278. 'Victoria River Notes' (from various correspondents), *Northern Territory Times*, July 15 1904; 'Out Nor West: A Land of Great Contrasts', *The Observer* (Adelaide), February 13 1926; S.E. Pearson, 'Pioneer Drovers', *The Pastoral Review*, July 16 1929: 653.
279. 'The Recent Record Droving Trips. Notes from diary and copies of some entries under dates therein concerning Skuthorpe's journey across the Territory with 3000 Wave Hill bullocks,' entry for May 4th 1904; B. Martin, 'Droving in Northern Territory', *The Pastoralists' Review*, June 15 1905: 294; it appears that by the time Skuthorpe's cattle were delivered at Narrabri, Dave Warneke and Oswald Skuthorpe had left and a man named Benson was in charge of one of the mobs ('A Long Droving Trip', *Northern Territory Times*, April 28 1905).
280. M. Mallison, June 27 1942. Mallison's story is based on an interview with Billy Miller (alias William Linklater). This was done nearly forty years after the event so must be treated with a degree of caution.
281. B. Martin, 'Droving in Northern Territory' (letter to the editor), *The Pastoralists' Review*, June 15 1906: 314; 'H7H' (Hely Hutchinson), March 15 1906: 39-41 and 'Record Droving Trips', *The Pastoralists' Review*, May 15 1905: 208.
282. 'H7H' (Hely Hutchinson), 'Odd Stock and Other Notes', *The Morning Bulletin* (Rockhampton), June 20 1905.
283. 'Correspondence. Long Droving Trips', *The Morning Bulletin* (Rockhampton), June 23 1905.
284. B. Martin, *The Pastoralists' Review*, June 15 1906: 314.
285. 'The Recent Record Droving Trips. Notes from diary and copies of some entries under dates therein concerning Skuthorpe's journey across the Territory with 3000 Wave Hill bullocks.' *The Pastoralists' Review*, June 15 1905: 294. The diary begins on May 4 1904 and it's virtually certain that it was kept by S.E. Pearson who joined Skuthorpe's team on Wave Hill station. In the same issue of the *Pastoralist's Review* (p. 276) there's a note to say that a map had been received from Pearson showing 'every creek, waterhole, and variety of feed en route' and that, 'It is, in fact, a diary of what one meets day by day en route.'
286. Ibid. It's apparent that the writer was with Skuthorpe's second mob because on June 24th when he was 'on 4 mile creek from Newcastle Waters', he refers to Warneke's mob as being 'near Montmona', a waterhole about 110 kilometres beyond Newcastle Waters on the road towards Queensland.
287. B. Martin, *The Pastoralists' Review*, June 15 1906: 314.
288. 'H7H' (Hely Hutchinson), 'Early Drovers in the Northern Territory – Leaves from the diary of Alfred Giles', *The Pastoralist's Review*, March 15 1906: 39.
289. Murranji Survey Plan made by Surveyor Scandrett in 1914. CP 607, Northern Territory Lands Department, Darwin.
290. T. Cahill, cited in the 'Government Resident's Report on the Northern Territory, 1905', *SAPP*, vol. 2, no. 45, 1906.
291. 'H7H' (Hely Hutchinson), 'Odd Stock and Other Notes', *The Morning Bulletin* (Rockhampton), June 20 1905.
292. According to Captain Bishop, cattle on the road would drink ten gallons (F. Bishop to the 'Government Resident' [actually the Northern Territory Administrator] October 6 1927, Wave Hill-Alice Springs Stock Route, NTRS F5, S258). However, Rodney Watson (pers. comm.), an experienced former drover who took cattle across the

Murranji Track in the 1940s and 1950s, a thirsty bullock would drink much more than ten gallons.

293. W. Steele, 'Pioneer Drovers – A Disappearing Band', *Queensland Agricultural Journal*, August 1 1929: 208.
294. 'A Long Droving Trip', *Northern Territory Times*, April 4 1905.
295. 'A Record Droving Trip', *The Observer* (Adelaide), February 25 1905.
296. 'Our Eastern Pastoral Letter', *Northern Territory Times*, January 18 1907.
297. 'H7H' (Hely Hutchinson), *North Queensland Herald*, January 22 1906.
298. 'Christmas at the Katherine', *Northern Territory Times*, January 12 1905.
299. Much of the Murranji country is limestone, sprinkled with sinkholes and underground cavities that reverberate when a mob of cattle or a motor vehicle passes overhead. This phenomenon has given rise among the Murranji drovers of the expression 'drummy ground' or 'hollow ground'.
300. Personal communication, Charlie Schultz.
301. Mounted Constable F.G. Burt, Temporary Inspector of Stock, in the 'Government Resident's Report on the Northern Territory, 1905', *SAPP* vol. 2, no. 45, 1906: 23-24; 'News & Notes', *Northern Territory Times*, July 14 1905.
302. *The Pastoralists' Review*, May 15 1906; 'A Narrow Escape', *Northern Territory Times*, April 20 1906; 'Stock Notes', *Northern Territory Times*, May 3 1907; 'A Long Droving Trip', *Northern Territory Times*, January 25 1907.
303. 'Stock Notes', *Northern Territory Times,* April 13 1906.
304. 'Stock Movements', *Northern Territory Times*, June 1 1906.
305. 'Station Life', *Northern Territory Times*, June 10 1910.
306. 'Cattle From The Territory. Drover's Graphic Story', *Adelaide Register*, June 4 1908: 5.
307. C. Noblett, 'Report of Sub-Inspector of Stock, Powell's Creek District', cited in 'Northern Territory, Report of the Government Resident for the year 1910', *CPP*, vol. 3, no. 66, 1911.
308. P. Woodley, *"Young Bill's Happy Days": Reminiscences of Rural Australia 1910-1915*, pp 348-387. (Reminiscences of T W Lavender, nd), Unpublished Masters thesis, Australian National University, Canberra, 1982.
309. Ibid: 351.
310. Ibid: 366.
311. Ibid: 371.
312. Ibid: 374.
313. Ibid: 374.
314. Telegram from the Northern Territory Administrator to unnamed person, June 14 1918, NAA, series A3, item 18/2017.
315. B. Buchanan, 1997: 116.
316. G. Buchanan, 1984 (1933).
317. 'Vanguard', 'North Australia: The Real Backblocks', *Cummins & Campbell's Monthly Magazine*, January 1934: 81.
318. Ernestine Hill to Billy Linklater, June 21 1946, Mitchell Library, CY 3480 Al 10/18.
319. E. Hill, 1951: 302.
320. George Farwell, March 15 1952: 241-45
321. 'Statement of Stock Treated at Public Dip', June 12 1967. File 331/7/8, 'Top Springs Dip (Pussycat)', Department of Primary Industries & Fisheries, Alice Springs.
322. Interview with Mick Coombes at Halls Creek, 1994.
323. L. Biltris, 1951: 44-45.

324. E.J. Connellan, *Failure of Triumph: the story of Connellan Airways*, Paradigm Investments, Alice Springs, 1992: 221.
325. A. Fleming, 'Tales of the Murrunji', *Brisbane Courier Mail*, August 11 1938.
326. *Macquarie Dictionary*, 1987: 975. It is also sometimes shown as 'Kingeemet' or 'Kingsmeet', versions that may have come about from the writers hearing Aborigines pronounce the name.
327. 'News and Notes', *Northern Territory Times*, June 7 1917.
328. Telegram from Smart, manager of Newcastle Waters, to the Northern Territory Administrator, J.A. Gilruth, February 1918, NTRS F5 S140.
329. 'Victoria River Notes', *Northern Territory Times*, May 11 1918. In the *Northern Territory Times* misspelled words, such as the word 'Murranji' here, become increasingly common as the First World War progresses and may be the result of wartime shortages; Frog Hollow was a section of Inverway station ('H.J.B.', *The Townsville Register*, October 10 1953).
330. J.M. Stuart, 1984 (1865): 306.
331. Recommendation 4 in a list of recommendations presented to the Royal Commission into the Northern Territory, in 'Report of the Northern Territory Commission together with Minutes of Proceedings, Evidence, and Appendices', *SAPP*, vol. 2, no. 19, 1895.
332. M.P. Durack to W. Griffiths (M.P.), November 29 1899, NAA ACT A1640/1 99/502.
333. W. Griffiths (M.P.), to 'the Minister for the Northern Territory', December 15 1899, NAA ACT series A1640/1, item 99/502.
334. Telegram from Government Resident Charles Dashwood to the 'Minister Controlling the Northern Territory', January 8 1900, NAA ACT, series A1640/1, item 99/502.
335. 'Pastoral', *Northern Territory Times*, May 2 1902.
336. B. Martin, *The Pastoralists' Review*, June 15 1906: 314.
337. T. Cahill to Government Resident C. Herbert, cited in the 'Government Resident's Report on the Northern Territory, 1905, *SAPP*, vol. 2, no. 45, 1906.
338. Government Resident's Report on the Northern Territory, 1906', *SAPP*, vol. 3, no. 45, 1907: 2-3.
339. 'Pastoral Notes', *Northern Territory Times*, March 23 1906.
340. 'News Jottings', *The Pastoralists' Review*, May 15 1906: 196.
341. H. Seal, cited in the 'Government Resident's Report on the Northern Territory, 1906', *SAPP*, vol. 3, no. 45, 1907; Government Resident Charles Herbert to the Minister Controlling the Northern Territory, August 22 1906, NAA, ACT, series A1640, item 1906/492.
342. 'N.A. League', *Northern Territory Times*, September 28, 1906.
343. Personal communication, Bill Cussens, Katherine, 1994. Bill was the son of a drover. He came to the Territory in 1933 and spent most of his life droving.
344. C. Herbert, 'Government Resident's Report on the Northern Territory, 1907', *SAPP*, vol. 3, no. 45, 1908: 2.
345. Ibid: 2.
346. Ibid: 25.
347. Mounted Constable J.L. Artaud, Temporary Inspector of Stock, January 1 1908, in 'Government Resident's Report on the Northern Territory, 1907', *SAPP*, vol. 3, no. 45, 1908; 'H7H' (Hely Hutchinson), 'Odd Stock and Other Notes', *The Morning Bulletin* (Rockhampton), June 20 1905.
348. 'News Jottings', *The Pastoralists' Review*, August 15 1907: 506.

349. 'Government Resident's Report on the Northern Territory, 1908', *SAPP*, vol. 3, no. 45, 1909.
350. Mounted Constable U.W. Holland to Inspector N. Waters, January 3 1910, cited in the 'Government Resident's Report on the Northern Territory, 1909', *SAPP*, vol. 3, no. 45, 1910.
351. 'Government Resident's Report on the Northern Territory, 1909', *SAPP*, vol. 3, no. 45, 1910.
352. 'News Jottings', *The Pastoralists' Review*, April 15 1910: 161.
353. 'Northern Territory. Report of the Government Resident for the year 1910', *South Australian Parliamentary Papers*, vol. 3, no. 66, 1911.
354. Temporary Inspector of stock, Mounted Constable C. Johnston, December 31 1905, cited in the 'Government Resident's Report on the Northern Territory, 1905', *South Australian Parliamentary Papers*, vol. 2, no. 45, *SAPP*, 1906.
355. 'Station Life', *Northern Territory Times*, June 10 1910.
356. Captain H.V. Barclay to Secretary, Department of External Affairs, August 3 1911, NAA ACT, series A3/1, NT 14/3682.
357. P. Donovan, At the Other End of Australia: The Commonwealth and the Northern Territory 1911-1978. University of Queensland Press, Brisbane, 1984: xiv, 2.
358. B. Strong, entry on H.V. Barclay in D. Carment, et al (eds.), *Northern Territory Dictionary of Biography: Volume One to 1945*, Northern Territory University Press, Darwin, 1990: 13.
359. Captain H.V. Barclay to Secretary, Department of External Affairs, August 3 1911, NAA ACT, series A3/1, NT 14/3682.
360. Captain H.V. Barclay, 'Report on Stock Route Victoria River-Newcastle Waters', August 3 1911, NAA ACT Item A3/1, Item 14/3682.
361. Memorandum, Instructions from E. Day, Crown Lands and Survey Department, to Surveyor A.B. Scandrett, May 16 1913, NTRS F9, 364/39.
362. A.B. Scandrett to the Chief Surveyor, Darwin, September 6 1913, October 14, 1913 and October 20 1913, NTRS, F9, 364/39.
363. A.B. Scandrett to the Chief Surveyor, Darwin, October 20 1913, NTRS F9, 364/39.
364. Ibid; the locations of Peak Knob and Flat-topped Hill as shown on the Flat Top Hill 1:100,000 map (sheet 5364, edition 1 1974) is incorrect. The correct location for Peak Knob is co-ords 900 526 and for Flat-topped Hill is co-ords 895 545. Both these hills have large stone surveyors' cairns built on them and are in the correct position relative to each other and to other cairns in the area, as shown on Scandrett's map.
365. A.B. Scandrett to the Chief Surveyor, Darwin, October 14 1913, NTRS F9, 364/39.
366. A.B. Scandrett to the Chief Surveyor, Darwin, March 6 1914. NTRS F9 364/39.
367. This story is told by Bill Harney (1952: 19), but elsewhere he provides different versions of the same tale (see W. Harney, *Content to Lie in the Sun*, Rigby Limited, Sydney, 1974 [1958]: 156).
368. Surveyor L.A. Wells, 'Report on Northern Territory Trigonometrical Survey Expedition', *SAPP*, vol. 3, no. 64, 1910.
369. 'Northern Territory. Officials at Variance', *The Age*, April 1 1916.
370. M. Travers, *Newcastle Waters*, Report prepared for the National Trust of Australia (N.T.), 1986: 16.
371. Copley Playford, Director of Lands and Mines, to the Government Secretary, February 23 1922, NAA ACT, series A1, item 1926/12258.

372. Ibid; 'Report of the Administrator for the Year Ended 30th June 1918', *CPP*, sessions 1917-19, vol., 6: 7.
373. Copley Playford, Director of Lands and Mines, to the Government Secretary, February 23 1922, NAA ACT, series A1, item 1926/12258.
374. Secretary of the Townsville Chamber of Commerce to F.W. Bamford, M.H.R., August 2 1918, NAA NT Series A3, Item 18/2017.
375. Administrator's Office to Hon. F.W. Bamford, MHR, August 28 1918, NAA ACT, series A3, item 18/2017.
376. 'Report of the Administrator for the Year Ended 30th June 1918'. *CPP*, sessions 1917-19, vol., 6: 7.
377. Ibid; 'Tenders for Bores on Stock routes', *Northern Territory Times*, November 9 1918.
378. S. Peacock to Commissioner of Lands, Darwin, April 30 1919. NTRS, series F5, P137; W.D. Bingle, secretary of 'Works and Railways', to the' Secretary, Commonwealth Treasury', NAA ACT series A571/56, item 21/7152.
379. Transcript of the taped memoir of William McDonald, in possession of his daughter, Jill Campbell, of Kybo station, Western Australia.
380. M. Terry, 1924.
381. National Archives of Australia (ACT), series A571/56, item 21/17152.
382. 'Territory Improvement', *The Graziers' Review*, November 14, 1921
383. Acting Administrator Stanisforth Smith, 'Annual Report of the Acting Administrator for the Year Ending 30th June 1920', *CPP*, session 1920-21, vol. 3, no. 28: 6
384. 'Report of the Administrator for the Year ended 30th June 1921', *CPP*, session 1922, vol. 2, no. 44: 14.
385. Memorandum from W.D. Bingle, Secretary Works and Railways, to Secretary, Commonwealth Treasury, May 14 1921, NAA ACT, series A571/56, item 21/7152.
386. Ibid.
387. S. Peacock to the Secretary, Home and Territories, October 29 1921. NAA ACT, series A1, item 1926/12258.
388. Notes of interview with S. Peacock. Interviewer, the Hon. R.W. Foster, M.P., January 10 1922, NAA ACT, series A1, item 1926/12258.
389. M. Nixon, 1978: 7.
390. Ibid.
391. List of specifications for bores 8 to 13. NAA ACT, series A1, item 1936/1701.
392. Notes of interview with S. Peacock. Interviewer, the Hon. R.W. Foster, M.P., January 10 1922, NAA ACT, series A1, item 1926/12258.
393. Peacock to the Secretary, Home and Territories, October 29 1921. NAA ACT, series A1, item 1926/12258.
394. S. Peacock to Northern Territory Administrator F.C. Urquhart, July 15 1924. NAA ACT, series A1/1, item 1926/12258.
395. S. Peacock to Senator Pearce, July 24 1923, NAA ACT, series A1, item 1926/12258; S. Peacock to Northern Territory Administrator F.C. Urquhart, July 15 1934, NAA ACT series A1926/12258; S. Peacock to the Secretary, Home and Territories, October 24 1925, NAA ACT, series A1/1, item 1926/12258.
396. S. Peacock to the Secretary, Home and Territories, October 24 1925. NAA ACT, series A1, item 1926/12258.
397. Ibid.
398. G. Edwards, Manager of the Australian Investment Agency (Vesteys), to the Secretary, Department of Home and Territories, June 18 1924. NAA ACT, series A1/1, item

1926/12258.

399. S. Peacock to the Secretary of Home and Territories, October 24 1925. NAA ACT, series A1/1, item 1926/12258.
400. Memorandum to the Secretary, Department of Home and Territories, May 27 1926, NAA ACT series A281/1, item DGW 27/1677.
401. Director General of Works to the Secretary, Works & Railways, July 31 1926. NAA ACT, series A281/1, series DGW 27/1677.
402. E. Stoddard to the Director General of Works, October 23 1926, series A281/1, item DGW 27/1677.
403. Personal communication, Louis Harmanis, Darwin, June 1991.
404. Report of the Administrator for the Year ended 30th June 1921. *CPP*, session 22, vol. 2, no. 44: 15.
405. S. Peacock to the Secretary, Home and Territories, October 29 1921. NAA ACT, series A1, item 1926/12258.
406. S. Peacock to Administrator F.C. Urquhart, July 15 1924. NAA ACT, series A1/1, item 1926/12258.
407. F. Bishop to the 'Government Resident', October 6 1927. NTRS F5 S258.
408. F. Bishop to the Northern Territory Administrator, April 29 1935, CRS, series F1, item 1940/508.
409. E.W. Stoddardt, April 6 1927, NAA ACT, series A1640, item 1906/492.
410. C. Schultz and D. Lewis, *Beyond the Big Run: Station Life in Australia's Last Frontier*, University of Queensland Press, Brisbane, 1995: 122.
411. Personal communication, Charlie Schultz.
412. Telegram from Captain H. V. Barclay to Department of External Affairs, August 3 1911, NAAC, A3/1 NT 14/3682.
413. Ibid.
414. Memo, Department of External Affairs, October 23 1911. NAAC, A3/1 NT 14/3682.
415. Ibid.
416. North Australia Commission to the Secretary, Home and Territories Department, February 11 1927, NAAC, A659 40/1/899.
417. C.W.D. Conacher to the Chairman, North Australia Commission, June 18 1928, NTRS F5 S258.
418. Ibid.
419. Ibid.
420. Secretary, North Australia Commission, to Assistant Secretary, Home and Territories Department, July 17 1928. NTRS F5 S258.
421. C. Abbott, Northern Territory Administrator, to A.S. Bingle, Australian Investment Agency, February 15 1941. NAA NT CRS F1 1940/508. Pastoral Lease 208N, held by Vesteys from March 7 1930 until surrendered on July 4 1947, was located between Newcastle Waters and Murranji Bore and surrounded No. 10 Bore (personal communication, Stuart Duncan at the Office of the Placenames Committee, Lands Department, Darwin).
422. V. Carrington, District Officer, to the Northern Territory Administrator, June 13 1941. NAA NT CRS F1 1940/508.
423. Ibid.
424. A.S. Bingle, Australian Investment Agency, to C. Abbott, Northern Territory Administrator, September 18 1942. NAA NT CRS F1 1942/112.
425. A. Rose, Chief Veterinary Officer, to Northern Territory Administrator, July 7 1947.

Murranji Stock Route — Deviation of Route at Newcastle Waters, file 331/5/73. DPI&F, Alice Springs.

426. Memo: Murranji No. 10 bore Stock Reserve, A. Rose, Chief Veterinary Officer, Animal Industry Division File No. 331/6/4. Murranji Stock Route — No. 10 Bore Stock Reserve. DPI&F, Alice Springs; Memo from A. Rose: No. 10 bore, Murranji — Stock and Quarantine Reserve. Murranji Stock Route — No. 10 Bore. File No. 331/6/4. DPI&F, Alice Springs; Memo from C. Mulhearn, Veterinary Officer: Proposed Quarantine Reserve — Lease No. 208, Murringi [sic]. August 4 1948. Murranji Stock Route — No. 10 Bore. File No. 331/6/4. DPI&F, Alice Springs.
427. A. Rose to Director of Lands, April 8 1954. Top Springs and Bore Quarantine and Holding Reserve. File 331/6/202. DPI&F, Alice Springs.
428. A. Rose (?) to Works Director, Department of Works, Elliott, May 14 1954, Top Springs and Bore Quarantine and Holding Reserve. File 331/6/202. DPI&F, Alice Springs.
429. A. Rose to A.S. Bingle, Australian Investment Agency, May 20 1954. Murranji Stock Route — General File. 331/4/15. DPI&F, Alice Springs.
430. *North Australian Monthly*, January, 1955; A. Rose to Director of Lands, October 7 1955. Top Springs and Bore Quarantine and Holding Reserve. File 331/6/202. DPI&F, Alice Springs.
431. Extract from the *Commonwealth Gazette*, August 2 1956. Top Springs and Bore Quarantine and Holding Reserve. File 331/6/202. DPI&F, Alice Springs.
432. E. Hill, 1951: 300.
433. 'H7H' (Hely Hutchinson), 'Early Drovers in the Northern Territory—Leaves from the Diary of Alfred Giles'. *The Pastoralists' Review*, March 15 1906: 39-41.
434. F. Bishop to the Government Resident, October 6 1927. NTRS F5 S258.
435. D. Lewis, *The Final Muster: A Survey of Previously Undocumented Sites throughout the Victoria River District*, 2000, pp. 203-208. Report prepared for the Australian National Trust (N.T.).
436. Information supplied by staff at the Australian National Dictionary Centre, Australian National University,
437. 'News from Outback', *Northern Territory Times and Gazette*, July 5 1927.
438. C. Conacher to the Chairman, North Australia Commission, June 18 1928,NAAC A659 40/1/899.
439. During an interview with former drover Reg Hart in 2004 he mentioned that a year or so before he came to the Territory in 1935 drover John Darcy lost his entire mob on the Murranji. Losing an entire herd wasn't a common occurrence so the drover mentioned in this passage almost certainly was Darcy.
440. A. Martin to J.W. Allen, Secretary, Northern Territory Pastoral Lessees Association, November 2 1931. NTRS, Northern Territory Cattlemen's Association Inc., PAC 106. vol. 39, 'Stock Routes and Reserves'.
441. Ibid.
442. J.W. Allen to H. Connell, Director, Works Department, April 9 1932. NAAC A284/1 B5244.
443. Memorandum from A. Percival, Assistant Secretary, Property and Survey Branch, Department of Interior, to Assistant Secretary, Works and Services Branch, December 2 1932. NAAC A284/1 B5244.
444. H. Rolland, Works Director, to Assistant Secretary, Works and Services Branch, Department of the Interior, June 16 1933. NAAC A284/1 B5244.

445. D.D. Smith, Resident Engineer, to Assistant Secretary, Works and Services Branch, Department of the Interior, April 16 1934. NAAC A284/1 B5244.
446. D.D. Smith, Resident Engineer, to Deputy Director-General of Allied Works, Alice Springs, January 7 1944. NAA NT, CRS F1 1943/10B.
447. F. Colson to the Resident Engineer, Alice Springs, October 12 1943. NAA NT CRS F1 1943/10B.
448. F. Colson to the Resident Engineer, Alice Springs, October 12 1943. NAA NT CRS F1 1943/10B; C. Abbott, Northern Territory Administrator, to Field Officer Clough, December 16 1943. NAA NT CRS F1 1943/10B.
449. D.D Smith, Resident Engineer, Alice Springs, to Deputy Director-General of Allied Works, January 7 1944. NAA NT CRF, series F1 item 1943/10B.
450. Haliden Hartt, 1944: 28.
451. C.N. Schultz to the Northern Territory Administrator, July 11 1948. NAANT CRS F1/0, Item 1947/198.
452. R.C. Jones, Director of Works, to The Government Secretary, Northern Territory Administration, September 7 1950.NAANT CRS F1/0, item 1947/198.
453. C. Abbott, Northern Territory Administrator, to Secretary, Department of the Interior, April 21 1938. NAAC A284/1 B5244.
454. D.D. Smith, Resident Engineer, Alice Springs, to the Northern Territory Administrator, June 13 1941.NAA NT CRS F1 1940/508.
455. *Hoofs and Horns*, July 1957: 6; October 1957: 10; April 1961: 59; September 1955: 8.
456. J.M.Stuart, 1984 (1865): 245.
457. G. Buchanan, 1984: 122.
458. L.A. Wells, 'Report on the Northern Territory Trigonometrical Survey Expedition', *SAPP*, No. 64, vol. 3, 1910
459. Captain H.V. Barclay to Secretary, Department of External Affairs, August 3 1911. NAAC, A3/1 NT 14/3682.
460. G. Farwell, March 15 1950: 242. Farwell only provides the name 'Sarli', but the Wave Hill Police Journal mentions 'Salie Mahomet' in a number of entries (Northern Territory Archives, F292, entries for September 1st 1932, April 13 1948 and January 19 1937 at which time he was at Inverway).
461. Lt.-Col. R.H. Weddell, 'Report on the Administration of the Northern Territory for the year ended 30th June 1932'. *CPP*, session 1932-34, vol. 3, no. 124: 35.
462. D.D. Smith, Resident Engineer, to Assistant Secretary, Works and Services Branch, Department of the Interior, April 16 1934. NAAC A284/1 B5244.
463. Lt.-Col. R.H. Weddell, 'Report on the Administration of the Northern Territory for the year ended 30th June, 1932', 47. *CPP*, session 1932-34, vol. 3, no. 124: 35.
464. J.W. Allen to Secretary, Department of the Interior, April 30 1936. NAAC A284/1 B5244.
465. J.W. Allen to Minister for the Interior, June 5 1936. NAAC A284/1 B5244.
466. J.W. Allen to Minister for the Interior, August 11 1936. NAAC A284 B5244.
467. D. Footell (Vesteys) to the Secretary, Northern Territory Pastoral Lessees' Association, July 15 1936. NTRS, Northern Territory Cattlemen's Association Inc. PAC 106. vol. 39, 'Stock Routes and Reserves'.
468. Memorandum from J. Carrodus, Secretary, Department of the Interior, to Assistant Secretary, Works and Services Branch. March 19 1937. NAAC A284/1 B5244; W. Middleton, Secretary, Australian, Investment Agency, to Secretary, Department of the

Interior, September 28 1937. NAAC A284/1 B5244.

469. F. Bishop to the Administrator of the Northern Territory, October 14 1936, NAA ACT, series A284, item B5244.
470. Report by E. Stoddart, Works Director, to Director-General of Works, Department of the Interior, April 7 1938. NAAC A284/1 B5244.
471. Report by F. Bishop to Northern Territory Administrator, Darwin, May 14 1938. NAAC A284/1 B5244.
472. The Australian Investment Agency to Secretary, Department of the Interior, June 20 1938. NAAC A284/1 B5244.
473. C. Abbott, Northern Territory Administrator, to Secretary, Department of the Interior, June 27 1938. NAAC A284/1 B5244.
474. Extract from report by F. Bishop, November 27 1939. NAAC A284/1 B5244.
475. Extract from Report of Chief Stock Inspector (D. Walker) to Director General of Health, November 6 1942. NAA NT CRS F1 1942/112.
476. W. Hare, *The Early History of Animal Industry In The Northern Territory*, Conservation Commission Of The Northern Territory, Government Printer, Darwin, 1985: 87
477. Charles Schultz to Chief Veterinary Officer, Colonel A.L. Rose, August 25 1948. Murranji Stock Route — General File, 331/4/15, DPI&F, Alice Springs.
478. Ibid.
479. Chief Veterinarian Colonel A.L. Rose to Charlie Schultz, March 29 1949. Murrangi Stock Route General File, 331/4/15, DPI&F, Alice Springs.
480. J.H. Whittem, Director of Animal Industry Branch, to the District Veterinary Officer (North), March 11 1959. NAANT, series F1/0, item 1951/763.
481. Murrangi Stock Route General File, 331/4/15. DPI&F, Alice Springs.
482. F. Bishop to the Government Resident, October 6 1927. NTRS F5 S258.
483. C. Conacher to the Chairman, North Australia Commission, June 18 1928, NAAC A659 40/1/899.
484. H. Rolland, Works Director, to Assistant Secretary, Works and Services Branch, Department of the Interior, June 16 1933. NAAC A284/1 B5244.
485. Letter from A. Moray, cited by W. Middleton, Secretary, Australian Investment Agency, to Secretary, Department of the Interior, April 18 1933. NAA ACT, series A284/1, item B5244.
486. F. Bishop to Northern Territory Administrator, April 29 1935. NAA NT CRS F1 1940/508.
487. J. Flemming, Chief Mechanical Engineer, to Assistant Secretary, Works and Services Branch, Department of the Interior, December 13 1935. NAA NT CRS F1 1940/508.
488. J.W Allen to Secretary, Department of the Interior, April 30 1936. NAAC A284/1 B5244.
489. J.W. Allen to Minister for the Interior, June 5 1936. NAAC A284/1 B5244.
490. Drover Saltmer to W. Carroll, July 8 1936. NAAC A284/1 B5483.
491. NAA ACT A284/1 B5483.
492. Telegram from D.D. Smith, Resident Engineer, July 28 1936. NAAC A284/1 B5483.
493. There's a bore on the south side of Yellow Waterhole, but if it was put down in 1936 or 1937 it's not mentioned in any documentation over the next thirty years.
494. Internal memo by chief Veterinary Officer, A.L. Rose, November 8 1948, Murrangi Stock Route General File, 331/4/15, DPI&F, Alice Springs.
495. Timber Creek Police Journal, August 11 1936. NTRS CRS F302.
496. N.C. Bell, Director of Mines, to the Acting Administrator. January 9 1937. NAA NT,

series F1/0, item 1936/456.

497. C. Birrell to Chief Clerk, Lands and Survey Branch, Darwin, December 24 1951. NTRS F28 Box 44, GL1364.
498. Telegram from D.D. Smith, November 23 1936, NAA ACT, Series A284/1, item B5483.
499. The Department of the Interior to the Secretary, Northern Territory Pastoral Lessees Association, March 17 1937. NTRS, Northern Territory Cattlemen's Association Inc. PAC 106. vol. 39, 'Stock Routes and Reserves'.
500. Photo of 'Set of three new 25,000 gall. tank No. 10 Bore Murranji Stock Route', DATE NAAC A284/1 B5244: D. D. Smith, Resident Engineer, to the Deputy Administrator of the Northern Territory, June 15 1936. NAAC A284/1 B5244
501. Memorandum from D.D. Smith, Resident Engineer, to Assistant Secretary, Works and Services Branch, Department of the Interior, October 21 1937. NAAC A284/1 B5244.
502. Report by A. Fleetwood, Engineer, Water, Supply and Sewerage, to Assistant Secretary, Department of the Interior, August 7 1936. NAAC A284 B5483; Administrator C.L.A. Abbott to The Secretary, Department of the Interior, May 12 1942, NAA NT CRS series F1, item 1942/112.
503. C. Conacher, Australian Investment Agency, to J. Carrodus, Department of the Interior, July 2 1936. NAAC A284/1 B5244.
504. Report by A. Fleetwood, Engineer, Water, Supply and Sewerage, to Assistant Secretary, Department of the Interior, August 7 1936. NAAC A284 B5483.
505. Resident Engineer D.D. Smith to His Honour the Administrator, May 30 1941. NAA NT F1, item 1940/508.
506. District Officer V.G. Carrington to the Northern Territory Administrator, June 13 1941, NAA NT, series F1, item 1942/112.
507. D.D. Smith, Divisional Works Officer, to the Chief Veterinary Officer, Animal Industry Division, July 13 1950, DPI&F, Alice Springs, file 331/4/15.
508. D.D. Smith, Resident Engineer, to the Northern Territory Administrator, October 25 1940. NAA NT CRS F1 1940/508.
509. A.S. Bingle, Australian Investment Agency, to C. Abbott, Northern Territory Administrator, November 4 1940. NAA NT CRS F1 1940/508; C. Abbott, Northern Territory Administrator, to Secretary, Department of the Interior, December 11 1940. NAA NT CRS F1 1940/508.
510. D.D. Smith, Resident Engineer, Alice Springs, to Secretary, Lands Department, Darwin, March 29 1941. NAA NT CRS F1 1940/508.
511. A.S. Bingle, Australian Investment Agency, to C. Abbott, Northern Territory Administrator, November 4 1940. NAA NT CRS F1 1940/508.
512. Report from Constable E. Morey, Newcastle Waters police station, to Administrator, September 29 1941. NAA NT CRS F1 1940/508.
513. C.L.A. Abbott to the Secretary, Department of the Interior, December 11 1940. NAANT CRS, series F1, item 1940/508.
514. V. Carrington, District Officer, to the Northern Territory Administrator, June 13 1941. NAA NT CRS F1 1940/508.
515. Report from Constable E. Morey, Newcastle Waters police station, to Administrator, September 29 1941. NAA NT CRS F1 1940/508.
516. Memo from A. Rose: No. 10 bore, Murranji — Stock and Quarantine Reserve, June 18 1948. Murranji Stock Route — No. 10 Bore. File No. 331/6/4. DPI&F, Alice Springs.

517. D.D. Smith, Resident Engineer, to the Northern Territory Administrator, October 25 1940. NAA NT CRS F1 1940/508.
518. Ibid; Field Officer W.L. Clough to the chief Clerk, Lands Department, 19-11-1940 NAA NT, F1 item 1940/508.
519. A.S. Bingle, Australian Investment Agency, to C. Abbott, Northern Territory Administrator, November 4 1940. NAA NT CRS F1 1940/508; a 'smash' is a 'rush' or stampede in which many cattle are lost, killed or injured.
520. Ibid.
521. D. McInnes, Field Officer, to the Chief Clerk, Lands Department, Darwin, December 4 1940. NAA NT CRS F1, item 1940/508.
522. C. Abbott, Northern Territory Administrator, to Secretary, Department of the Interior, December 11 1940. NAA NT CRS F1 1940/508.
523. A. Martin to Lord Luke, July 21 1941. Bovril Australian Estates Ltd.: Records, Correspondence between Australian Mercantile Land and Finance Co. Ltd., Sydney, and B.A.E. Ltd., London, and station manager. Noel Butlin Archives, 119/6.
524. F. Bishop to the Government Secretary, Darwin, May 21 1941. NAA NT CRS F1 1940/508.
525. Telegram from C.L.A. Abbott to Department of Interior, cited in Abbott to V.G. Carrington, June 7 1941, NAA, NT, series F1, item 1940/508.
526. A.S. Bingle to Administrator Abbott, September 18 1942, NAA NT, series F1, item 1942/112.
527. Telegram from C.L.A. Abbott to Department of Interior, cited in Abbott to V.G. Carrington, June 7 1941, NAA, NT, series F1, item 1940/508.
528. Report from C. Abbott, Northern Territory Administrator, to Secretary, Department of the Interior, July 15 1942. NAA NT CRS F1 1942/112.
529. A.S. Bingle, Australian Investment Agency, to Government Secretary, Alice Springs, March 25 1942. NAA NT CRS F1 1942/112.
530. Ibid.
531. A.S. Bingle, Australian Investment Agency, to Administrator, March 20 1942. NAA NT CRS F1 1942/112.
532. A.S. Bingle, Australian Investment Agency, to Administrator, March 20 1942. NAA NT CRS F1 1942/112; Telegram from A. Martin, manager of VRD, to Administrator (?), April 1942. NAA NT CRS F1 1942/112; Timber Creek Police Journal, July 27 1942. NTRS F302.
533. P. Donovan, 1984: 135.
534. A. Martin, manager of VRD, to Lord Luke, Chairman of Bovril, April 27 1942. Bovril Australian Estates Ltd. Records, Correspondence between Australian Mercantile Land and Finance Co. Ltd., Sydney, and B.A.E. Ltd., London, and station manager, Noel Butlin Archives,119/6.
535. 'Attorney for N.A.' to Lord Luke, Chairman of Bovril, April 27 1942. Bovril Australian Estates Ltd. Records, Correspondence between Australian Mercantile Land and Finance Co. Ltd., Sydney, and B.A.E. Ltd., London, and station manager. Noel Butlin Archives, 119/6.
536. 'Attorney for N.A.' to Lord Luke, Chairman of Bovril, July 4 1942. Bovril Australian Estates Ltd. Records, Correspondence between Australian Mercantile Land and Finance Co. Ltd., Sydney, and B.A.E. Ltd., London, and station manager. Noel Butlin Archives, 119/6.
537. Personal communication, Charlie Schultz, Yankalilla, 1991; A. Martin, manager

of VRD, to Lord Luke, Chairman of Bovril, September 23 1943. Bovril Australian Estates Ltd. Records, Correspondence between Australian Mercantile Land and Finance Co. Ltd., Sydney, and B.A.E. Ltd., London, and station manager. Noel Butlin Archives, 119/6.

538. 'Report on Inter-Departmental Conference On Supplying Civilians In Northern Territory And Problems Arising Therefrom', February 15 1943. NAA NT CRS F1 1943/10B.
539. A.S. Bingle, Australian Investment Agency, to C. Abbott, Northern Territory Administrator, September 18 1942. NAA NT CRS F1 1942/112.
540. Interview with Bill Cussens in Katherine, 1994.
541. A.S. Bingle, Australian Investment Agency, to Government Secretary, Alice Springs, April 10 1942. NAA NT CRS F1 1942/112.
542. W. Littlejohn to Government Secretary, Alice Springs, June 6 1942. NAA NT CRS F1 1942/112.
543. F. Clough, to Government Secretary, April 7 1942. NAA NT CRS F1 1942/112.
544. C. Abbott, Northern Territory Administrator, to Secretary, Department of the Interior, May 5 1942. NAA NT CRS F1 1942/112; W. Clough, Field Officer, to Government Secretary, Alice Springs, May 20 1942. NAA NT CRS F1 1942/112.
545. W. Littlejohn, to Government Secretary, Alice Springs, June 6 1942. NAA NT CRS F1 1942/112.
546. D. McIndoe, to A.S. Bingle, Australian Investment Agency, June 22 1942. NAA NT CRS F1 1942/112.
547. Report from C. Abbott, Northern Territory Administrator, to Secretary, Department of the Interior, July 15 1942. NAA NT CRS F1 1942/112.
548. A.S. Bingle, Australian Investment Agency, to C. Abbott, Northern Territory Administrator, September 18 1942. NAA NT CRS F1 1942/112.
549. Government Resident Charles Dashwood to C.C. Kingston, the Premier of South Australia, January 20 1896, NAA ACT, series A/1640 item 96/35.
550. 'Western Australian Boundary. From Tennant's Creek to Sturt's Creek', *South Australian Register*, October 10 1896.
551. C. Chewings, 'A Journey from Barrow Creek to Victoria River', *The Geographical Journal*, vol. 76, no. 4, October 1930: 316-338; *The Pastoralists' Review*, July 15 1909.
552. R. Kimber, *Arltunga Man: Walter Smith Australian Bushman*, Hesperian Press, Perth 1986: 107-108; R. Kimber, entry on Joe Brown in D. Carment, et al (eds.), 1990: 39-41; Timber Creek Police Journal, January 17 1935. NTRS F292.
553. Notes of Deputation which waited upon Minister for Home Affairs (Hon. S.L.A. Abbott) at Wave Hill, 16th June, 1929. NTRS, series F5 item S258.
554. Geo. A. H., Secretary, to Assistant Secretary, Department of Home Affairs, September 23 1930, NTRS series F5, item S258; Mounted Constable T. White to N. Bell, Chief Warden of Mines, June 5 1931, NTRS, series F5, item S258;
555. C. Abbott, Northern Territory Administrator, to A.S. Bingle, Australian Investment Agency, December 21 1942. NAA NT CRS F1 1942/112.
556. A.S. Bingle, Australian Investment Agency, to C. Abbott, Northern Territory Administrator, January 2 1943. NAA NT CRS F1 1943/10B.
557. Ibid.
558. Personal communication, David Nash; Taped interview with Stan Jones, manager of Gordon Downs station from 1952 to 1964, Katherine, August 2000.
559. A.S. Bingle, Australian Investment Agency, to C. Abbott, Northern Territory

Administrator, September 8 1942. NAA NT CRS F1 1940/508.

560. A.S. Bingle, Australian Investment Agency, to C. Abbott, Northern Territory Administrator, September 18 1942. NAA NT CRS F1 1942/112.
561. A.S. Bingle, Australian Investment Agency, to Secretary, Department of the Interior, December 7 1942. NAA NT CRS F1 1942/112.
562. A.S. Bingle, Australian Investment Agency, to C. Abbott, Northern Territory Administrator, December 8 1942. NAA NT CRS F1 1942/112.
563. List of essential and desirable requirements for east-west stockroute, drawn up by Abbott, Northern Territory Administrator, 1943, NAA NT CRS F1 1943/10B.
564. A.S. Bingle, Australian Investment Agency, to C. Abbott, Northern Territory Administrator, September 18 1942. NAA NT CRS F1 1942/112.
565. Ibid; C. Abbott, Northern Territory Administrator, to A.S. Bingle, Australian Investment Agency, December 21 1942. NAA NT CRS F1 1942/112; List of essential and desirable requirements for east-west stockroute, drawn up by Abbott, Northern Territory Administrator, 1943, NAA NT CRS F1 1943/10B; A.S. Bingle, Australian Investment Agency, to C. Abbott, Northern Territory Administrator, January 2 1943. NAA NT CRS F1 1943/10B.
566. Report on Inter-Departmental Conference On Supplying Civilians In Northern Territory And Problems Arising Therefrom. February 15 1943. NAA NT CRS F1 1943/10B.
567. F. Colson to the Resident Engineer, Alice Springs, October 12 1943. NAA NT CRS F1 1943/10B; C. Abbott, Northern Territory Administrator, to Field Officer Clough, December 16 1943. NAA NT CRS F1 1943/10B.
568. Report on Murranji from W. Clough, Field Officer, to Administrator, October 5 1943. NAA NT CRS F1 1943/10B.
569. Memorandum from W. Haslam, Deputy Director-General of Allied Works for Northern Territory, to Government Secretary, Alice Springs, June 16 1943. NAA NT CRS F1 1943/94; Report on Murranji from W. Clough, Field Officer, to Administrator, October 5 1943. NAA NT CRS F1 1943/10B.
570. Report on Murranji from W. Clough, Field Officer, to Administrator, October 5 1943. NAA NT CRS F1 1943/10B.
571. D.D. Smith, Resident Engineer, to Deputy Director-General of Allied Works, Alice Springs, May 19 1944. NAA NT CRS F1 1943/10B.
572. W. Scully, Minister for Agriculture and Commerce, 1944. NAA NT, series F1, item 1943/10B.
573. C. Abbott, Northern Territory Administrator, to Deputy Director-General of Allied Works, Alice Springs, March 17-3 1944. NAA NT CRS F1 1943/10B.
574. Drover's schedule from Vesteys, May 16 1944. NAA NT CRS F1 1943/10B.
575. D.D. Smith, Resident Engineer, to Deputy Director-General of Allied Works, Alice Springs, May 19 1944. NAA NT CRS F1 1943/10B.
576. Drover's schedule from Vesteys, June 12 1944. NAA NT CRS F1 1943/10B.
577. Circular letter, Animal Industry Division, Alice Springs: The Regulation of Cattle Movements During the Droving Season of 1947. NAA NT CRS F1 1946/100 Pt 2.
578. '91 Mobs listed to leave Territory', *Northern Territory News*, June 18 1953.
579. Tentative Droving Programs for 1957, 1961 and 1963. NTRS 1718.
580. C. Conacher to the Chairman, North Australia Commission, June 18 1928, NAAC A659 40/1/899.
581. W.G. Middleton, Secretary of the Australian Investment Agency Ltd. (Vesteys), to The

Secretary, Department of the Interior, April 18 1933. NAA ACT, series A284/1, series B5244.

582. Report by A. Fleetwood, Engineer, Water, Supply and Sewerage, to Assistant Secretary, Department of the Interior, August 7 1936. NAAC A284 B5483.
583. Vesteys' manager A.S. Bingle to The Government Secretary, Northern Territory Administration, March 25 1942, NAA NT, series F1, item 1942/112.
584. Ibid.
585. A. Rose, Chief Veterinary Officer, to Field Officer Clough, June 4 1946. NAA NT CRS F1 1946/100 Pt 1.
586. Circular letter, Animal Industry Division, Alice Springs: The Regulation of Cattle Movements During the Droving Season of 1947. NAA NT CRS F1 1946/100 Pt 2.
587. 1947 Droving Season – Tentative program. NTRS, Northern Territory Cattlemen's Association Inc. PAC 106, A1/2A.
588. J. Carrodus Secretary, Department of the Interior, to the Administrator, April 16 1946. Murranji Stock Route General File, 331/4/15. DPI&F, Alice Springs. NTRS
589. J.W Allen to Secretary, Department of the Interior, April 30 1936. NAAC A284/1 B5244; The Australian Investment Agency to Secretary, Department of the Interior, June 20 1938. NAAC A284/1 B5244.
590. M. Terry, 1927: 89.
591. List of essential and desirable requirements for east-west stockroute, drawn up by Abbott, Northern Territory Administrator, 1943. NAA NT CRS F1 1943/10B.
592. Note by A. Rose re stockroute improvements, nd., Murranji Stock Route — General File, 331/4/15. DPI&F, Alice Springs.
593. A. Rose to C. Schultz, March 29 1949. Murranji Stock Route — General File. 331/4/15. DPI&F, Alice Springs; Minute to various Government Departments, from A. Rose, June 24 1949. Murranji Stock Route — General File. 331/4/15. DPI&F, Alice Springs; NTRS F1 1946/100 Pt 2
594. A.L. Rose, chief Veterinary Officer, to The Government Secretary, N.T. Administration, September 3 1948, Murranji Stock Route — General File. 331/4/15. DPI&F, Alice Springs
595. A. Rose, Chief Veterinary Officer, to Northern Territory Administrator, August 6 1947. Murranji Stock Route — Deviation of Route at Newcastle Waters, File 331/5/73. DPI&F, Alice Springs.
596. Copy of stockroute deviation sign. Murranji stock Route — Deviation of Route at Newcastle Waters, File 331/5/73. DPI&F, Alice Springs; A. Rose, Chief Veterinary Officer, to Northern Territory Administrator, July 7 1947. Murranji Stock Route — Deviation of Route at Newcastle Waters, File 331/5/73 DPI&F, Alice Springs; A. Rose, Chief Veterinary Officer, to Northern Territory Administrator, August 6 1947. Murranji Stock Route — Deviation of Route at Newcastle Waters, File 331/5/73. DPI&F, Alice Springs.
597. J. Althans to A. Blain, MHR, Canberra, May 7 1947, and H.W. Byers to A. Blain, MHR, Canberra, June 9 1947. Murranji Stock Route — Deviation of Route at Newcastle Waters, file 331/5/73. DPI&F, Alice Springs.
598. A.J. Rose, Chief Veterinary Officer, to Northern Territory Administrator, July 7 1947. Murranji Stock Route — Deviation of Route at Newcastle Waters, file 331/5/73. DPI&F, Alice Springs.
599. A.J. Rose, Chief Veterinary Officer, to Northern Territory Administrator, August 6 1947. Murranji Stock Route — Deviation of Route at Newcastle Waters, file

331/5/73. DPI&F, Alice Springs.

600. A.J. Rose, Chief Veterinary Officer, to the Government Secretary, Northern Territory Administration, September 3 1948. Murranji Stock Route — Deviation of Route at Newcastle Waters, file 331/5/73. DPI&F, Alice Springs
601. W.J. Davidson, Chief Clerk, to Newcastle Waters Ltd., February 9, 1951, NAA NT series F1/0, item 1951/763.
602. J. Whittem to Assistant Administrator, Darwin, December 10 1958. Murranji Stock Route — Deviation of Route at Newcastle Waters, file 331/5/73. DPI&F, Alice Springs.
603. 'Mulga Wires', *Hoofs and Horns*, August 1951: 44-45; Extract from Monthly Report by C, H, Brown, for the Month of September 1950, Murranji Stock Route — General File, 331/4/15. DPI&F, Alice Springs.
604. 'Mulga Wires', *Hoofs and Horns*, June 1951: 40 and August 1951: 44-45.
605. Extract from Monthly Report by C.H. Brown, for the Month of April, 1951, 16-5-51. Murranji Stock Route — General File, 331/4/15. DPI&F, Alice Springs.
606. 'Mulga Wires', *Horns and Horns*, August 1951: 45
607. 'The Week in North Australia', *Northern Territory News*, March 7 1952.
608. D. Lewis, *Slower than the Eye Can See: Environmental change in northern Australia's cattle lands*, Tropical Savannas CRC, Darwin, 2002: 32-34.
609. 'Territory Letter', *Horns and Horns*, July 1953: 46.
610. 'The Week in North Australia', *Northern Territory News*, July 17 1952.
611. 'Mulga Wires', *Hoofs and Horns*, March 1954: 43.
612. 'Mulga Wires', *Hoofs and Horns*, July 1955: 8.
613. '91 Mobs listed to leave Territory', *Northern Territory News*, June 18 1953.
614. 'Mulga Wires', *Hoofs and Horns*, July 1957: 6.
615. 'Mulga Wires', *Hoofs and Horns*, October 1957: 10.
616. 'John Stockman' (Constable Bert Mettam), 'Territory Letter', *Hoofs and Horns*, April 1961: 59.
617. 'John Stockman' (Constable Bert Mettam), 'Territory Letter', *Hoofs and Horns*, September 1955: 8
618. R. Marsh to Director of Animal Industry Division, Alice Springs, May 13 1958. Top Springs Dip (Pussycat) File 331/7/8. DPI&F, Alice Springs.
619. Personal communication, former drover Ian McBean.
620. 'Mulga Wires', *Hoofs and Horns*, 1958: 58.
621. J. Maddock, *A History of Road Trains in the Northern Territory, 1934-1988*, Kangaroo Press, Sydney, 1988: 105-109.
622. W. Hare, 1985: 59.
623. 'Mulga Wires', *Hoofs and Horns*, January 1954: 43.
624. C. Brown: Duplication of Bores — Barkly and Murranji Stock routes. Murranji Stock Route — General File. 331/4/15. DPI&F, Alice Springs.
625. Tentative Droving Program, 1961. Northern Territory Archives, NTRS 1718.
626. Tentative Droving Program, 1963, in W. Hare, 1985: 44.
627. Only two mobs traveled over the Murranji in 1967 (personal communication, Noel 'Pic' Willetts, July 2005). Pic's statement is confirmed in file 331/7/8, 'Top Springs Dip (Pussycat)', held at the Department of Primary Industries and Fisheries, Alice Springs, which contains two 'Statements of Stock Treated at Public Dip', one for Willetts and one for Mick Coombes. Their combined herd amounted to the figure cited here.

628. Top Springs Quarantine Reserve, 1977. Murranji Stock Route — No. 10 Bore. File No. 331/6/4. DPI&F, Alice Springs.
629. F.C. Rideout, Project Officer, to Director of Animal Industry Branch, Darwin, November 16 1978. Murranji Stock Route — General File. 331/4/15. DPI&F, Alice Springs.
630. R. Wright, Lands Allocation Branch, Department of Lands, to Secretary, Department of Primary Production, Darwin, July 9 1981. Murranji Stock Route — General File. 331/4/15. DPI&F, Alice Springs.
631. D. Tabrett to Assistant Director of the Land Development Branch, Department of Lands, Darwin, 1981. Murranji Stock Route — General File. 331/4/15. DPI&F, Alice Springs.
632. Personal communication, Stuart Duncan at the Office of the Placenames Committee, Lands Department, Darwin.
633. An entry in the Timber Creek Police Letter Book (March 12 1903) and others in the Timber Creek Police Journal (August 18 1902, August 24 1902, November 3 1902, March 12 1903 and June 17 1903) make it virtually certain that Campbell, Martin and Fleming were partners on Illawarra station. Mounted Constable E. O'Keefe, cited in 'Government Resident's Report on the Northern Territory, 1905' (*SAPP*, vol. 2, no. 45, 1906, p. 23), states that Fleming and Martin had dissolved their partnership.
634. C.E. Gaunt, 'Old Time Memories: The Birth of Borroloola', *Northern Standard*, October 16 1931.
635. *Northern Territory Times & Gazette*, September 15 1888.
636. C.E. Gaunt, 'Old Time Memories: The Lepers of Arnhem Land and Sketches', *Northern Standard*, July 10 1934.
637. Report on NT Stations. H.W.H. Stevens to Goldsbrough Mort & Co. Ltd., January 8 1891. Goldsbrough Mort and Co. Ltd: Head Office, Melbourne: letters received from HWH Stevens, Port Darwin, re NT property and butchering business, 1889-1892. Head Office, Melbourne: letters received from H. W. H. Stevens, Port Darwin, re NT property and butchering business, 1889-1892. Noel Butlin Archives, 2/872.
638. T. Meldrum to drover J.A. Davis, July 6 1897. Goldsbrough Mort and Co. Ltd: Head Office, Melbourne: letters received from H. W. H. Stevens, Port Darwin, re NT property and butchering business, 1889-1892. Noel Butlin Archives, 872.
639. Timber Creek Police Journal, June 27 1899.
640. Ibid: May 15 1902, May 30 1902; W.F. Buchanan was the brother of Wave Hill pioneer, Nat Buchanan, and was the outright owner of Wave Hill from 1894 (*Northern Territory Times and Gazette*, February 23 1894).
641. Timber Creek Police Letter Book, June 27 1903, photocopy held at the Berrimah police station, Darwin.
642. Department of Lands – Land Administration Branch, office copies of pastoral permits - 1902-1922, Northern Territory Archives Service, F670 vol. 1, pastoral lease 2198. They obtained additional leases 2212 and 2213 on January 1 1902, and lease 2214 on January 4 1902 (information from the Office of the Placenames Committee, Lands Department, Darwin).
643. Timber Creek Police Letter Book, July 27 1903, photocopy held at the Berrimah police station, Darwin.
644. M. Mallison, *Sydney Morning Herald*, June 27 1942; Timber Creek Police Journal, March 31 1902, August 18 1902. NTRS F302.
645. 'H7H' (Hely Hutchinson), 'Odd Stock and Other Notes', *The Morning Bulletin*

(Rockhampton), June 20 1905.
646. Timber Creek Police Journal, November 3 and 4 1902. NTRS F302.
647. T. Ronan, *The Deep of the Sky: An Essay in Ancestor Worship*, Cassell Australia, Melbourne, 1963: 179.
648. Timber Creek Police Journal, March 31 1902. NTRS F302.
649. Timber Creek Police Letter Book, March 12 1903, photocopy held at Berrimah police station, Darwin; 'A Narrow Escape', *Northern Territory Times*, April 20 1906.
650. Timber Creek Police Journal, May 11 1909, NTRS F302.
651. E. Hill, 1951: 324.
652. F. Burt, Temporary Inspector of Stock, Victoria River District, December 30 1905, in 'Government Resident's Report on the Northern Territory, 1906', *SAPP*, vol. 2, no. 45, 1906: 23.
653. 'The Victoria River Survey', *Northern Territory Times*, March 23 1906.
654. W. Steele and C. Steele, *To the Great Gulf: The Surveys and Explorations of L.A. Wells*, Lynton Publications, Adelaide, 1978, p. 129.
655. Timber Creek Police Journal, April 25 1909, July 3 1909. NTRS F302.
656. Report of the Inspector of Police for 1913, in Government Resident's Report on the Northern Territory, p. 38. *CPP*, session, vol. 2, 1914-15-16-17.
657. Files at the Office of the Placenames Committee, Darwin.
658. T.D. Bancroft, internal memo, Department of External Affairs, October 23 1911. NAA ACT, series A3/1, item 14/3682.
659. M. Nixon, *The Rivers of Home: Frank Lacy – Kimberley Pioneer*, Vanguard Service Print, Perth, 1978: 7.
660. W. Braitling to Secretary, Home and Territories, May 5 1921. NAA ACT, series A1 series 1930/2585; Memo from Acting Director of Lands and Mines to Government Secretary re Volkman (and Braitling), August 21 1922. NTRS F28 GL336.
661. W. Braitling, entry on W. Braitling in D. Carment, et al (eds.), *Northern Territory Dictionary of Biography, Volume One: To 1943*, Northern Territory University Press, Darwin, 1990: 33-34.
662. W. Braitling to the Secretary, Department of Home and Territories, May 4 1922. NAA, ACT, series A1, item 1930/2585.
663. W. Braitling to E. Copely Playford, Director of Lands and Mines, July 21 1922, NTRS f28, GL 336.
664. W. Braitling to Copley Playford, Director of Lands and Mines, July 21 1922. NTRS F28 GL336; W. Braitling to Director of Lands, Darwin, June 18 1923, NTRS F28 GL336.
665. W. Braitling to the Secretary, Department of Home and Territories, May 4 1922. NAA ACT. A1 1930/2585; M. Terry, 1925: 202.
666. W. Harney, 1957: 183-84.
667. M. Terry, 1927: 89.
668. W. Braitling, Application for Pastoral Licence, July 21 1922, NTRS F28 GL336.
669. W. Braitling to the Secretary, Department of Home and Territories, May 4 1922, NAA ACT. A1 1930/2585.
670. M. Terry, 1925: 196.
671. Memorandum from Accountant, Home and Territories Department, December 23 1926. NAAC A1/1 1930/2585; W.W. Braitling to L.H. Giles, August 20 1927. NAA ACT, series A1, item 1930/2585.
672. W. Braitling to L.H. Giles, June 26 1926, NAA ACT, series A1/1, item 1930/2585.

673. 'Notes from Never Never', *Northern Territory Times*, September 2 1927.
674. D. Carment, et al (eds.), *Northern Territory Dictionary of Biography, Volume One: To 1945*. Northern Territory University Press, Darwin, 1990: 33-34.
675. Telegram from W. Braitling to Director of Lands, Darwin, October 18 1928, NTRS F28 GL336.
676. J. Ditchfield, *Angels Don't Go Droving*, Central Queensland University Press, Rockhampton, 2003: 47.
677. Dick Scobie, interviewed at Charters Towers, December 1994.
678. Ibid.
679. Department of Lands – Land Administration Branch, Correspondence files, 'GL' series (Grazing Licences), 1912 – 1972. F28 GL1200.
680. Dick Scobie, interviewed at Charters Towers, December 1994.
681. Department of Lands – Land Administration Branch, Correspondence files, 'GL' series (Grazing Licences), 1912 – 1972. F28 GL 1296.
682. Dick Scobie, interviewed at Charters Towers, December 1994.
683. Ibid.
684. Department of Lands – Land Administration Branch, Correspondence files, 'GL' series (Grazing Licences), 1912 – 1972. F28 Box 59 GL1724.
685. 'John Stockman' (Constable Bert Mettam), 'Territory Letter', *Hoofs and Horns*, August 1959: 46.
686. Dick Scobie, interviewed at Charters Towers, December 1994.
687. General Inspection Report by G. A. Buchanan, October 29 1952. NTRS F28 Box 42 GL 1296.
688. P. Sutton, 1983: 130; this word is pronounced 'Pahn-jahk'.
689. A colour photograph of this sinkhole entrance has been published in O. Ruhen, *et al*, *This Is Australia*, Paul Hamlyn Pty Ltd, Sydney, 1975: 228. This book (p. 229), and the *Murranji Land Claim* book (Northern Land Council, Darwin, 1983: 130), both state that the grooves were caused through the rubbing of innumerable hair belts.
690. A.L. Rose to the Government Secretary, N.T. Administration, September 15 1948, NAA ACT series F1/0, item 1947/198.
691. Report by Pastoral Inspector Egan, December 2 1958. NTRS F28 Box 42 GL 1296.
692. Memorandum from C. Brown to Director of Animal Industry, October 10 1957. Murranji Water Hole. Murranji Stock Route, General File 331/5/72. DPI&F, Alice Springs.
693. 'Coachers' are quiet and easily managed cattle used by musterers to decoy other cattle, and to help control them.
694. Dick Scobie, interviewed at Charters Towers, December 1994.
695. Ibid.
696. Personal communication, Long Captain Marajala, Murranji Track, 1991.
697. Dick Scobie, interviewed at Charters Towers, December 1994.
698. Ibid.
699. 'Broke his neck twice and survived to tell', unprovenanced newspaper article, nd.
700. Memorandum to Director of Native Affairs, 'Victoria River Downs Station Inspection 7th April to 15th April 1952', NAA NT CRS F1, item 52/758.
701. Sid Hawks, interviewed in Darwin in October 1998.
702. 'John Stockman' (Constable Bert Mettam), 'Territory Letter', *Hoofs and Horns*, May 1951: 47.
703. C.R. McKellar to The Secretary, Commonwealth Railways, May 11 1929, NAA SA,

Series B300/2, item 7257.

704. This line was probably followed by Wason Byers and his prospecting party when they travelled into the southern Murranji-Tanami country in 1955 ('Territory Letter', *Hoofs and Horns*, September 1955: 8; personal communication, David Nash, who spoke with Liebeknecht, a member of Byers' party).
705. 'A Drama of the Outback', *Sydney Morning Herald*, October 15 1954.
706. *North Australian Monthly*, January 1955: 26.
707. A. Rose to Director of Lands, October 7 1955, Top Springs and Bore Quarantine and Holding Reserve, File 331/6/202, DPI&F, Alice Springs.
708. C.J. Hawks to the Minister for Lands, April 1955, NTRS Box 52, GL 1555.
709. Department of Lands – Land Administration Branch, Correspondence files, 'GL' series (Grazing Licences), 1912 – 1972. F28 GL 336 transferred from Braitling to Bovril, 1/11/28.
710. Assistant General Manager of Australian Mercantile Finance Company, to the Director of Lands, Darwin, June 18 1952. NTRS F8 Box 52 GL 1555.
711. Department of Lands – Land Administration Branch, Correspondence files, 'GL' series (Grazing Licences), 1912 – 1972. F28 Box 58 GL 1703.
712. Sid Hawks, interviewed in Darwin in October 1998; Wave Hill Police Journal, October 3 1960, Northern Territory Archives, F292.
713. R. Bucknall, entry on Thelma Hawks in D. Carment and H. Wilson (eds.), *Northern Territory Dictionary of Biography*, vol. 3, Northern Territory University Press, Darwin, 1996: 151.
714. Personal communication, Rodney Watson. Rodney is a former drover himself who drove cattle along the Murranji Track many times and who helped the Hawks build their first store.
715. K. White, *True Stories of the Top End*, Indra Publishing, Briar Hill, Victoria, 2005: 48-50; 'Police man charged', *NT News*, December 16 1981 and December 17 1981.
716. F.G. Brown, *The Lost Mines and Treasures of Northern Australia*, Gemcraft Publications Pty. Ltd., East Malvern, 1983: 60-62.
717. Interview with Dick Scobie, Charters Towers, December 1994.
718. J. Weir to Mines Branch, Darwin, 1974. Top Springs and Bore Quarantine and Holding Reserve. File 331/6/202. DPI&F, Alice Springs.
719. B.L. Rideout, Chief Inspector of Stock, to Assistant Secretary, Mines Branch, December 4 1974. Top Springs and Bore Quarantine and Holding Reserve. File 331/6/202. DPI&F, Alice Springs.
720. N.C. Bell, Director of Mines, to the Acting Administrator. January 9 1937. NAA NT, series F1/0, item 1936/456. This correspondence indicates that Kaczinski was working for J. Gorey, who had the contract to sink the bore at Murranji Waterholes.
721. W.G. Woolnough, 'Supposed Oil Indications at Murranji Waterhole, Northern Territory', NAA NT series F1/0, item 1936/456.
722. 'John Stockman' (Constable Bert Mettam), 'Territory Letter', *Hoofs and Horns*, September 1955: 8.
723. Personal communication, David Nash, 1992.
724. The only book produced by a drover about his experiences on the Murranji Track is *Fifteen Hundred Down The Murranji*, written by Bob Lunney and published in 1997 (Crawford House Publishing Pty. Ltd., Bathurst). This deals with Bob's trip from Willeroo to Rocklands with drovers Bob and Les Little in 1956. However, there are other books by or about former drovers which deal with the Murranji in passing or

as a minor part of the whole, for example, *The Boss Drover and His Mates* (A. Ingham, Halstead Press, Sydney, 1996).

725. Haliden Hartt, 1944: 25-28.
726. W. Harney, 1957: 183-84.
727. C. Schultz and D. Lewis, 1995: 123-24; D. Lewis, entry on Charlie Schultz in D. Carment and H. Wilson (eds.), *Northern Territory Dictionary of Biography*, vol., 3, 1996: 290-292.
728. Interview with Charlie Schultz, Yankalilla, 1991.
729. Ibid.
730. Interview with Reg Hart, Hendra, Qld, September 2004.
731. Interview with Bill Cussens in Katherine, 1994.
732. Ibid.
733. Ibid.
734. Interview with Edna Jessop at Mt. Isa in 1995.
735. Ibid.
736. Interview with Edna Jessop at Mt. Isa in 1995.
737. Edna pronounced it 'More-in-jeye'.
738. Interview with Edna Jessop at Mt. Isa in 1995.
739. Interview with Kelly Dixon at Camooweal, December 1997.
740. Ibid.
741. Ibid.
742. C.L.A. Abbott to The Secretary, Department of Interior, July 15 1942, NAA NT, CRS series F/1, item 1942/112.
743. Interview with Kelly Dixon at Camooweal, December 1997.
744. Interview with Scotty Watson, Alice Springs, September 2000.
745. To 'track-ride' is to follow horse or cattle tracks to determine how far out the animals have gone, usually with the intention of turning them back if they have gone too far.
746. Ibid.
747. Personal communication, Rodney Watson, September 2005.
748. Rodney Watson, interviewed by Judith Hozier for the Stockman's Hall of Fame, c1990.
749. Interview with Eugene Kostin, Brunette Downs, July 1999.
750. Ibid.
751. Interview with Charlie Yeeda at Halls Creek, 1994.
752. Ibid.
753. Ibid.
754. Ibid
755. Interview with Mick Coombes at Halls Creek, 1994.
756. Ibid.
757. Ibid.
758. These sites were gazetted on June 17 1998. *Northern Territory Government Gazette*, No. G23.
759. Noel 'Pic' Willetts, oral history interview, NTRS, TS 356, tape 2.
760. Personal communication, Long Captain Marajala and Nugget Kiriyalangungu.
761. D. Lewis, letter to the editor of the *Stockman's Hall of Fame paper*, December, 2000.
762. Statement of Stock Treated at Public Dip, June 20 1967. Top Springs Dip (Pussycat), File 331/7/8, DPI&F, Alice Springs; personal communication G. Coleman, Regional Stock Inspector, Alice Springs, 1991.

INDEX

Books by
Darrell Lewis

Roping in the History of Broncoing

The Murranji Track